THE
BETTER HOME
BOOK

THE
BETTER HOME
BOOK

HOW TO KEEP YOUR HOUSE
CLEAN, SAFE AND BEAUTIFUL

NINA GRUNFELD

KEY PORTER BOOKS

First published in Great Britain in 1990 by
Conran Octopus Limited, 37 Shelton Street,
London WC2H 9HN

Published in Canada in 1991 by:
Key Porter Books Limited
70 The Esplanade
Toronto, Ontario
Canada M5E 1R2

Canadian Cataloguing in Publication Data

Grunfeld, Nina
  The Better Home Book

ISBN 1-55013-303-9

1. Dwellings – Maintenance and repair – Amateurs'
manuals. 2. Home economics. I. Title.

TX323.G78 1991   643'.7   C91-093095-3

Printed and bound in Hong Kong

The author would like to thank Nicky Stephens, Terry Ray, Phil
James and Ira Wijeratne for getting on with it while I was
writing about it and for passing on their hints. Also to my
mother-in-law for sharing her flower arranging expertise.

I also want to thank everyone who worked on the book,
especially Polly Powell and Helen Lewis for doing so much in
advance (and afterwards) and Sarah Riddell for keeping me
going.

Lastly, thanks to Mike Wilks and Judy Piatkus for starting
my "homecare" career, to Dasha Shenkman for being such a
good friend and especially to Jane O'Shea for thinking of me.

As usual, with love to Nicholas.

The publisher would like to thank Carole McGlynn, Sandy
Shepherd and Diana Craig for their help in the production of
this book, and Richard Eckford, Vanessa Luff and Ron
Hayward Partnership for providing the illustrations.

The step-by-step projects on pages 177, 179, 186, 187, 189
were styled by Debbie Patterson and photographed by Geoff
Dann; the fabric was painted by Tabby Riley and the furniture
was painted by James Finlay. The Conran Shop and Distinc-
tive Trimmings kindly lent items used in the photographs.

Contents

INTRODUCTION

Your home is the most expensive purchase you will ever make, and it deserves the best treatment you can give it. The Better Home Book is an essential reference source for all homeowners and will help you look after and treasure everything inside your four walls.

The first section of the book, "Prevention and Protection," will show you how to get organized and will help you plan both your time and your home so that cleaning and maintenance become as quick and as simple as possible. Included is all-important advice on stain removal, spring cleaning, instant tidying and closet design.

The second section, "Home Repairs," is essential reading for anyone who wants to carry out simple repairs around the home. It will save you money and time – why wait for the plumber or decorator when we show you how to do the simple work yourself? Hints on repairing chipped paintwork, reducing drafts, clearing a blocked toilet and cleaning a gilt frame are included – plus a list of what not to attempt yourself!

The third section, "The Safe Home," tackles the inherent dangers in the home. It will help you make your home safer, not only against the potential perils of fire and water, but also against burglars and disease. There is a comprehensive section on insurance, with room-by-room advice on how to make your home a safer place to be.

The fourth section, "The Beautiful Home," is filled with inspirational ideas and hints on how to make the best of your home – essential for people bored with what they have, but who don't want to spend a fortune on changing it: tips on reusing old curtains, adding appropriate period moldings, painting floors, walls and ceilings, and advice on using color to astonishing effect.

Where possible, I have tried to give ecologically sound alternatives. These may well sometimes conflict with the options that are most convenient for you. You must make up your own mind what you should do, but it is important that you are aware of all the alternatives and the effect that your decision will have on both your time and the environment you and your family live in.

The book is filled with fun and easy boxes to inspire you. There are boxes filled with "green" information, boxes to alert you to potential dangers, "Golden Rules" to save you time and money, step-by-step boxes to guide you through practical jobs and ergonomic boxes to help you become more efficient in the way you do your tasks.

The Better Home Book does not concern itself with the structure of your home. Instead it deals with tasks inside your home that you will be able to tackle yourself. You should be able to implement most of the suggestions given in this book, but always make sure you fully understand the instructions before you begin. If manufacturers have supplied you with care or operating instructions, always read them first and, if you are at all worried or unsure about anything you are about to do, consult the experts. All the methods given in this book have been effective, but there is no guarantee that they will be wholly effective. It is essential to follow the instructions given on products.

If at any stage you feel you need expert help, first ask friends if they can recommend anyone. If they can't, find three or more relevant firms in your local newspaper or telephone directory. If possible, choose companies that are members of trade associations and always meet an employee from the company before deciding to use it. Ask for a written estimate before employing a firm, and compare estimates carefully – always read the small print.

Enjoy caring for your home – you'll soon notice the results.

Nina Grunfeld

7

PREVENTION AND PROTECTION

Storage

Whether you like putting things away or not – and who does? – it is impossible to tidy up if there is nowhere to put anything. Some people, even when they have plenty of cupboards, never manage to keep their home tidy. They find it easy to take a book off the shelves and impossible to put it back – and they are not helped if the shelves can be reached only with a stepladder.

Having enough storage space does not mean that everything has to be put away. An overly-tidy home neither looks nor feels very welcoming. But too much clutter means it is impossible to do anything without moving something first. There is a balance between the two and one that you will feel at ease with when you find it.

Before you begin cleaning or attempting to tidy up your home, you must first have somewhere to put things. Everything in your home should have its own space that is easy to get at; otherwise there is no incentive to be tidy. If you have to move a heavy mattress out of the way before you can open the trunk to get at the blankets stored there, you will never use the trunk. First decide what you need to store and then find a unit to house it.

Most items are best kept off the floor, to make vacuuming or cleaning easy, and shelves and cupboards that do not require you either to stretch or to stoop are by far the most tempting to use.

ROOM BY ROOM

Even if you do not yet own many of the items listed below, it is better to allow for more, rather than less, storage space in your home. Most families have changing needs and often harbor at least one hoarder.

All kinds of objects can be turned into storage containers. Empty shoe boxes are ideal for the bathroom (for medicines – kept safely out of children's reach, for makeup, for summer-holiday lotions etc); a stack of cardboard boxes can hold photographs, bills and newspaper clippings; glass jars can store safety pins, paperclips and beads; plastic buckets can hold cleaning materials; and old baskets can contain fruit, vegetables or dried flowers.

Garden shed/Garage
- Baby carriages, bicycles
- Barbecue
- Garden furniture & tools
- DIY equipment & materials
- Car-repair equipment
- Spare sets of keys
- Cage, basket, tank
- Pet food

Cellar
- Logs
- Wine
- Non-perishable food

Hall closet/Corridor
- Overshoes, boots, umbrellas
- Coats & hats
- Letters to be mailed/received by mail
- Library books to be returned

- Sports equipment (summer/winter)
- Telephone, answering machine

Attic/Storage room
- Trunks, suitcases
- Christmas decorations
- Old children's clothes, toys & equipment (waiting for next baby/child)
- "Out of season" clothes

Kitchen
- Utensils, pots, pans
- Cutlery, dishes
- Food (perishable/nonperishable)
- Cookbooks and home-care books
- Notes to yourself (shopping lists, emergency telephone numbers, etc)

Large cupboards
- Broom closet (brooms, vacuum cleaner, etc; spare toilet paper & paper towels; string; used plastic & string bags; iron; ironing board)
- Linen cupboard (sheets, towels, pillowcases, old curtains, tablecloths, spare bedding, rugs)

Utility/DIY room
- Washing machine, spin dryer
- Soap powders
- Spare fuses, lightbulbs, plugs
- Candles, matches, vases
- Tape measure, screwdriver, hammer, etc (if not in garage)

Bathroom
- Dirty laundry
- Brushes (hair, tooth, clothes)
- Makeup, other toiletries
- Cleaning equipment
- Medicines

Living room
- Television
- Video, video cassettes
- Stereo system
- Records, compact discs, cassettes
- Books
- Musical instrument/s
- Any collection/s
- Photographs in/not yet in albums
- Old newspapers, magazines
- Presents waiting to be given

Dining room/Study
- Glasses, china
- Cutlery
- Pens, pencils, etc
- Daily correspondence
- Typewriter/word processor/fax
- Accounts
- Old letters you want to keep
- Address books
- Filing cabinets

Bedroom
- Clothes
- Jewelry
- Loose change (and other contents of pockets)
- Spare handbags
- Sewing machine, sewing basket, spare safety pins, etc
- Shoes, shoe-cleaning equipment
- Books

Nursery/Playroom
- Toys
- Books
- Homework
- Children's works of art
- Children's clothes
- Games

Kitchen storage **112–3**
Chilled kitchen storage **114–5**
Planning your bathroom **118–9**

Furniture **184–5**

PREVENTION & PROTECTION

When to get rid of things

Some things are just dangerous to keep: old medicines and food long past its expiry date should be thrown away. So should shoes that cannot be resoled and that no longer give your feet any support. Old catalogs can be a disappointment when the prices have soared and the goods are unavailable. There is a philosophy that says whenever you buy anything new you should throw away whatever it is replacing. Most of us would find that difficult, if not impossible, to follow, but we can try.

It may help you to get rid of possessions you have not used for at least a year if you sell them or give them to charity, rather than just throw them out. Most charities are keen to have anything you no longer need. Old magazines might be welcomed by hospitals and old toys by children's hospitals; most clothes, unless they are rags, are also useful for resale, although often shoes are not.

GOLDEN STORAGE RULES

- Store items as near as possible to where they are most often used.
- Store articles in frequent use at waist height, or just above.
- Where possible, do not stack articles.
- Avoid storing anything in an inaccessible place: getting something out should not be a struggle.
- Do not hang more than one item (brush, utensil, belt) on a single hook.
- Label all boxes and wrapped articles.

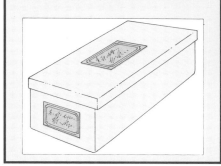

Above Pots and pans can be hung on hooks above the work surface within easy reach.

Below A wall of bookshelves and cupboards with sliding doors is ideal in a small room.

THE LINEN CUPBOARD

Bed and table linen should be stored in a separate cupboard. Sort linens into three categories: much-used, little-used and reserve, and store on separate shelves. Shelves should be made of slatted wood and placed about 2 ft (60 cm) apart.

FREE-STANDING STORAGE

If you are lucky enough to own or find some beautiful pieces of furniture that can be used effectively for storing things, keep them. They can be moved from wall to wall, room to room or even home to home and will always add visual interest. The disadvantages are that they are not usually as space-efficient as built-in furniture and can be more difficult to clean.

Some free-standing furniture is specifically designed for one-room living where space is at a premium. Convertible sofa-beds can be found with extra space in the base for storing bedding. There are tables that drop down from the wall for meals and can be pushed back up again afterwards, and chairs that can be folded and hung on the wall.

NOT WHAT IT SEEMS

This built-in cupboard has been effectively designed to suit the style of the room. The sides have been recessed to make the wardrobe appear free-standing and the height has been kept below that of the picture rail to avoid making the room look smaller.

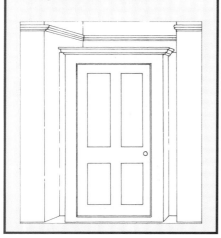

Above Displaying china on dresser shelves is a decorative solution to the storage problem.

Right If you can find one, an old drawer unit like this keeps everything tidied away.

FREE-STANDING OR FITTED?

- Do you want to be able to take the storage units with you when you move or are you happy to leave them?
- Will they increase the value of your home if they are built in?
- What do you need to store? You may find it difficult to find suitable free-standing furniture for stereo equipment, tennis rackets, skis, etc.
- What space do you have? If space is restricted, remember that a free-standing piece takes up more room than a fitted unit.
- What is your budget? If it is strictly limited, you may be able to find a free-standing piece costing less than a purpose-built storage unit.

FITTED STORAGE

Walk around your home and assess it carefully. Are there large spaces over some of your doors, or under or over the stairs, as well as the more obvious alcoves that could be filled with cupboards or shelves? Lofts and cellars make useful storerooms, although not if they are damp. Remember that building-in a cupboard can change the shape and proportions of your room – for better or for worse. Picture the finished result before you start work, and consider making cupboards three-quarter height so they do not overpower the room.

Always bear in mind the character of the room. Do several different drawings first and, if you are working in an old house, try to find out what style of cupboard would have been originally used in a home of this period. Or maybe you can turn a small storage room into a large walk-in cupboard instead of having a number of smaller cupboards.

Ready-made and purpose-built

Ready-made units are usually found only in kitchens and bathrooms. Whereas they may be easy to clean and look neat and streamlined, they are inflexible in their design. Often you may find potentially useful spaces left without a cupboard because the manufacturer simply does not make one of that particular size.

Purpose-built cupboards are used mainly in bedrooms, but there is no reason why they should not be fitted elsewhere. Half-height ones with shelving above are useful for storage space in living rooms and look very elegant built into alcoves or centered on a wall so that a recess appears on either side of it. Folding doors take up less space than conventional side-hanging doors, as do sliding doors and roll-down fronts, or you could simply use a curtain.

Top A wall of built-in wardrobes, cupboards and drawers provides generous storage.

Above Purpose-built shelving looks tidy and makes good use of available space.

SHELVING

Before you attach shelving or any other wall-hung units to your walls, check the construction of the wall and its load-bearing capacity. On a stud wall, for example, you must fix the shelves to the wall studs, not to the drywall surface. Also find out where pipes and electric cables run so that you do not drill into them. Make sure that the shelves themselves are going to be well supported. A wall-fixed batten running behind the entire shelf will give a lot of extra support, and a strip of thicker wood along the front of a thin shelf will make it look more substantial as well as strengthening it.

Items stored on high shelves should be lightweight or infrequently used. Ideally shelves should be 4–12 in (10–30 cm) wide or items become difficult to reach.

STORING BOOKS

Adjustable shelving is useful for storing books as they generally range in height from 7 to 14 in (17 to 34 cm). Allow about 6 in (15 cm) of shelf for every six paperbacks. Leave at least 1 in (2.5 cm) space between the top of your books and the bottom of the shelf above to help you pull them out easily. Six average-size paperbacks weigh about 2½ lbs (1.2 kg).

Above When filling your shelves, store lighter or less frequently used items at the top — it is difficult to stretch and lift something heavy at the same time!

AWKWARD SPACES

Most awkward spaces can be used for storage, provided that they have adequate ventilation and are waterproof and well lit. If you are planning to use your attic for storage, make sure that there is easy access into it. The joists should be strong and covered with a cheap, but strong, wooden sheeting to allow you to walk between them.

Spaces over doors can be filled with either a cupboard or shelves, but should not hold objects you need on a daily basis. Bookshelves surrounding a door look welcoming; just make sure the books above the door are ones you will not need to reach often.

If cellars are dry, they are useful for storing anything from unused furniture to nonperishable foods, as well as wine. If they are damp, most items will eventually suffer.

Right The recesses on either side of the fireplace in an attic are "dead" space and are really useful only for storage.

ON WHEELS

Heavy or bulky objects stored under shelving could be put on castors and pulled out to avoid back strain.

UNDER THE EAVES

The sloping spaces in attics do not provide enough headroom for standing and are really useful only for storage.

Make sure cupboards you have fitted into these recesses are well made and will not leak or let in large amounts of dust. Good lighting is essential as they can be very deep.

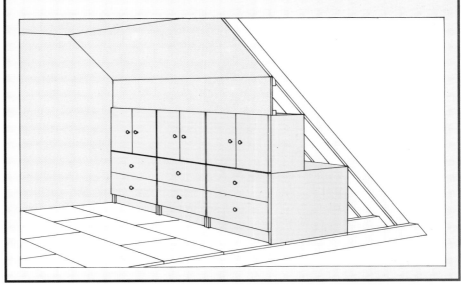

CLOSET DESIGN

The more flexible your closet or wardrobe is, the better. If shelves can be moved up and down and drawers added or removed, you will be able to change it around as your needs change. If the wardrobe is backless, make sure the wall paint will not rub off on clothes.

Drawers and shelves can be kept clean by lining them with wallpaper, old wrapping paper or special drawer liners. Coat hangers should ideally be the old-fashioned large wooden ones, or padded, and should fit the garment well.

Look after your clothes and they will last much longer. Turn evening dresses, and anything made of velvet, inside out before hanging. Hang shirts, but fold knitwear. Fold trousers on the crease and hang them upside-down on special trouser hangers. Hang skirts from loops sewn into the waistband. Always wash clothes or have them dry-cleaned before storing them away.

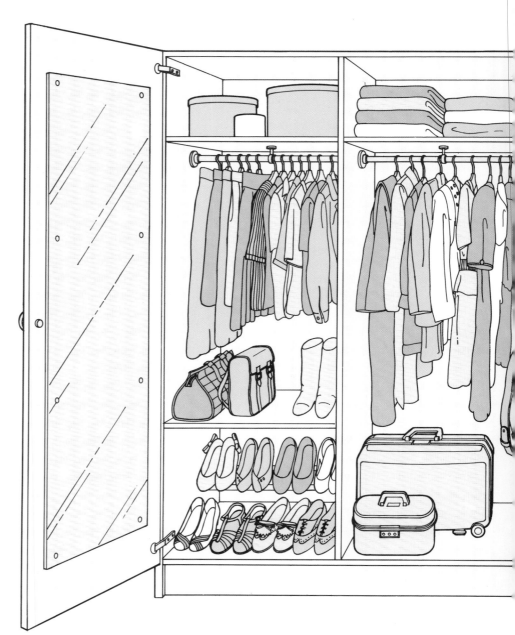

> Do not pack clothes tightly or they will crease. They also need room to breathe.

> Allow space for "out of season" clothes to be kept in plastic bags.

> A full-length mirror can be fixed to the inside of a door. If both doors are used you can see your back as well as your front. If you use only one door, it should not, when open, face the window. Light from the window should shine on you, not on the mirror.

MOTH REPELLENTS

Instead of using mothballs, which contain toxic chemicals, wrap clothes in newspaper or scatter them with orange peel or lavender flowers.

> Shoe racks should be placed off the floor so that the air can circulate fully round them. Make shoe racks out of two parallel rods 5 in (12 cm) apart.

> A compartment that can house briefcases and suitcases at the bottom of the cupboard is useful.

Woolens can be kept on the top shelf or in pull-out drawers in the underwear section.

Shelving for hats should be generous enough to allow room for them to be kept in hatboxes: laying a hat on a flat surface may damage its brim. Shelves can also be used for handbags and knee-length boots. Shelves should be at least $1\frac{1}{2}$ ft (45 cm) apart, and you should try not to fill them too full or they quickly become untidy.

As clothes can be heavy, rails need to be supported every $2\frac{1}{2}$ ft (75 cm). Allow approximately 3 ft (90 cm) of hanging rail for a man and 5 ft (152 cm) for a woman; a child needs slightly less. The usual height of a hanging rail is about $5\frac{1}{2}$ ft (168 cm) from the ground. Jackets, skirts, shirts and light sweaters can be hung from rails $3\frac{1}{4}$ ft (99 cm) high. Rails should be placed about 1 ft (30 cm) away from both the wall and the cupboard door to allow enough space for coat hangers. Hanging clothes parallel to the wall on extending rails saves space but can be infuriating to use as clothes are hard to reach and remove.

Hanging all clothes of a certain type (shirts, skirts, dresses, etc) together – possibly even in color ranges – saves time when looking for what to wear in the morning. It also prevents fluff from a garment of one color settling on a garment of another color. Space above or below short clothes can be used for extra shelving.

Underwear, socks and tights can be kept in shallow pull-out drawers below eye level so they are easy to find.

A man can hang ties and belts on a rack on the inside of one door. A woman may find a rack useful for hanging belts or small bags. Belts can also be hung by their buckles on small hooks.

General Cleaning

GETTING ORGANIZED

Every day, set aside some time to make a list of what you hope to achieve that day or week. Ticking completed items off gives such satisfaction and compiling the list helps you realize what your priorities are. Spend an evening working out a permanent list of tasks to be done around your home and subdivide them into "everyday," "once a week" or "once every two weeks" and "once a year."

Your household already has a system, even though you may not be aware of it. You probably wash the dishes after each meal (or at least within 24 hours) and you may well take out the garbage every day or stack your newspapers for recycling rather than throwing them away. Start noticing and rationalizing what you do when and what you do not do at all, and bear in mind that most tasks only get worse if left to pile up.

Organize your housework to make it as easy as possible for yourself. For example, if you leave things that are in the wrong room on the "flightpath" to their correct home, they are more likely to get taken there.

If you can do a messy job in the kitchen, or better still in the garden, take it there and then you will have less to clean up afterwards. If you are feeling energetic, it saves effort to clean adjoining rooms at the same time. Never clean if you do not feel like it; it may put you off for another day.

The kitchen

Most of the housework you will have to do on a regular, everyday basis will be in the kitchen, preparing and cleaning up after meals. Being organized about this and establishing a routine can do a lot to make this daily chore easier to cope with. For example, put everything away as soon as you have finished using it, clean up messes and spills immediately and wipe over worktops once you have finished cooking – they just get more difficult to deal with later.

In the kitchen, line shelves and drawers with wipe-clean paper and replace it when dirty. Wash dishes, pots, pans and cooking utensils as you cook, or soak them, and use nonstick pans. Soak plates and cutlery from the first course while you are eating your second course, and so on. Wash glasses first and then wash dishes, from cleanest to dirtiest. Make sure your drainer is large enough so that you can leave everything to drain dry except silver and glasses, which should be dried with a clean linen tea towel.

Buy as many labor-saving devices as you can afford and then use them. If you have a dishwasher (very time-saving) make sure you have enough dishes, glassware and cutlery to fill it and some spare to use while the machine is full. Time yourself doing certain tasks you find boring, such as emptying the dishwasher; you will be amazed at how little time they take. Swill sinks with water after use and buy a sink (and basin) strainer to stop food bits and pieces or loose hairs clogging up your drains.

The bathroom

Use bubble bath rather than soap in your bath: you will not have a dirty ring afterwards and both you and the bath will be clean. Better still, save water and use the shower. Before you put clothes into the washing machine, use them to dust a bit of your room. Have laundry baskets to put dirty clothes into the moment they are removed so that piles of laundry are not left lying on the floor. Similarly, put away clean clothes when they are dry (and ironed, if necessary).

The bedroom

In the bedroom, use a duvet and fitted undersheet on your bed. Buy mini bookshelves rather than bedside tables to avoid large piles of books gathering that have to be lifted when you want to clean. Keep curtains off the floor. Trailing ones may be fashionable, but you have to lift them when vacuuming and the bottoms get dirty very quickly. Choose soft furnishing fabrics and blankets that can be put in the washing machine or dry-cleaned. Choose colors and textures that do not show the dirt and, if you have pets, leave towels on favorite pieces of furniture for them to lie on. There is nothing more infuriating and time-consuming to remove than pet hairs on furniture.

Furniture and floors

When buying furniture, try to avoid fiddly pieces with built-in dust-traps. Choose furniture that is easy to move or clean under and does not need to be polished. Have as few *objets d'art* lying around as possible. Although open fires are cosier, they are more difficult to keep clean than gas or electric fires.

Use wall-to-wall carpets wherever possible; it is easier to vacuum than to clean a smooth floor, even if it is sealed with clear polyurethane lacquer, and carpets are more luxurious to walk on. Old wooden floors have years of dust under them that will continually rise to the surface, so cover them with carpet.

INSTANT TIDYING FOR WHEN VISITORS COME

- Straighten crooked pictures
- Empty all wastepaper baskets
- Remove old newspapers and magazines
- Empty ashtrays
- Plump cushions
- Throw away dead flowers
- Open the windows and air the room
- Clean up any spills
- Clean and relay yesterday's dead fire
- Sweep up the crumbs and fluff on visible bits of the carpet
- Put a new toilet roll in the holder and fold your bathroom towels neatly
- Shut the kitchen and bedroom doors

BASIC CLEANING EQUIPMENT

Cleaning is easier if you have the right equipment. Keep equipment clean and in good working order. Wash bristle brushes with soap, not detergent, and leave them to dry naturally. Hang all brushes; do not leave them resting on their bristles.

To save time and energy, buy one basic set of cleaning equipment and products for each floor of your house.

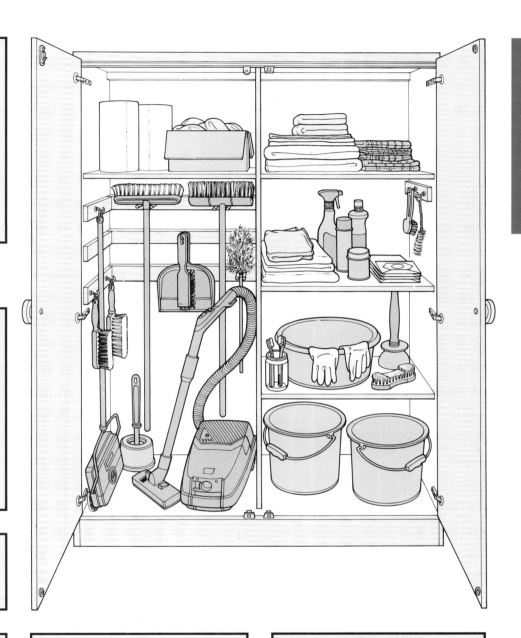

Brushes
- Scrub brush (for floors and other hard tasks)
- Toilet brush and stand
- Old toothbrushes (for cleaning taps)
- Bottle brush (if you have a small baby, buy a special bottle brush)
- Dishwashing brush or scouring pads
- Dustpan and soft brush
- Stiff brush (for carpet edges and stairs)
- Soft hearth and flue brush (if you have an open fire)

Brooms
- Long-handled soft broom (for hard floors)
- Hard broom (for outside)

Carpet cleaners
- Vacuum cleaner plus attachments (upright cleaners are the quickest for large expanses of carpet; cylinder models are easiest for stairs, hard floors and curtains)
- Carpet sweeper (for antique rugs and instant sweeping)
- Carpet shampooer and electric floor polisher (unless essential, rent rather than buy)

Rags and cloths
- Paper towels
- Old cotton sheets, shirts, socks, etc (useful for rags)
- Cotton dusters
- Floor cloths
- Dish cloths
- Disposable sponge cloths (a luxury for dishes and floors)
- Chamois leather (another luxury useful for windows)
- Tea or dish towels

Mops
- Dust mops or feather duster
- Squeeze mop or cotton floor mop

Miscellaneous
- Plastic dishwashing container
- Plastic buckets
- Large garbage can
- Rubber gloves
- Suction plunger

CLEANING MATERIALS

Playing it safe: family

Always keep cleaners well away from children and never transfer them into other containers as you may forget what is in them.

Always follow manufacturers' instructions and use all cleaning materials with care. If you have to use powerful cleaners, open the windows wide, wear rubber gloves and avoid any contact with your skin or eyes. If strong cleaning materials do get on your skin or into your eyes, wash or rinse with lots of cold water at once. Should you or your child accidentally swallow any cleaning products, check the poison information on the bottle or box, or call poison control.

Do not mix cleaning products. Take special care when using drain or toilet-bowl cleaners: if mixed with liquid bleaches they give off a chlorine gas.

If a manufacturer recommends a particular cleaning agent to be used with his equipment, check if your guarantee will be lost if you use another brand.

Playing it safe: environment

Use materials sparingly: some pollute the environment; some can harm you. Many aerosols contain chlorofluorocarbons (CFCs) that damage the protective ozone layer around our planet. If you must use aerosols, buy only non-CFC brands. Pouring bleach, scouring powder, paint thinner or many other leftover cleaning solutions down the sink or drain contributes to the contamination of our drinking water. If you continue to use toxic products, take any remains to a hazardous-waste collection center, if one exists near you. Otherwise change to natural, nontoxic household products where you can.

There are many "green" cleaning materials coming on to the market that will help protect the environment. There are also safe alternatives. The choice of materials is yours, but if you use these methods, wherever possible, much pollution can be avoided.

Basic checklist

Highly polished surfaces are most attractive when they are kept looking shiny and glossy. Different kinds of material – from wooden floors to man-made laminates – dictate the type of cleaner to use.

For clothes
- Laundry products (see page 46)
- Stain-removal kit (see page 50)

For surfaces
- Scouring powder (for removing grease and dirt from hard surfaces; cleans by rubbing away the surface and can damage it)
- Nonabrasive scouring cream (milder than scouring powder, but may not be suitable for cleaning plastic)
- Disinfectant (for killing or halting the growth of bacteria. Some are poisonous; use with care and sparingly)
- Household chlorine bleach (read instructions; use carefully and sparingly)
- Washing soda (for dirty paintwork, cleaning drains and dishwashing; read instructions before use)

For dishes
- Dish detergent (mild)
- Dishwasher powder and salt and rinse aid (for dishwashers)
- Steel-wool pads (cut them in half so they last longer; wear rubber gloves when using)

For polishing

- Floor polish (rub spirit-based polishes in; leave water-based ones to dry – they leave a shiny film without rubbing. Apply water-based polishes every six weeks, and occasionally strip old polish off with polish stripper and start again)
- Polish stripper (for removing build-up of water-based floor polish)
- Nonslip floor polish (for kitchens, bathrooms, utility rooms and other wet areas)
- Beeswax (thin down to pasty consistency with vinegar before applying to floor; leave to dry and then polish)
- Furniture polish (wax pastes need elbow grease but are good for antiques. Creams need light rubbing only; some can also be used for glass and paintwork)

For special use

- Toilet-bowl cleaner (a mixture of bleach and disinfectant: follow instructions. For daily cleaning, not hard-water stains)
- Oven cleaner (for removing burned-on grease; use with care)
- Descaler (for kettles and irons in hard-water areas)
- Bath-stain remover (for removing hard-water stains from baths, sinks, toilet bowls, etc)
- Furniture cleaner
- Carpet shampoo
- Upholstery shampoo
- Metal polishes (for hard metals such as brass or soft metals such as silver or chrome; also Silver Dip for cutlery)
- Graphite cream (polish for cast-iron stoves and grates)
- Glass cleaner (for windows, mirrors, etc)
- Household soap (for washing hands and pure bristle brushes)
- Water softener (for some dishwashers in hard-water areas to prevent the build up of scum)

For you

- Hand cream (for when rubber gloves are not enough)
- Dirty-hand cleaner or hand-barrier cream (for DIY enthusiasts)

TAKING THE STRAIN

Always be aware of the movements your body is making. Try to use the correct muscles for each task. Even with a simple task like pouring, keep your elbow close to your body and notice how it lessens the strain on your arms and shoulders.

When lifting a heavy object, bend your knees and keep your spine straight so you use your stronger leg muscles rather than putting strain on your spine.

When pushing or pulling, get as close as possible to the object so you use the force of your entire body and put the strain on your legs and not on your arms.

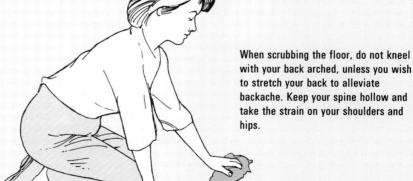

When scrubbing the floor, do not kneel with your back arched, unless you wish to stretch your back to alleviate backache. Keep your spine hollow and take the strain on your shoulders and hips.

REGULAR CLEANING

Once a week

- Every Monday morning, write all your letters and pay your bills.
- Empty wastebaskets around the house. Save time by going round with a large plastic bag and emptying all the baskets into it.
- Clean and disinfect the entire bathroom.
- Change the towels, washcloths, bathmats, the dish towels from the kitchen and all the bed linen. Tidy the wardrobe and closet.
- Hand-wash anything you need to, such as woolens and other delicate items, or take things to the dry-cleaners.
- Wash hairbrushes and combs.
- Clean and disinfect the kitchen thoroughly, including the garbage pail.
- Put salt and rinse aid in the dishwasher, and water softener, if necessary.
- Shake the doormat outdoors and sweep the front steps.

THE ERGONOMICS OF CLEANING

To avoid strain and possible accidents, always clean when you are feeling relaxed, not tense or tired and likely to make mistakes. Use calm, regular circular strokes when cleaning rather than short, jerky movements.

Find ways of saving time and energy. Never go anywhere empty-handed; put things you want to move in a place where you will trip up over them unless you pick them up; move the garbage bag around the house rather than carrying all your wastepaper baskets to the bag. Keep a set of cleaning materials and equipment in a convenient spot on each floor and try to run up and down the stairs as little as possible.

Never stand when you can sit. Never sit when you can lie. If you must stand, keep your feet slightly apart with one foot just in front of the other.

WHAT A WASTE

- Recycle items (plastic bags, food waste for compost, clothes, building materials, etc) wherever possible
- Buy and return refillable or returnable bottles and deposit nonreturnable bottles in your recycling depot. Avoid nonreturnable plastic bottles
- Take large unwanted metal items to scrap yards

- Buy recycled paper goods and save all your paper for recycling
- Give magazines to hospitals, doctors, dentists, etc
- Buy as little packaging as possible – choose loose vegetables rather than packaged ones
- Campaign for a hazardous-waste collection in your area

- Clean all table tops and other surfaces to remove marks.
- Quickly dust each room from top to bottom, and from the top of each piece of furniture to the bottom, including upholstered furniture and blinds, and then vacuum.
- Vacuum or sweep the stairs and hall thoroughly.
- Empty the vacuum cleaner and carpet sweeper.
- Shake out your pets' beds and mats and clean any cages, fish tanks, etc.
- Starting in spring, begin regular maintenance in the garden. In summer, you will have to mow the lawn regularly as well.

Every other week

- Clean the filters in the washing machine and spin and/or tumble dryer.
- Thoroughly clean any open shelves in the kitchen and bathroom.
- Clean the kitchen sink drain by pouring boiling water and a handful of washing soda down it.
- Clean and polish any hard floors (or have them sealed so they do not need polishing).
- Polish old brass door hardware, including that on the front door. Most modern brass does not need polishing. See if any silver or other metal objects you have need cleaning and use the appropriate polish.
- Clean one room thoroughly. Do a different room every other week until you have cleaned your entire home, and then take two weeks off.

Cleaning difficult items

Regard hard or unpleasant cleaning jobs as a challenge; that way they will be more fun. A toilet can be cleaned easily, but never attempt the job without first putting on rubber gloves. Time yourself when laying your open fire and see if you can beat your record next time. Listen to the radio if it relaxes you and makes you feel you are accomplishing two things at once. Better still, get your partner to clean something else at the same time and you will be working twice as fast.

A few tips

- Never scrub dirty windows or mirrors with a dry cloth or soap.
- Avoid cleaning windows when the sun is shining or in frosty weather. Use warm, rather than hot water and a chamois leather or a rubber blade on a handle for large plate-glass windows.
- Always cover the floor below the radiator when cleaning it. Use a special vacuum-cleaner attachment, a feather duster or a stick covered with a rag to clean the crevices.
- Clean decanters by swilling with a denture-cleaning tablet dissolved in water, or vinegar and salt.
- Artificial plastic flowers can be cleaned by shaking them vigorously in a bag filled with salt.

Right In rooms like this with a large expanse of glass, windows must be kept sparkling clean as any dirt will show.

SPRING CLEANING

"Spring" cleaning was far more relevant before the days of gas and electric heating when spring was the time you began to get rid of the memory of winter soot and dirt. Even now, spring is the time you begin to feel like cleaning as the sun starts shining and revealing dirt and dust you had not noticed for a few months. But depending on how much energy you have and how many items there are requiring cleaning, "spring" cleaning can take place once a year or every three months.

The amount of occasional cleaning you have depends on how regularly and how often you clean during the year. Some jobs, such as cleaning bedcovers, servicing electric blankets or having your furnace checked, are best done in spring, when the weather is getting warmer and you no longer need the benefits of such items. But spring cleaning should not become a chore; do it only when you feel like it. If you force yourself to clean just because you feel you should, the work will seem more of a grind, you are more likely to be careless and have accidents, and you will simply end up becoming resentful about the whole process. One word of warning: always finish one job before you start the next, otherwise you may never finish anything. In your initial rush of enthusiasm, don't be tempted to try to do everything at once. It is far better to complete a few smaller jobs than to end up with a houseful of unfinished larger jobs that you will only have to return to later.

> **Bathroom**
> **Clean the shower curtains**

Kitchen
- Have the kitchen range and any other gas appliances serviced
- Clean the filter on the stove hood
- Clean the fridge and defrost the freezer, after using as much of the contents as possible. Upright freezers should be defrosted every three months; chest freezers need this attention only every six months
- Clean out your kitchen cupboards, checking all expiry dates. Throw out anything that is old. Empty out and wash all spice jars and glass bottles that are on display, then refill
- Sharpen all your knives, scissors and gardening equipment

Bedroom
- Air mattresses, pillows and duvets in the sunshine and then vacuum them
- Have any feather pillows and quilts professionally cleaned and, if necessary, have them refilled too
- Put winter clothes and blankets in mothproof storage to prevent damage during the summer

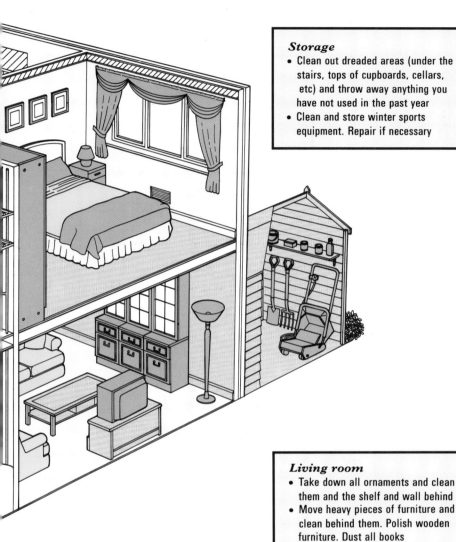

Storage
- Clean out dreaded areas (under the stairs, tops of cupboards, cellars, etc) and throw away anything you have not used in the past year
- Clean and store winter sports equipment. Repair if necessary

Living room
- Take down all ornaments and clean them and the shelf and wall behind
- Move heavy pieces of furniture and clean behind them. Polish wooden furniture. Dust all books

General
- Go through all your drawers, desks and cupboards and ruthlessly throw things out that you no longer want
- Wash all paintwork, especially tops of things (picture frames, doors, windows, cupboards, etc)
- Clean all light fittings, lamps and shades
- Clean all electric (toasters, electric blankets, etc) and electronic equipment (stereos, televisions, etc) and have them serviced or repaired if necessary

- Shampoo dirty carpets and clean all your loose rugs
- Take down all pictures and clean the walls behind them. Wash all washable walls, starting at the bottom and working your way upwards
- Wash or dry-clean curtains, loose covers, blankets, bedcovers and cushion covers
- Oil all doors that squeak, all furniture castors that stick and all metal curtain rails. Rub other curtain rails and drawer runners with candle wax or furniture polish for smoother running

JOBS FOR THE AUTUMN

- Clean out the garden shed and oil and store garden tools. Get the lawnmower serviced. Repair any summer sports equipment, if damaged
- Check there are no holes in your roof; get inside the attic to look. If tiles or shingles have fallen off, replace them. Check the garage and garden shed roofs too: it is much better to take precautions now, rather than wait for damage by winter weather
- Find and fill all wall, ceiling and floor cracks, both indoors and out. If they are large and persistent, call a professional to check the cause
- Make sure damp patches and mysterious stains are kept under control
- Clean out drains and gutters and put a wire "bird cage" on top of outlets to stop future blockages. Find out if gutters and downpipes can cope with heavy rain by tipping a bucket of water down them. Replace them if necessary
- Make sure outdoor pipes are drained of water and taps turned off so the pipes cannot freeze during winter. Find out where your supply valve is and how to turn it off
- Clean radiators, drain them if necessary and check that your central-heating system is working before winter begins
- Replace the washers on any taps that are dripping. Make sure none of your bathroom fittings are leaking
- Have your chimneys swept, if you have open fires, in preparation for the winter. Look to see if your chimney stacks are leaning or cracking and have them repaired if necessary
- See if brickwork needs repointing and that outside woodwork is not rotting and letting in damp. Repaint woodwork and walls every three to five years
- Have your burglar alarm serviced. Darkness provides a convenient cover for burglars

Room by Room
KITCHENS

A country kitchen may appear a far more relaxed place in which to cook and entertain, but a fitted kitchen is infinitely easier to keep clean. There are easy-to-wipe surfaces, no hidden nooks and crannies and no cracks to harbor dropped food. Whichever style you opt for, it is essential to keep a kitchen scrupulously clean as it is a potential breeding ground for germs. You will probably also want to equip it with the latest in modern appliances. Unfortunately, the more technology you have, the more there is to go wrong; so make sure you look after appliances correctly. The better you maintain equipment, the longer it lasts.

Hygiene

Check food cupboards and your fridge regularly to see that food expiry dates, including those on dry goods, have not passed. Wipe greasy and sticky bottles with detergent solution.

Work surfaces

In a fitted kitchen the work surfaces may well be plastic laminate, which is easy to keep clean as long as you wipe up spills at once. Stains can be removed with a nonabrasive cream or mineral spirits. Do not use a laminated surface as a cutting board.

Teak, maple or mahogany work surfaces should be rubbed in the direction of the grain with linseed oil, roughly every six months. Very hot pots can burn wooden surfaces, so treat them with care. Wooden chopping boards should be scrubbed in the direction of the grain. Do not soak them or dry them near the heat or they may warp and become unusable.

Electrical appliances

The element in your electric kettle must always be covered with water before you turn the kettle on (but do not overfill or you may blow a fuse). In hard-water areas place a marble in the kettle to keep it from furring up, or use filtered water. If the furring is not yet too bad, add lemon juice or vinegar to the water in the kettle and boil, repeating with fresh solutions until the scale has disappeared. Rinse before using.

Every now and again remove the crumbs of bread from inside your electric toaster by turning it upside down or unscrewing the bottom, making sure you have first unplugged it. Never try to remove crumbs or a piece of toast from the toaster with a metal object while the toaster is plugged in.

Electric mixers and blenders should not be run for too long at a time or the motor may burn out.

Regularly dismantle and clean, or replace, the filter of your exhaust fan and wipe the fan blades with a damp cloth. Never let water come into contact with the motor: switch off and unplug the fan before cleaning it. Make sure it is dry before turning it on.

Above Metal storage drawers can be easily cleaned with a nonabrasive detergent.

Left A country kitchen has a variety of surfaces, making it harder to keep clean.

CLEANING FIXTURES AND APPLIANCES

Safety first
For all household appliances always follow manufacturers' care instructions.

Microwave ovens
Wipe inside with a damp cloth after use. Never place metal items in a microwave.

Ovens
Catalytic linings in modern ovens help keep them clean. Never use abrasives on nonstick surfaces. Instead, use a plastic- or nylon-mesh pad. Never use aerosol oven cleaner on warm glass. Clean glass doors with bicarbonate of soda. Old-fashioned ranges are more or less self-cleaning: the heat burns off spills and grease spots. Always make sure the pilot light is relit after cleaning.

Sinks and drainers
Never use abrasives or vinegar in your stainless-steel sink. Keep it clean with dishwashing liquid and rinse and dry it after use. Clean stubborn stains on your vitreous enamel sink with a bleach solution. If your drain is grease-blocked, pour a handful of washing soda down it, followed by 1 quart (1 l) of boiling water.

Stove tops
Keep gas or electric rings clean. Mop up spills the moment they occur. Always turn electricity off before cleaning. Make sure the pilot lights on your gas-stove top are always relit after cleaning or after a heavy spillage.

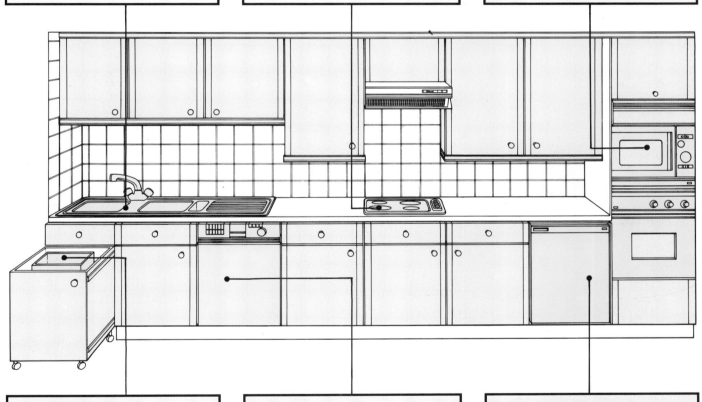

Garbage cans
Both the garbage can and the bin in which you keep the compost should be regularly washed and disinfected. Even if a plastic liner bag is used, a lot of dirt will somehow seep through. Try to have three bins: one for paper (to be recycled), one for compost (for the garden) and one for the garbage collector.

Dishwashers
Unless you have small children, leave the dishwasher door open between washes so air can circulate around the machine. Empty the dishwasher filter after each use and keep the dishwasher topped up with salt, rinse aid and water softener, if necessary.

Fridges and freezers
Clean the outside of fridges and freezers with a warm detergent solution and then dry. Defrost fridges and freezers regularly, and wash out with moistened bicarbonate of soda. Then rinse and dry well. Never try scraping ice off the inside walls or putting saucepans of hot water inside to speed up the defrosting process.

BATHROOMS & UTILITY ROOMS

General principles 106–7
Bathrooms 116–7

Bathrooms 164–5

THE "GREEN" BATHROOM

- Clean the inside of the toilet by applying a paste of borax and lemon juice to the wet surface. Leave for two hours and then scrub
- Clean mirrors with a mild vinegar solution or cold tea
- Use vinegar or lemon juice to remove hard-water deposits on taps

The bathroom is usually one of the easiest rooms, as well as one of the most important, to keep clean. Wash bathmats once a week as well as towels and washcloths. Empty the wastebasket regularly.

Baths and basins

Rinse the bath and basin well with fresh water every time you finish using them. At least once a week, clean both thoroughly. Clean fiberglass baths and basins regularly with a nonabrasive cleaner so that heavy soiling never builds up. For heavy soiling, soak with a solution of lukewarm water and biological detergent. Rinse well afterwards.

Acrylic baths and basins must also be cleaned with a nonabrasive cleaner, but stubborn stains and scratches can gently be removed with metal polish. Regularly remove limescale deposits with diluted lemon juice. Cast-iron baths and basins can be cleaned with mild abrasive liquid cleaners, but use with care as harsh abrasives can ruin the surface forever. Mild under-tap stains may be removed with lemon juice. More stubborn stains will need a proprietary cleaner; check with the manufacturer. Bidets should be cleaned as frequently as baths and basins.

Drains and overflow exits should be cleared and cleaned frequently. Hairs and soap buildup can cause obstructions. Buy a hair trap for the basin and shower plug-holes.

Scrub discolored sealants with a nonabrasive cleaner, using an old toothbrush. If stains are impossible to shift, regrout.

Taps and towel rails

Chrome taps and other fittings (grabrails, towel rails, etc) should be regularly wiped over with a damp cloth and some detergent, then rinsed and dried. Proprietary chrome cleaners can be used to restore shine. Bear in mind that such cleaners are often environmentally "unfriendly," however, and elbow grease is often just as effective.

Toilets

Keep the toilet clean at all times. Wipe the outside, seat and handle regularly with disinfectant and, once a week, clean the inside thoroughly (see box). If the toilet bowl is cracked, it will be a breeding ground for germs and you may find it safer to buy a new toilet. Wooden seats are more romantic but less hygienic than plastic ones. If your toilet is blocked, get a plumber as soon as possible. Avoid throwing too much paper, etc, down the toilet. Disinfect the toilet brush regularly and keep it out of the reach of small children.

Showers

Clean the rose of the shower head by taking off the shower head and cleaning it from the inside to remove any loose limescale. Use a pin to clear blocked holes, then reassemble the rose, making sure it is watertight. In hard-water areas, this needs to be done frequently.

Wash shower curtains with soapsuds or a mild detergent, then rinse and dry naturally. Never rub, squeeze or wring them. Remove any mildew with a mild bleach solution. Wash shower doors with detergent or vinegar solution.

Glass, wood and tiles

Mirrors, windows, wooden windowsills and tiles should be regularly wiped dry to prevent the buildup of moisture. Remove hairspray from mirrors with a little methylated spirit. Buff mirrors with a soft cloth.

Utility-room equipment

Have washing machines and spin and tumble dryers serviced regularly, and use the washing powder or liquid the manufacturer recommends, in the correct amount. Clean the filter regularly. If your washing machine is not situated on the ground floor, it is worth sitting it in a small metal box with an overflow pipe in case it floods.

Never overload machines, as you could damage the motor. Unless you have small children, leave machine doors open when machines are not in use to allow air to circulate. Wash soap compartments occasionally and wipe the rubber door seal dry, as water can rot the rubber. Remove fluff from tumble-dryer filters regularly.

If your steam iron needs to be used with distilled water, then do so, or it will need descaling. If any materials have burned onto the base, remove with metal polish (if chrome), fine steel wool or abrasive powder (if aluminum) and a soapy sponge or nylon-mesh pad (if nonstick).

Above Utility-room machines need little regular cleaning except for drying rubber door seals and removing fluff from filters.

Far left The bathroom is an easy room to keep clean since so many of the surfaces are hard and easily washable.

LIVING ROOMS, HALLS & STAIRS

The living room will be easier to clean if you have planned it well. Plain colored upholstery shows the dirt far sooner than heavily textured or patterned fabrics. Blended materials are easier to clean and harder wearing than all-wool fabrics. A close weave of fabric generally gives better wear than a loose weave, and loose covers that can be dry-cleaned are very practical. You could always have covers fitted on your chairs for winter and loose covers made in a different fabric for the summer to go over them. Twice as expensive initially but they will last at least twice as long – and you will not get bored with your purchases as quickly. Why not have winter and summer curtains as well? Remember to vacuum upholstery and curtains regularly.

Every now and again move your furniture around the room so that the carpet underneath does not get heavily indented, or use castors on the legs of very heavy pieces. Always get help moving furniture: it may either do damage to your back or harm the item.

Light and heat

The sun is a very strong bleaching agent. Do not leave any wooden or upholstered pieces of furniture, photographs or paintings in bright sunlight for too long or colors will fade (or darken): the sun will make dark wood lighter and light wood darker. Draw the curtains on sunny days or use roller blinds to diffuse the light.

Keep wooden furniture, especially antiques, away from radiators or other direct heat sources. Use a humidifier or stand saucers of water under each piece of furniture or hang special water containers over the radiators. Heat will cause wood to dry out, and perhaps to crack and shrink. This is almost inevitable in a centrally heated house, but you can minimize the damage.

ANTIQUE FURNITURE

Most antique furniture needs only to be dusted, so use a clean duster often and pick up the dust, rather than just pushing it around. Never use modern furniture cream or furniture polish on antique furniture. For very occasional use, rub in a small amount of beeswax, building up the shine by buffing with a soft cloth and plenty of "elbow grease."

Be careful of any area that is cracked or where bits of veneer or molding are lifting or dropping off; even a duster with a loose thread can cause considerable damage. If antiques are damaged, get them professionally repaired as soon as possible.

Hall and stairs

It is very important to keep the hall and stairs clean because this is where dirt first enters the house. An extra large doormat that can regularly be taken outside and shaken is essential. Even better is the Eastern idea of leaving your shoes by the front door.

To clean the hall thoroughly, start by removing any exposed obstacles – coats, hats, bicycles, strollers, etc. Then work from the topmost landing down toward the hall, brushing or vacuuming the stair carpet – a portable vacuum cleaner is ideal for this task – and sweeping and polishing the stair edges and banisters. Once on the ground floor, restore everything to its proper place. Finish by cleaning the telephone.

Left Living rooms can be kept presentable with regular dusting of furniture and hard surfaces, vacuuming of soft furnishings and keeping the fireplace, if any, swept and clear of ash.

Above A hard floor in an entrance hall, like this attractive checkered one, is a practical alternative to carpeting as it is easier to wipe up muddy footmarks and to keep it clean.

DINING ROOMS & STUDIES

A dining-room is often a convenient room to double as a study. Having a separate desk or table to work on is ideal, but otherwise spread out over the dining-room table, making sure you have protected it well first, especially if it is valuable. Using a full-size heat-proof cover under a tablecloth makes sense. Or cover the entire table with a sheet of plywood or formica that can be lifted off when the table is needed. Lay a piece of fabric under the wood to ensure the table is not scratched.

Dining-room table

Dining-room tables are made of many different materials and, sadly, the more beautiful, the more sensitive they are. As a general rule, stand vases, glasses and hot cups, mugs, dishes and plates on mats so any heat or liquid cannot damage the surface of the table. Also, line the underneath surface of any ornaments or objects (including your type-writer) with a piece of felt.

French-polished furniture is very delicate and can easily be damaged by liquid, so protect it carefully or wipe any spills up at once. Even if your table surface is a plastic laminate and seems more robust, hot dishes should not stand on it, nor should bread or anything else be cut on it as scratches cannot be removed. Wipe up anything spilled, especially any red stains (berry juice, red wine, etc) immediately.

Above The table in this spacious dining room has been covered with a cloth to protect the surface.

Living rooms & studies 122–3

Style & color 166–75
Furnishings 176–83
Furniture 184–9
The indoor garden 190–5
Entertaining 196–9

PREVENTION & PROTECTION

Working surfaces

If your desk or table top is fake leather, it should be cleaned by gently wiping it with an almost dry cloth dipped in the suds of a detergent (not soap) solution and polished afterwards with a soft cloth. If it is real leather, use soapsuds. Spilled ink is a problem. Rub the stain cautiously with mineral spirits, but be careful as mineral spirits can remove the color from the leather. Every now and again, feed real leather gently with leather restorer but be careful to avoid touching any gilt decoration.

Any typewriters, computers or other office equipment in your home should be kept covered as much as possible to avoid the buildup of dust. Also avoid spilling any liquid over a keyboard as it will damage the works. Make sure that your machines are regularly serviced and overhauled so that they are kept in good working order.

YOUR FILING SYSTEM

Keep locked away:
- Personal (birth, marriage certificates, passport, etc)
- Legal (will, lease, etc)
- Health (list and dates of family illnesses, medical cards, etc)
- Investments (details of shares, etc)
- Bank (statements, unused checkbooks, etc)
- Insurance (property, contents, etc. Photograph all your valuables and keep photographs of them here)

Keep safely:
- Credit cards (statements, etc)
- Home (all finances)
- Gas, electricity, water, telephone, etc (bills and correspondence)
- Guarantees and operating instructions (for all household appliances)
- Decoration (receipts from furniture, carpets, etc, you have bought; names, numbers and swatches of paint and paper used in your home, etc)
- Personal finance (anything concerning tax, benefits, etc)
- Work (invoices)
- Receipts (any you can offset against taxes)
- Stores (statements and correspondence)
- Car (insurance, license, etc)
- Travel (foreign addresses, travel agents, etc)
- Children (school reports, health, baby-sitters' telephone numbers, etc)
- Pets (licenses, inoculations, etc)
- Hobbies (catalogs, newspaper cuttings, invoices, etc)
- Pending (correspondence you need to reply to; things you are deciding whether or not to keep, etc)

BOOK RULES

Never:
try to make an open book lie flat or you may break the spine;
store books over a radiator or in a very dry room;
pack books too tightly on a shelf or stack too many on top of each other or you may damage their bindings;
pull a book out of a bookcase by the top of its spine or by gripping it tightly with your fingernails or you could damage its binding;
open a valuable book quickly or you could break its spine;
use self-adhesive tape for repairing books – the glue will stain the paper and make it brittle;
allow children to scribble on books.

Right An ingenious solution for where to store all the paraphernalia of the "home office." If carefully thought out, it is possible to keep the typewriter or word processor, files and so on, in a compact space, and yet have them accessible.

BEDROOMS

We spend one-third of our lives in our bedroom, even though most of that time we are asleep. A calm, tidy bedroom is conducive to a good night's sleep, so keep it simple and uncluttered.

Find some attractive bowls to put your jewelry in when you remove it at night or it can get left on the top of dressing tables or chests of drawers and look untidy. Hang up your clothes as soon as you remove them, or drop them straight in the laundry basket.

MATTRESS CARE

- Always follow manufacturers' care instructions and never expect miracles: ring marks may remain after cleaning
- When you buy a new mattress, remove the polyethylene or plastic wrapper and buy a cover of plain or quilted cotton to cover the mattress with. They are easy to wash and will help preserve the mattress. Use a rubber sheet over the mattress if the bed is being slept in by a bed-wetting child or an incontinent adult
- Never roll or bend a spring mattress, just turn it over weekly for the first six weeks and then every three months after that. Reverse the mattress from head to foot at the same time
- Do not allow children to bounce on the bed and sit on the edge as it can damage the springs
- Clean the mattress monthly with a soft brush; using a vacuum cleaner may pull the mattress cover out of shape
- To clean stains from a mattress, tip it on its side. Urine stains should be immediately sponged with cold dishwashing-liquid solution and then rinsed with cold water and a little disinfectant. Blood stains should be sponged with cold, salt water, and well rinsed. Try not to overwet the mattress, and dry it thoroughly before making the bed again. Use upholstery shampoo on stubborn stains

It is important that the bed is comfortable and clean. A great deal of dust can be avoided by using a bedspread. Pillows can be covered with two pillowcases, the top one opening on the other side from the bottom one. Washing bedding regularly and airing your bed every morning will keep it feeling fresh. Bed-making is easier if your bed is on castors. Fitted sheets and duvets also make bed-making quicker.

Sheets are made in many different fibres. Nylon and polyester are cheaper and easy to wash and dry, but need to be washed frequently. A cotton polyester mix feels almost like cotton but needs no ironing. Cotton and linen feel crisp and cold to the touch, and are softer when ironed. Linen is quite heavy when wet. Flannelette is soft and warm, but needs to be washed frequently.

Cleaning bed linen

This can begin once winter is over. Untreated woolen blankets should only be dry-cleaned. Blankets made of synthetic fibers can often be put in the washing machine or dry-cleaned.

Down- and feather-filled duvets and pillows should be taken to a specialist cleaner, whereas other natural-fiber fillings can be dry-cleaned. Duvets and pillows filled with synthetic fiber must be washed or taken to a specialist cleaner; they should never be dry-cleaned. Foam-filled pillows can be washed in warm, soapy water, then rinsed well and dried thoroughly.

Above Fresh air must be allowed to circulate in the bedroom.

NURSERIES & PLAYROOMS

Children generally do not mind how tidy their bedroom, nursery or playroom is – it is only you who cares, so tidy it yourself if you want it to look nice. It is better not to force small children to help tidy, or it may put them off doing it when they get older.

When children are young, the floor space should be kept as clear as possible for them to play in. Take out only a few different toys at a time, rather than their entire toy collection, or they will get bored with everything very quickly. As long as you change toys every day, a few toys will keep their interest for a long time – and there will not be so much clearing up at the end of each day. As children grow older and collect more possessions, they need more storage space and furniture, such as a desk and chair on which to do their homework.

Plastic and wooden toys of children up to nine months old should be washed once a week in a mild disinfectant solution. Soft toys should also be cleaned regularly; follow manufacturers' care instructions. Cleaning toys also gives you a chance to check that they are still safe. Baby equipment, such as high chairs, should also be kept meticulously clean and safe.

Wash children's bedding and nightclothes every few days. Wash those of bed-wetters every day.

Keep the diaper-changing area clean and tidy, and store any medical supplies out of reach. Keep a special bucket with a sterilizing solution in the bathroom for cloth diapers, which should be washed daily, and throw disposable diapers immediately in the garbage or burn them. If your child uses a potty, keep it in the bathroom and wash it with a disinfectant solution after use.

PUTTING TOYS AWAY

Make it as easy as possible for yourself – and your child – to put toys away. Large baskets and plastic bins or cardboard boxes (useful for building bricks, wooden railway pieces, soft toys etc) can be stored away in a corner; shoe bags (for construction kits and other sets) can be hung on hooks within a child's reach. Shoe boxes and plastic jars have myriad uses for storing smaller items. (Jigsaw puzzles are best kept in their original boxes.)

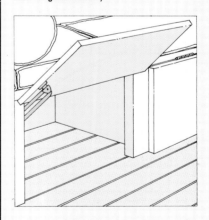

A separate toy cupboard with easy-to-reach shelving is ideal. But, for really fast tidying, build floor cupboards with flip-up lids so you can sweep toys away.

Left A large box for storing toys is essential for keeping a child's room tidy.

General cleaning 18–25
Stain removal 50–1
A–Z of stain removal 52–3

Preparation 78–9
Painting 80–1
Wallpapering 82–3

Around the Home
WALLS & CEILINGS

Plan ahead for easier wall and ceiling cleaning. Light colors show up dirt and stains far more than dark colors, and nonwashable coverings are obviously more trouble than painting your walls with a washable surface. Regular dusting or light vacuuming will help keep walls and ceilings clean. If they do get soiled, and are covered with anything other than paint, read any manufacturer's care instructions before cleaning. Even then, test cleaning methods on an unseen part of the wall or ceiling before removing your stain so that, if your method causes any damage, it will not be visible.

Many stains on wallpapers and painted walls can be removed by gently rubbing with a piece of stale white bread. Or you can make a wallpaper-cleaning dough by mixing 3 tablespoons of flour with 1½ tablespoons of mineral spirits and 1½ tablespoons of water, kneading well for a few minutes, and then rubbing gently along the wall with long, sweeping movements.

Cork

Cork should never be overwet, but just sponged gently with warm, mild detergent solution.

Fabric (including silk)

Always follow the manufacturer's care instructions and never use spot remover or upholstery cleaner. Instead, dab general stains with baby powder, leave for a couple of hours and then gently brush it off. Never attempt to clean silk yourself. Always consult a specialist dry-cleaner.

Grasscloth and burlap

Never use water. Dab stains with baby powder, as for fabric above. Remove general stains on burlap by rubbing gently with a piece of stale, white bread, as for wallpaper.

Paint (water-based)

Keep clean by dusting regularly and using a mild solution of dishwashing liquid on any stains. Rinse and dry well afterwards. Never use abrasive powders and always keep water clean and rinse thoroughly with cold water. If you are cleaning an entire wall or ceiling, cover electric sockets and switches and remove any paintings, sconces, etc. Clean small areas (about 2 ft [60 cm] square) at a time, and rinse and dry each area before moving on to the next bit of wall. Repaint whitewashed (distempered) walls when badly stained.

Paint (oil-based)

Rub with dishwashing-liquid solution or a hot, mild washing-soda solution. Tackle general stains with a liquid nonabrasive cleaner and a soft nail brush.

Polystyrene/Styrofoam (expanded)

Sponge tiles with a warm, mild detergent solution, never anything stronger. Rinse well afterwards and leave to dry naturally. Do not apply pressure or dents will be left. If badly stained, paint with a water-based paint.

Tiles (aluminum and ceramic)

Clean white grouting with an old toothbrush dipped in mild bleach solution and then rinse well. Use a detergent solution for colored grouting. Clean the tiles with a mild detergent solution, then rinse and dry with a chamois leather.

Tiles (mirror)

Wipe with a chamois leather wrung out in a mild vinegar solution.

Wallpaper (nonwashable)

Never use water on nonwashable wallpaper; instead, rub any general stains with stale white bread and rub light smudges and pencil marks with an eraser. Food and grease stains, as well as candle-wax stains, can be removed by placing a piece of blotting paper over the stain and covering it carefully with a warm iron, which will draw the grease out and into the paper. Remove any traces of grease with moistened borax or bicarbonate of soda or with liquid dry-cleaner.

Wallpaper (textured and embossed)

Never press textured wallpaper too hard or overwet it. Clean regularly by brushing or lightly vacuuming and sponge general stains with a little mild detergent solution. Dab grease stains with baby powder. Leave for two hours for the grease to be absorbed and then gently brush the powder off.

Wallpaper (washable)

Treat washable wallpaper with care, as you would water-based paint. Always test any stain-removing materials first and never overwet the surface or the paper will peel.

Wallpaper (vinyl "scrubbable")

Although they should not be overwet, vinyl wallcoverings are tougher and can be washed with a mild solution of dishwashing liquid; stains can be gently "scrubbed" with a liquid nonabrasive cleaner. Crayon marks can be removed with silver metal polish and felt-tip pen stains with neat dishwashing liquid or methylated spirit. Never use ammonia, acetone, abrasives or nail-polish remover on vinyl.

WALLPAPER CARE SYMBOLS

 Spongeable

 Washable

 Super washable

 Scrubbable

PROTECTING PAINT FINISHES

Having decorated your walls lovingly you do not want them to get dirty.
- Varnish provides a protective surface that can be wiped clean.
- In heavily used areas, such as hall-ways, a thin plexiglass sheet attached to the wall provides durable covering.
- A chair rail will prevent chairbacks from scuffing the wall and can become a decorative feature.

Above The cool classic effect of marbling creates interest in an area that is normally neglected, such as landings and stair wells. If you are doing it yourself, use an oil-based paint, which can be cleaned more easily (with mild detergent) than water-based types.

FLOORS

If you dread cleaning floors, choose your surfaces carefully. If children eat in the dining room, do not choose a carpeted floor, but a parquet or cork one. Very light-colored carpets, unless heavily textured, show the dirt quickly. A patterned carpet does not show the dirt as much as a plain one. A marble floor may last for years, but will be colder on your feet than linoleum.

Sweep hard floors regularly, sometimes as often as after every meal if you have small children, and wash them frequently. If you spill something on your floor, you must first scrape off or wipe up any deposit and then tackle the remaining mark. Many floors come with their own proprietary cleaner, or at least their own manufacturer's care instructions. Check these before cleaning.

Cement, concrete and stone

These floors should be regularly scrubbed with detergent or washing-soda solution. Stubborn stains can be treated with a strong bleach solution and then rinsed well with clear water. Never use soap or abrasives; never use acid on limestone. Polishing a stone floor can make it beautiful, but slippery.

Cork

A heavily soiled sealed cork floor can be lightly sanded to remove the surface dirt and then resealed (for care of sealed cork floors, see Plastic films/seals, below). Sponge unsealed tiles gently with a warm, mild detergent solution. Do not overwet them or they may crack. Polish unsealed tiles, but not sealed tiles.

Linoleum

Linoleum should always be kept as dry as possible. Never leave oil or water standing on it and dry well after washing regularly with a liquid nonabrasive cleaner, or washing-soda solution, and then rinsing. Rub scuff marks with an emulsion floor polish and remove crayon marks with silver metal polish. Polishing linoleum will add an extra seal to prevent dirt penetrating the surface.

Marble

Marble stains easily, so wipe up spills at once with warm, soapy water, rinse well and buff with a soft cloth. Wash regularly with a mild liquid abrasive cleaner, then rinse and dry. Never use strong detergents, oil, gasoline or mineral spirits on marble. If the floor becomes badly stained, the surface can be carefully removed by machine grinding but this is a job for a professional.

Above Marble floors are long-lasting and look beautiful. The disadvantages of marble are that it stains easily and can be cold and hard underfoot. It is also one of the most expensive floor coverings.

CLEANING CARPETS

New carpets will shed fluff at first, which should be removed regularly with a carpet sweeper. Once the carpet has been down for six weeks, you can start using a vacuum cleaner daily or weekly, depending on the use the carpet gets.

Antique rugs must be professionally cleaned. Never vacuum; instead, use a carpet sweeper.

Below Quarry tiles and glazed or ceramic tiles require different cleaning techniques. Ceramic and glazed tiles should be regularly cleaned with a mild detergent. Remove general stains by scrubbing with a bicarbonate of soda and bleach paste, iron-based stains with a gentle abrasive cleaner, lime stains with neat vinegar. Mop up general stains on quarry tiles with a liquid abrasive cleaner, and treat white patches with a vinegar solution.

Below Wooden floors should never be allowed to get overwet: always wipe up spills at once. Very stained wood can be sanded. Sealed wood can be rubbed with cold tea or cleaned with a liquid abrasive cleaner; untreated wood should be scrubbed with scouring powder or cleaned with detergent and a little water. Clean waxed wood with a mild detergent solution or fine steel wool dipped in a beeswax-and-turpentine solution, then polish.

Plastic films/seals

Wipe up spills immediately and clean regularly with a detergent solution. Apply a little emulsion or paraffin polish two or three times a year and shine before it dries.

Rubber

Wash rubber only when necessary. Remove fat, grease, oil, gasoline, alcohol and fruit-juice splashes at once and never use detergent, gasoline, wax polish or mineral spirits on your rubber floor. Simply wash with soapy water and then rinse, and rub off any scuff marks with a mild abrasive liquid.

Rugs (antique, dhurries, fur, Oriental, shaggy, skin)

Always have these professionally cleaned.

Rush and sisal matting

Never overwet or use any detergent, ammonia, washing soda, household soap or strong alkalis on it. Vacuum frequently and tackle nongreasy stains with the foam or lather of carpet shampoo and greasy stains with an aerosol spot remover. Lift loose unbacked mats occasionally to sweep the floor under them. Mist rush matting occasionally with cold water, using a plant sprayer.

Slate

Wash regularly with washing-soda solution and rinse well. Use a proprietary cleaner for more stubborn stains. Do not use soap on slate floors as the scum will be impossible to remove.

Vinyl

Clean regularly with warm soapy water or a little liquid abrasive cleaner, but only if necessary. Rub stubborn marks gently with fine wire or steel wool. Always rinse well and never use gasoline, lighter fluid, mineral spirits or wax polish on vinyl. In winter, keep a vinyl floor warm as cold makes it brittle.

Energy saving 62–3
Electrics 76–7
Metals 102–3

LIGHTING

If you keep bulbs and shades clean, you will have a lighter home for less money. Shades need to be dusted regularly and cleaned according to their surface. Keep a large supply of all the bulbs you need and a list of what they all are for when you need to replace them.

Once a month, unplug the lamp, remove the bulb and take off the shade. Wipe the bulb and dry it thoroughly before replacing. Clean the base of the lamp: porcelain, china and glass bases can be cleaned with a damp cloth dipped in a mild dishwashing-liquid solution and carefully rinsed and dried well afterwards. Marble and alabaster bases just need wiping with a damp cloth. Lacquered metal bases just need dusting; otherwise clean with the appropriate metal polish.

Lampshades

Fabric (nylon, rayon, cotton, etc) shades can be dipped repeatedly in warm soapy water, rinsed in clear warm water and left to dry naturally in a hot place. This should be attempted only if the frame of the lampshade is plastic rather than metal, as metal can rust, and only if the fabrics are sewn rather than stuck together, as water can soften the glue and cause the lampshade to become unstuck. Before you start dipping, you must also be sure that your washable fabric shade has a washable lining. If you are unsure or your shade is valuable, have it professionally dry-cleaned.

Plastic shades can be dipped in warm, soapy water as well. Do not rinse them, but leave a little of the soap on the shade to make it dirt-resistant. Glass shades should be treated with care. Always put a plastic bowl in the sink first, in case the shade slips out of your hands when wet.

Some shades are fragile. Paper shades should just be dusted – buy another shade when the first becomes worn and dirty. Silk shades should be professionally cleaned before they begin to look dirty, as should any fabric shades that are hand-painted.

Metal shades need only be regularly dusted and fiberglass shades should just be carefully wiped with a damp cloth. Rub buckram (stiffened cloth) shades with turpentine and clean metallic paper shades by rubbing with a mixture of 1 tablespoon (15 ml) of turpentine and $\frac{1}{4}$ pint (150 ml) of paraffin, and then wiping it off.

SAFETY FIRST

- Never touch a light or a live socket with wet hands
- Switch off and unplug lamps before you clean them or their shades
- If cleaning wall or ceiling lights, first turn electricity off at the fuse box
- Make sure your stepladder is steady and that you are wearing nonslip shoes before climbing on the ladder to clean ceiling lights
- When taking down bowl shades from the ceiling to clean them, make sure there is someone to take the shade from you. Do not climb up and down ladders, holding fragile shades
- While cleaning light fittings, always make sure that wires are unfrayed and secure. Rewire if necessary
- Never put back a lampshade that is scorched without first making sure that the shade is on straight and that the lightbulb is not too strong
- If you are removing lightbulbs from a light to wash them, make sure they are completely dry before replacing them or you could get an electric shock

Left Concealed lighting is more gentle on the eye.

CLEANING LIGHTS

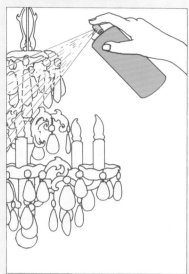

Crystal chandeliers
Wear cotton gloves and dip your fingers into a solution of ammonia to which you have added a little dishwashing liquid. Rub the crystal clean. Or use a special spray cleaner.

Candlesticks
Never scrape wax off candlesticks with a knife or you may scratch the surface. Either put them in the freezer for half an hour and then peel the wax off (this does not harm silver) or pour warm water into the candleholder and remove the wax with a soft cloth once it has softened.

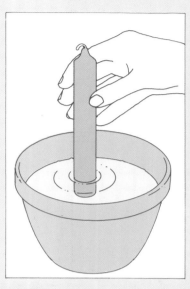

Candles
Sponge candles with methylated spirit to clean them. To make candles fit candlesticks, dip the ends in hot water until they are soft enough to be molded into shape.

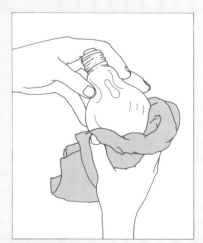

Lightbulbs
Once a month, remove all your lightbulbs and clean them with a damp cloth. Before replacing them, rub a few drops of your favorite perfume onto the bulb. The lit bulb will fill the room with a delicate smell.

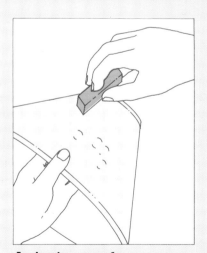

Imitation-parchment lampshades
Rub imitation-parchment shades clean with an eraser.

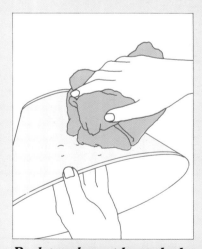

Real-parchment lampshades
Wipe real-parchment (vellum) shades clean with a solution of 1 tablespoon (15 ml) soap flakes, 1 tablespoon (15 ml) water and 2 tablespoons (30 ml) methylated spirit.

FURNITURE & SOFT FURNISHINGS

Manufacturers of modern pieces of furniture often provide care instructions, which should be followed. Antique furniture should always be professionally restored, and you should carefully identify your surfaces before cleaning them.

Upholstery

Taking precautionary action may prevent your getting nervous about your furniture, especially your upholstery. Certain fabrics – patterned and those with a thick weave – show dirt and stains less easily than pale, finely woven fabrics. Otherwise protect upholstery by spraying it with a fabric protector or fit loose covers that can easily be machine-washed or taken to the drycleaner. Replace loose covers that have been laundered while they are slightly damp; they are easier to get on and will mold into shape better.

Regularly remove all cushions and beat upholstery to bring the dirt and grit to the surface. Then vacuum with a nozzle attachment. To freshen up upholstered covers, rub them over with a soft pad of clean white material dipped in pure alcohol – which will clean any grease stains before evaporating – or use a proprietary upholstery cleaner.

If you do spill something on your sofa or armchair, do not panic. Remove the surface deposit first and blot dry with a clean, white cloth and then tackle the stain, making sure you do not overwet the upholstery. Follow any manufacturer's care instructions, check on the properties of the fabric before starting cleaning and test your cleaning product on an unseen corner first. Never use household detergent on upholstery, and do not use methylated spirit on acetate or triacetate, modacrylic or rayon upholstery. Always consult professional upholstery cleaners for antique furniture and for cleaning tapestry covers and velvet, or velveteen, upholstery.

Leather

Sponge leather upholstery clean with a soft cloth wrung out in pure soap-flake solution (and do not rinse afterwards) or use a damp cloth rubbed over a bar of glycerine soap. Occasionally feed

Above Loose cushion covers and seat covers are much easier to clean than fitted ones, and if made from a serviceable, preshrunk cotton can be put in the washing machine. Clean cane furniture by dusting or wiping it with a mild soapy solution with a little ammonia added to it.

leather with a special hide cleaner. Never overwet leather upholstery or use detergent, dry-cleaning fluid, gasoline or ammonia on it. If leather pieces are valuable or nonwashable, do not attempt to clean them yourself, but consult a professional upholstery cleaner.

Bamboo, basketware and cane

Regularly dust or vacuum bamboo, basketware and cane furniture. Bamboo should be scrubbed gently with warm soapy water plus a little borax, then rinsed with cold salt water and left to dry. Never use detergent on bamboo. If basketware and cane furniture is varnished, wipe it with mild soapsuds to which you have added a little ammonia. If unvarnished, scrub lightly with warm, salt water. Always rinse well with cold water to restore the stiffness, then wipe off excess moisture and leave the piece to dry naturally.

Glass, mirror and metal

Glass tabletops and mirrors can be cleaned by rubbing with vinegar or alcohol and then drying with a paper towel and buffing with newspaper. Using a cotton cloth leaves a "lint" on glass, so always use paper or a linen cloth for drying.

Metal furniture should be cleaned with dishwashing-liquid solution or the appropriate metal polish. Rub rust stains with turpentine to remove them.

Plastic

Plastic surfaces, such as acrylic, plexiglass and polyurethane, should never be cleaned with abrasives, chemicals, acids, petroleum, bleach or disinfectant, spot removers or acetone, as these could scratch, or otherwise damage, the surface. Do not dust them with a dry cloth either as it will make them even more static. Instead, wash with a warm (not hot), mild liquid-detergent solution or buy some special antistatic polish or other proprietary cleaner.

Wood

Wooden furniture needs special attention, depending on the finish and on the age of the piece. All wood furniture needs to be carefully dusted, but, unless they are antique, regularly used pieces, such as dining-room tables, may need polishing every week or so. Other pieces of furniture may well need to be polished only every six months or so. Make sure you are using the correct polish: old-fashioned beeswax is best for antique furniture. Never use too much water on wood or use oiled or treated dusters on waxed furniture. If there is a buildup of old polish, this can be removed with a proprietary cleaner.

Use a proprietary stain remover to get rid of coffee cup or glass stains.

Curtain care

Curtains should be washed or dry-cleaned according to the fabric they are made of and whether or not they are lined and interlined. Some curtains can be gently washed in the machine, but always hand-wash or dry-clean delicate fabrics and follow any manufacturer's care instructions. Remove hooks, curtain weights, etc, from curtains before washing and test fabrics in discreet spots before plunging them in the bath. Never soak rayon curtains or iron plastic shower curtains. Large, heavy curtains are impractical to clean at home, and are best left to professionals.

Although they look attractive, curtains that bunch on the floor get dirtier more quickly than those that hang clear.

CLEANING BLINDS

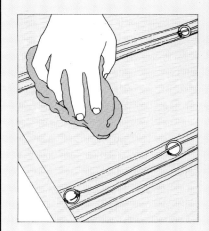 

Roller and Roman blinds made from a washable fabric can be taken down from the window and gently scrubbed with warm soapy water. Then rinse them in cold water and dry them naturally. If they are made from a nonwashable fabric, you can clean them by rubbing with dry flour using a rough flannel cloth.

Dust Venetian blinds regularly with a feather duster to keep them clean – this may help to cut down on the amount of major cleaning you have to do! When they get very dirty, take them down, put them in the garden and hose them down,

scrubbing with a brush and some soap at the same time. Do not put them in the bath as they may scratch its surface.

If you cannot remove them, put on a pair of old cotton gloves, and wash the blinds with your fingers. To clean wooden venetian blinds, dip gloved fingers in liquid furniture polish and rub one slat at a time, changing the gloves frequently. Painted and plastic blinds should be washed with mild soapy water, using the same technique. If the soapy water has little effect, try paint thinner or mineral spirits.

Regular cleaning 22–3
Bathrooms & utility rooms 28–9
Stain removal 50–1

Your responsibility 70
Safety with water 71
Electrical maintenance 76–7

Laundry

As with everything else, if you want to save time when washing, check the care labels on items before you buy them. Avoid garments that have to be dry-cleaned or hand-washed and ideally buy drip-dry items to save ironing.

Sorting your washing

Before you begin your washing, look at the care label in each of your clothes, sheets, etc, and sort the items into piles, depending on the wash suggested by the care label. You can wash clothes with different care labels together, providing you use the lower of the two recommended temperature washes, but in the long term this will affect the quality and wear of your clothing.

If washed with colored clothes of the same fabric, whites will gradually become gray; and if mixed with non-colorfast clothes of the same fabric, colorfast fabrics will soon look dull. Sorting your washing correctly takes a minute and ensures that your clothes will be clean, and that the colors will not run or creases set into the fabric. Basically your piles should look like this: whites together, reds and browns together, blues and blacks and greens together, hot-wash items together, hand-wash items together, etc.

Will it run?

If an article has no label, hand-wash it at first in cool water. The next time you wash it, increase the temperature of the water slightly. If it seems to withstand this treatment, try the gentlest machine-wash setting. If you are not sure whether a fabric is colorfast or not, leave a piece of wet cotton batting on an inconspicuous part of the garment for a few minutes. If any dye comes off on the cotton batting, the garment is best hand-washed on its own, or dry-cleaned professionally.

Always wash dark red and dark blue cotton articles separately when they are new as these colors often bleed at first. If you do have an accident in the washing machine and all your wash turns pale blue, remove the item that has bled and immediately put the rest of the wash through the same wash cycle again. It may help to remove the color.

Delicate fabrics

If garments are antique, very delicate, irreplaceable or very expensive, wash them by the correct method or by hand in cool water or take them to be professionally dry-cleaned. Loose covers, net curtains and washable suits are best washed with care. If in any doubt, it is always best to go to a specialist cleaner. Embroidered textiles, tapestry, needlework and pile fabrics, such as velvet, velveteen, chenille and delicate silk damask, should all be dry-cleaned.

If the manufacturer suggests dry-cleaning a garment it is because the colors will run in water or because the fabric will shrink enormously or because trimmings, pads, etc, will not wash. It may be that the manufacturer is just playing safe, but unless you are prepared to risk ruining the item by hand-washing it, have it dry-cleaned.

Loading the washing machine

Most weekly washes divide into two or three groups. When loading your washing machine, do not exceed the manufacturer's recommended weight for the machine and certainly never force clothes in until the drum is tightly packed or clothes will be badly washed and very creased. Most towels and cloth diapers are very absorbent, so reduce the load if it is all or part towels or diapers. Also reduce the load for man-made and drip-dry noniron fabrics according to the manufacturer's instructions.

Before washing

Before you start washing, make sure all the pockets are empty and that all holes and tears are mended, as washing will make them bigger. Close zippers and hooks, open shirt buttons, as they are more difficult to open before ironing when the shirt is still damp, and put stockings and tights in a pillowcase to stop them wrapping round everything and each other.

Some woolens, even when labeled hand-wash, can be machine-washed on a low temperature. Some machines even have a wool label setting especially designed for this. Wrap woolens in a towel before putting them in the washing machine as this keeps them in shape. Do not dry woolens in a dryer unless the care label on the garment says it is safe to do so.

Pre-soaking

While the first wash is on, remove any stains from items due for the second wash. If collars and cuffs are very soiled, scrub them lightly by hand first with a bar of household soap and a nail brush before putting them in the machine with the rest of the wash; or use a stain remover. Often pre-soaking really dirty items, like tablecloths, napkins and badly soiled sports clothes, in a plastic bucket filled with a warm-water proprietary prewash product is the best way to begin to clean them.

Never soak silks, woolens, leather, fabrics with flame-resistant finishes, drip-dry or noncolorfast fabrics. Never put biological detergents in metal buckets, or soak metal zippers in a biological-detergent solution as it will cause the metal to rust. Never soak whites and colored fabrics together in case colors run – there is nothing more frustrating than seeing a favorite white item come out of the wash tinted a delicate shade of pink or blue!

Hot wash

Boil handkerchiefs, facecloths and babies' diapers every few washes to keep them clean or soak them in diaper-sterilizing solution before putting them in the washing machine (diapers should be soaked before every wash). Always rinse diapers well, as any remaining soap can irritate your baby's skin.

Drying clothes

Dryers are expensive to run and waste energy, and clothes do not smell as fresh afterwards. If you must use a dryer, use it on the cool setting. Most fabrics will crease less in a cool tumble and there is less danger of shrinkage. Woolens and other knitted fabrics should not be tumble dried at all.

Useful tips
- Most fabrics need less ironing if you give them a good shake, stretch them to remove creases and then hang them up, either indoors or outside. Hanging pleated skirts and other items on hangers can also reduce ironing
- Lay knitted fabrics flat on a towel to dry having first pulled them gently into shape

- Fabrics you wish to iron later, such as silks, chiffons, cottons, crepes and linens, should not be allowed to dry out completely. They could all be rolled together and left for a few hours to dry out a little and then ironed
- Nylon is discolored by the sun, and wool and silk are weakened. Dry them indoors

WASHING SYMBOLS AND CARE LABELS

Always use the recommended-care label advice to achieve the best results and help make your clothes look good and last longer.

Red = Do not do/use   Amber = Use caution   Green = Go ahead

 Do not wash. RED

 Hand wash gently in lukewarm water. AMBER

 Machine wash in lukewarm water (up to 40°C, 100°F) at a gentle setting (reduced agitation). AMBER

 Machine wash in warm water at a gentle setting (reduced agitation). AMBER

 Machine wash in warm water (up to 50°C, 120°F) at a normal setting. GREEN

 Machine wash in hot water (not exceeding 70°C, 160°F) at a normal setting. GREEN

 Dry on flat surface after extracting excess water. AMBER

 Tumble dry at low temperature and remove article from machine as soon as it is dry. Avoid over-drying. AMBER

 "Drip" dry – hang soaking wet. GREEN

 Tumble dry at medium to high temperature and remove article from machine as soon as it is dry. Avoid over-drying. GREEN

 Hang to dry after removing excess water. GREEN

 Do not use chlorine bleach. RED

 Use chlorine bleach with care. Follow package directions. AMBER

 Do not iron or press. RED

 Iron at a high temperature (up to 200°C, 390°F). For example, this is recommended for cotton and linen. GREEN

 Do not dry clean. RED

 Dry clean, tumble at a low safe temperature. AMBER

 Dry clean. GREEN

WASHING MATERIALS & EQUIPMENT

There is such a wide range of both washing materials and fabrics available on the market that it can be confusing. To complicate matters further, several entirely new ranges of environmentally (and physically) safe products are appearing on the market. If these are available to you, use them, otherwise follow the guide below. Always read any instructions given on the item you wish to wash, as well as those on the product and on your washing machine.

Washing powders

Washing powders can be soap powders, synthetic detergent powders or a blend of the two. Some are best for hard-water and some for soft-water areas. They are used for normal machine-washing, although some have less lather than others so are better in certain types of washing machine. Read the package and your washing-machine manual for further information.

Many washing powders work better in hot water, which is a waste of energy. Many contain pollutants that can cause eczema and other skin problems. Use environmentally safe products when available. If you must use detergents, experiment by using less than the recommended amount. Soap powders are less effective in hard-water areas, so it is better to use synthetic detergent powders than to add more soap powder. Add water softener to your wash for more effective cleaning rather than extra detergent. You may find that you need less than you thought.

Biological (enzyme) detergents

These are designed for removing protein stains, such as blood, eggs, fruit, etc, that cannot be removed by other washing powders. The enzymes work by breaking down proteins. They can be used for soaking items and they can also be used for washing, although the enzymes become ineffective at temperatures higher than 140°F (60°C).

Soap flakes

These produce a lot of foam, which is excellent for hand-washing lightly soiled articles, woolens and other delicate fabrics, especially in soft-water areas. For hard-water areas, use synthetic detergent flakes/liquid. Do not use soap flakes for machine-washing as they produce too much foam.

Bleach

Soaking white fabrics for an hour in a bucket of cold water to which a tablespoon of bleach has been added can make them noticeably whiter. Always read manufacturers' instructions before using bleach and use with care. A mild solution of hydrogen peroxide is safer than chlorine-based bleaches, which can damage or destroy silk, wool, leather, rayon, elastane and resin-treated fabrics, as well as cottons with special finishes. Never use undiluted bleach and always rinse well after use.

Fabric softener

Fabric softener (or conditioner) is added to the final rinse, and its effect lasts only until the next wash. It works by coating fibers with a material that makes them feel soft. It also reduces the static electricity that causes man-made fibers to cling. Fabric softener contains enzymes that can be harmful to, or may irritate, some skin, especially that of babies. Never use fabric softener undiluted, and make sure detergent is completely removed from the item before you apply the fabric softener or a chemical reaction is produced that reduces the effect of the softener. For a natural softness that will irritate no one, hang washing outside to dry.

Starch

Sprays or powders applied before ironing will stiffen cotton or linen fabrics.

THE "GREEN" WASH

Although enzymes do provide an effective washing agent, many people are allergic to them, and they can cause both skin and breathing problems. Bleaching agents can also irritate the skin. On a global scale, the phosphates found in detergents will overfertilize algae, which will multiply and clog up the Earth's water. This overproduction of algae has serious consequences because it reduces the oxygen supplies needed by fish and plant life and this eventually causes them to suffocate.

With increasing awareness of environmental issues, there are now many phosphate-free, biodegradable washing products on the market, suitable for both machine- and hand-washing, which will neither irritate your skin nor pollute the waters. Another alternative is to make your own environment-friendly washing agent. You can make your own soft soap for hand-washing by dissolving 2 cups of grated bar soap in 1 gallon (4.5 l) of hot water. Simmer for ten minutes and leave to cool before using. Or, if you prefer, you could use plain, unperfumed soap flakes.

If you have to deal with badly soiled garments, using bleach or detergent is not the only solution. Pre-soak heavily stained garments in a mild borax solution (1 tablespoon borax to 1 gallon [4.5 l] water), which will deodorize as well as remove stains. Another clever trick is to try adding 1 teaspoon of white vinegar or baking soda to each machine load of washing to freshen clothes and to remove smells. To save energy, hand- and machine-wash with cold or cool water whenever possible.

If you have blankets, duvets and pillows dry-cleaned, make sure you air them thoroughly when you get them home and before you use them. The fumes are toxic. Always get the above items professionally dry-cleaned: the fumes left in items cleaned in dry-cleaning machines cannot be removed.

WHICH MACHINE?

When choosing equipment for washing and drying clothes, you need to answer the following questions:

- What space have you available?
- How much do you want to spend?
- How large is your weekly wash?
- Is there a setting for economy-load washes?
- How much time do you want to spend washing?
- Do you have many woolens and other delicate items to wash?
- Can you do a separate spin for hand-washed items?
- Can you use the detergent of your choice in the machine?

- Do you want to be able to dry items as well or have you got somewhere to hang them up to dry?
- How easy is it to get your machine serviced?
- Will they service your washing machine if it is installed in a bathroom?
- How easy is it to clean the filter?
- Is the hose long enough? (If not, will they extend it for you before you buy?)
- Can you move the machine easily? Has it got castors? (Avoid machines that have to be bolted to the floor.)
- Are the instructions easy to follow?
- Have you asked friends what washing machine/dryer they would recommend?
- Have you done sufficient market research?

Choosing a washing machine and dryer

There are two main types of washing machine; semi- and fully automatic. Twin-tubs are semi-automatic, which means they are cheaper but that you have to work a lot harder. Both the washtub and spin cycles are loaded from the top and are useful for people with small washes as they do not take large loads or very bulky items.

Fully automatic machines are usually large enough to take a family wash, and some of them incorporate dryers. Front-loading automatic machines are the most expensive, but all you have to do is select the setting. Top-loading machines will carry out all the same washing processes but you have to change the controls from one cycle of the wash to the next.

Wringers can be bought both free-standing or attached to a washing machine and are either hand-operated or electrical. They do not get clothes dry enough for ironing.

A spin cycle will remove excess water from items and speed up drying. Some spin cycles will rinse as well.

Dryers are expensive to run but they can make ironing easier by reducing the wrinkling of clothes. Do not install a dryer in a room where ventilation is a problem as they generate a lot of moisture, or else choose a model with a moisture-collecting chamber. Do not overload your dryer, and remember to remove any fluff from the filter after use.

Unsightly appliances can be tucked away into cupboards. However, you may need to install special outlets and waste pipes.

HAND-WASHING & IRONING

Sort out your hand-wash according to the colors and fabrics of the items you wish to wash, referring to any care labels for guidance.

Soak all items, apart from those made of wool, silk, noncolorfast or flame-proof fabrics, for a few hours before washing to loosen the dirt. Make sure the detergent or soap powder has thoroughly dissolved before putting the garments in. If you are soaking garments in biological detergent, use a plastic bucket and do not soak any clothes or cushions with metal zippers.

Woolens

Wash woolens in a warm solution of soap flakes with as much lather as possible. Knead and gently squeeze the lather through the garment; do not rub. Be as quick as you can and try not to stretch the garment. Rinse in warm water, using the same movements as for washing. Add a splash of vinegar to the final rinse to help remove soap. Squeeze the garment gently to remove excess water, then lay it flat on a towel, and gently pat the garment into shape. Lay another towel flat on top and then roll

the sandwich up so it looks like a sausage and stamp on it to remove as much water as possible. Unroll the towels, remove the garment and place it flat on another towel to dry naturally away from a direct heat source. When nearly dry, press with a cool iron.

Blankets

Wash blankets in a bath or large basin so they will not crease. Squeeze out water before drying, but do not wring or twist. Hang the blanket lengthways on a line to dry, so that as much of the blanket as possible is supported.

Permanent-press and drip-dry

Wash garments with permanent-press or drip-dry finishes separately in warm water. Rinse them in warm water and put them on a hanger to dry or simply fold them to drip-dry. Do not use hot water and do not spin, wring or squeeze the fabric while it is wet or they will be pulled out of shape.

Wash acrylics as for wool.

Do not wash elastic and elasticized

Above Hanging newly washed sheets on a line leaves them virtually crease-free.

STARCHING

Starch is normally used to stiffen cotton and linen fabrics only. There are three methods of starching: using hot or cold water or an aerosol.

Hot-water starch is made by mixing starch powder with boiling water to produce a whitish mixture. You dip the clothes into the mixture, making sure the starch has been evenly absorbed by the fabric. Then iron the fabric while still damp. Cold-water starch is used in exactly the same way.

Aerosol starch is convenient, but expensive. The result lasts only until the garment is next washed, but it is ideal for freshening up clothes between washes or if you only have one or two items that need starching.

---

items in hot water or they will shrink. Do not wring or pull them when wet either or they will stretch. Remove excess moisture by spinning them in the washing machine or rolling in a towel.

IRONING

As with most other household jobs, the equipment used for ironing is of vital importance, both for the finished result and for your health. Make sure the height of the ironing board can be adjusted so that you can iron comfortably both sitting down and standing up. Cover the board with a thick pad, which should be wrinkle-free, and buy two ironing-board covers so that one is always clean. A sleeve board and pressing cloth are both useful, but not essential, as is a cord holder, which will prevent the cord falling onto the board and getting in the way. If you do not use a cord holder, put the cord behind you and to your working side.

Choosing an iron

There are many different types of irons to choose from. Steam irons are heavier than nonsteam irons, but essential if you tend not to find time for ironing until items have dried out. Choose one that can get into corners easily; an open handle can do this better but is less balanced and less easy to grip than a closed handle. Preferably your iron should be capable of both dry and steam ironing and should have a wide range of temperatures, to suit each fabric type. A spray attachment is also useful for dry ironing.

Rotary irons are expensive and take up space. They will save time if you have a lot of linen to iron and, with practice, can also be used for shirts.

Golden rules

Before ironing, check attached care labels to find out what setting to use and make sure articles are at the right stage of dampness (see box). Start by ironing items that need a cool iron and, if you think your iron may be too hot, test it on a seam or hem. If the iron starts sticking to the material, let it cool down.

With large and awkward garments, first iron all the double parts (pockets,

IRONING DIFFICULT FABRICS

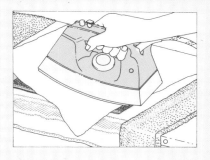

Embroidery

Lay a bath towel on the ironing board and cover it with a clean dish towel. Place the embroidery face down on it. Put a clean, damp cotton or linen cloth on it and iron quickly with a hot iron.

Woolen coats and suits

Put the garment on the ironing board, right side up, place a damp cloth, preferably a pressing cloth, over it and iron with a medium-hot iron. Remove the now dry cloth, lift the garment, and with the back of a clothes brush beat the steam out of it so it will not mark or shrink. Repeat the process on the rest of the garment.

Velvet

If possible, iron velvet face down on a velvet board, or cover your ironing board with some velvet of the same color. Otherwise cover the ironing board with a thick towel, turn the garment inside out, and iron the velvet lightly on the wrong side with a warm iron.

seams, hems, etc) on the wrong side of the material. Then turn the garment over onto its right side and iron all the small, fiddly parts (collars, cuffs, sleeves, belts, etc) before ironing the main part of the article.

Iron the collars of shirts and blouses first until quite dry. Start on the wrong side and then turn over onto the right side. Begin ironing at the center of the collar and work the iron outwards, first to one tip, then to the other. Next iron the cuffs, again first on the wrong side and then on the right, and then iron the sleeves (right side only), making sure you do not iron a crease into them. Iron the yoke, if any, then iron the main part of the shirt or blouse, beginning at the buttons on the front and working round the shirt until you reach the buttonholes on the other side. Always iron into gathers and pull pleats into shape and then iron on top. When ironing circular tablecloths, mats, etc, iron from the outside and work toward the center. When ironing handkerchiefs, iron round the hem first and then iron over the whole surface.

After ironing, leave clothes to air and become bone dry before wearing them or putting them away. Never rest the iron with the sole plate down; rest it on its heel and do not walk out of a room leaving the iron on.

HOW WET?

When you begin ironing, make sure that all articles are the correct dampness. Most articles should be slightly damp (see below for those that should not). If they are too dry you will not get rid of all the creases and will not achieve a good finish; if they are too wet you will waste time and energy. A steam iron or water spray will help to dampen articles that are too dry.

Fiber	Damp/Dry	Temperature
Acetate	Damp	Cool
Acrylic	Dry	Cool
Angora	*Do not iron*	
Cotton	Damp	Hot
Cotton, drip-dry	Dry	Cool
Linen	Damp	Hot
Mohair	*Do not iron*	
Nylon	Dry/Damp	Cool
Polyester	Dry/Damp	Cool
Silk	Damp	Warm
Polyester	Dry	Warm
Triacetate	Dry/Damp	Cool
Viscose rayon	Dry/Damp	Warm
Wool	Dry/Damp	Cool

Stain Removal

Materials for the job

- Absorbent materials (soft white cloths, paper tissues, small sponges, blotting paper, cotton batting)
- Clothes brush
- Fine sandpaper for suede cleaning
- Spatula (useful for scraping off solid spills)

Cleaning products

Absorbent powders
(Fuller's earth, French chalk, powdered starch, talcum powder)
These can be difficult to remove from dark, nonwashable fabrics and should not be used on carpets.

Acetic acid
(White vinegar is diluted acetic acid; lemon juice can often be used instead)
Never use acetic acid on acetate or triacetate fabrics. Always test first.

Acetone
(Nonoily nail-polish remover contains acetone and can be used as a substitute)
Inflammable; toxic fumes. Always test before using. Harmless to most fabrics. Never use on acetate, triacetate, modacrylic, viscose, rayon, or on acrylic or modacrylic carpets. Use amyl acetate instead (see below).

Ammonia
Always follow instructions and test fabric for colorfastness before using. Poisonous; toxic fumes. Never use undiluted. If spilled on skin, wash immediately with white vinegar or lemon juice. Use white vinegar (see Acetic acid above) or lemon-juice solution if ammonia may affect the color of the article. Never use on silk, wool or their blends, nor on woolen carpets. Always rinse well after use; never let it dry on the fabric.

Amyl acetate
Inflammable; toxic fumes. Always test before using. Use on acetate, triacetate, modacrylic, viscose rayon instead of acetone.

Bleach
(See Chlorine bleach and Hydrogen peroxide below)

Borax
Harmless to most fibers. Can be used directly on white fabrics; otherwise dilute with water. Always test before using.

Chlorine bleach
Never use undiluted. Treat fabric several times with a weak solution rather than once with a strong one. Never soak fabrics in chlorine-bleach solution for longer than 30 minutes. Always rinse well after use; always test before using and follow instructions carefully. Never mix with other cleaning agents. Poisonous. Never use on silk, wool, leather, linen, viscose, rayon, elastane or on drip-dry or deep-colored cottons, or on articles with flame-proof or crease-resistant finishes. Never use in a metal bucket or on garments with metal zippers. Hydrogen peroxide is a safer bleach to use.

Detergents (biological)
Always test before using and follow instructions. Make sure your family is not allergic to this product and do not use if you have small children. Never use on protein fibers, wool or silk or noncolorfast, flame-resistant or rubberized fabrics. Never soak zippers or other metal fastenings.

Detergents (nonbiological)
Follow instructions. Use lather only on nonwashable items.

Eucalyptus oil
For oil and tar stains. Use undiluted. May smell during and after use.

Glycerine
Use diluted with warm water to soften old stains. Rinse well after use. Safe on most fabrics.

Glycerine soap
Always follow instructions.

Hydrogen peroxide
A mild bleach. Always follow instructions and test before using. Never use on nylon or flame-resistant fabrics.

Lemon juice
Useful to stop process started (discoloration, burning, etc) by strong alkalis such as ammonia.

Lighter fluid
Inflammable. Always use undiluted and test before using. Useful as weak grease solvent. Never use on acetate, triacetate, modacrylic, viscose or rayon fabrics.

Methylated spirit
Inflammable; poisonous. Use undiluted and always test first. Never use on acetate, triacetate, modacrylic, viscose or rayon fabrics.

Nail-polish remover
(See Acetone above)

Soda syphon
Plant spray will do as a substitute for squirting water.

Spot remover
A grease solvent (aerosol, liquid or paste) that may work on other stains. Apply only to dry surfaces and always follow instructions. Treat fabric several times with a weak solution rather than once with a strong one. Inflammable. Never use on leather, suede, rubber, plastics or waterproofed fabrics.

Turpentine
Inflammable. Always test before using. Never use on acetate, triacetate, modacrylic, viscose or rayon fabrics.

White vinegar
(See Acetic acid above)

Stain-removal methods

There are four basic methods of removing stains, and the one you choose depends on the article stained, on the fabric stained and on the stain itself. These are referred to in the text opposite as methods 1 to 4.

Method 1 (spot-cleaning)

This method can be used to remove stains from carpets (but not rubber-latexed or foam-backed) and fitted upholstery as well as from loose fabrics. Test cleaning agents first on a hidden part of the fabric before beginning stain removal. Wait 15 minutes to see if fabric is damaged. If it is, consult professional dry-cleaners.

First remove any surface deposit from the stain. Then, if possible, put a wad of clean white cotton batting or a similar absorbent pad under the fabric with the wrong side of the fabric facing upwards. Saturate another clean pad with the recommended spot remover and begin removing the stain, working from the outside of the stain toward the center to avoid making rings. Change pads on both sides frequently and blot the stain dry after each application of spot remover.

If you cannot get to the back of the stain, use the same method, working from the front and using pads on the front of the fabric only. Never pour the spot remover directly onto the surface and always use it sparingly. Do not rub too hard.

Method 2 (absorbent)

This method cannot be used on carpets as the absorbent material can often not be removed later.

First remove any surface deposit, then spread the fabric as flat as possible. Apply the recommended absorbent powder thickly over the stain and flatten it gently. Remove the powder by brushing, shaking or vacuuming as soon as it is saturated and reapply as necessary. Be careful about applying absorbent powders to dark, nonwashable fabrics as they can be difficult to remove.

Method 3 (wet-cleaning)

This method can be used to remove stains from most fabrics, as well as from upholstery and carpets. Test any cleaning agents used on a hidden part of the fabric before using it.

On **washable fabrics**, once you have removed the surface deposit, rinse quickly with cold or warm water. Then soak the fabric in a solution of the recommended cleaning agent. If the stain persists, sponge it a little on the wrong side of the fabric using a clean white absorbent pad on both sides of the fabric, one for absorbing the stain and the other for applying the cleaning agent. Rinse with clean water and blot dry. Never soak wool, silk, noncolorfast or flame-proof fabrics.

On **nonwashable fabrics**, after you have removed the surface deposit, sponge the stain gently with cold water. Then, if possible, stretch the stained part of the fabric over a bowl and pour cold water over the stain from a height of 2–3 ft (60–90 cm).

On **upholstery and carpets**, remove the surface deposit and blot the stain. Then sponge the stain lightly with either foam shampoo or the foam of a solution of either upholstery or liquid carpet shampoo and warm water. Blot often and be careful not to overwet the upholstery or carpet. Then rinse by sponging gently with cold water. Never use household detergent on upholstery or soap, soap powder or soda on carpets.

Method 4 (boiling water)

This method can be used only on white and colorfast linens.

Stretch the stained fabric over a basin and sprinkle the stain with a little detergent or dry borax. Pour boiling water through the stained part of the fabric from a height of 2–3 ft (60–90 cm) and then rinse the fabric well.

GOLDEN RULES FOR REMOVING STAINS FROM FABRICS

- Act fast. The faster you act, the milder the remedy needed
- Make sure you know exactly what you are going to do before you begin
- Remove surface deposit and blot dry
- For grease stains, cover with an absorbent powder. Never use an absorbent powder on carpet
- For fruit/wine stains, cover with salt. Never use salt on a carpet
- For other stains, rinse with cold water and blot dry
- Always follow manufacturers' care instructions, if available
- Always follow instructions on cleaning products carefully
- If necessary, test cleaning product first in an inconspicuous place
- Be careful. If in doubt or unable to identify a stain, consult professional cleaners
- Once a stain has been removed, dry quickly and evenly with a hair-dryer or fan heater to prevent a ring appearing – unless the fabric is one that is not intended to be dried next to a direct heat source
- After treating the stain, launder, dry-clean or shampoo as usual
- If the stain persists, consult professional cleaners

SAFETY FIRST

- Be careful when storing and using cleaning agents. Some are highly inflammable and poisonous. Some can burn the skin, so protect your hands when using them
- Label all agents clearly
- Always follow any instructions given, and use cleaning agents in small quantities
- When following instructions on cleaning products, keep to one set of measures (either metric or imperial) as the conversions may not be exact
- Always test the cleaning agent first in an inconspicuous place to make sure it will not damage the fabric or remove any color
- Thoroughly clean any equipment used during stain removal
- Never use cleaning fluids near an open flame, or smoke while using
- Keep windows open when removing stains
- Never mix cleaning agents. Thoroughly rinse the first one out before applying the second
- Keep all cleaning agents out of the reach of children

A–Z OF STAIN REMOVAL

Although these methods have been effective, there is no guarantee that they will be wholly successful. Many items may benefit from washing, dry-cleaning or gentle bleaching after the stain has been partially removed.

Always make sure that the cleaning product is suitable for the material. If in any doubt, have items professionally dry-cleaned.

Before starting, read the Golden Rules box and Stain Removal Methods on page 51.

Acids *(acetic, hydrochloric, sulfuric, etc)*
Strong acids may cause permanent damage. Rinse with cold water at once (Method 3), then sponge with ammonia or bicarbonate-of-soda solution (Method 3) and rinse.
Carpets: apply weak solution of borax (Method 3). Use with care.

ADHESIVES
Some adhesives now have their own solvent; if possible use these, following instructions.

Adhesives *(clear or contact)*
Use nonoily nail-polish remover, acetone or amyl acetate (Method 1).

Adhesives *(epoxy resin)*
Stains cannot be removed once dry. Use acetone or amyl acetate (Method 1). Use lighter fluid on synthetic fabrics (Method 1).

Adhesives *(latex)*
Remove at once with a damp cloth. If dry, use spot remover or turpentine (Method 1).

Adhesives *(model-making cement)*
Stains cannot be removed once dry. Use spot remover or amyl acetate (Method 1).

Adhesive tape
Use spot remover (Method 1).
Carpets: if stains are indelible, trim carpet with scissors.

ALCOHOL

Alcohol *(beer)*
Use detergent or upholstery or carpet shampoo (Method 3). Sponge dried stains with white-vinegar solution (Method 3).

Alcohol *(spirit)*
Use detergent or borax solution. If necessary use hydrogen-peroxide solution (Method 3).

Alcohol *(wine)*
Washable fabrics: pour white wine on red wine stain or cover with salt (Method 2). Use boiling water (Method 4) or soak in biological-detergent or borax solution (Method 3). If necessary use spot remover (Method 1).
Nonwashable fabrics: sponge with warm water, then use hydrogen-peroxide, borax solution or upholstery/carpet shampoo (Method 3). Use glycerine solution on dried stains.
Carpets: flush with soda water or warm water or white wine for red wine stains (Method 4). Blot. Shampoo. Sponge dried stains with methylated spirit (Method 1). Test first.

Alkalis *(ammonia/washing soda)*
Strong alkalis may cause permanent damage. Sponge at once with cold water. Use lemon-juice or white-vinegar solution (Method 1).

*Animal stains (see **Vomit**)*

*Antiperspirant (see **Deodorant**)*

*Baked beans (see **Beetroot**)*

*Ballpoint (see **Ink**)*

*Battery acids (see **Acids**)*

*Beer (see **Alcohol**)*

Beetroot
Use biological-detergent solution (Method 3). If necessary, use spot remover (Method 1).

Blood
Washable fabrics: soak immediately in cold water then wash in cold biological-detergent solution or with upholstery shampoo (Method 3). Remove dried blood with the above method. If badly stained, try using ammonia (Method 3), then wash as above. Never use hot or boiling water on blood stains as it sets the stain.
Nonwashable fabrics: blot or brush off surplus. Sponge with cold water plus ammonia, or upholstery or carpet shampoo (Method 3), then rinse.
Upholstery: rub lightly with a paste of cornflour and cold water. Brush off when dry. Repeat.

*Boot polish (see **Grease**)*

*Burns (see **Scorch marks**)*

*Butter (see **Grease**)*

Candle wax
Fabrics: remove deposit. Place blotting paper over (and under if possible) fabric and press quickly with a warm iron, changing the paper often until the wax is absorbed. Remove color traces with methylated spirit or spot remover (Method 1).
Upholstery/carpets: chill wax deposit with an ice cube, then scrape off wax. Remove color traces as above.

Carbon paper
Use methylated spirit or spot remover (Method 1).

*Cat mess (see **Vomit**)*

Catsup
Washable fabrics: use biological-detergent solution (Method 3).
Nonwashable fabrics: remove deposit and wipe with cold water. When dry use spot remover (Method 1).

Chewing gum
Chill with ice cube to harden (or put in freezer). Scrape off then use spot remover (Method 1).

Chocolate/Cocoa
Use biological-detergent or borax solution (Method 3). If necessary, use spot remover (Method 1).
Upholstery: use spot remover (Method 1).

*Chutney (see **Jam**)*

*Cod liver oil (see **Grease**)*

*Cologne (see **Perfume**)*

*Coffee (see **Tea**)*

*Cosmetics (see **Makeup**)*

Crayon
Use spot remover or lighter fluid (Method 1).

Cream
Washable fabrics: use biological-detergent or borax solution (Method 3). Use spot remover (Method 1) if necessary.
Nonwashable fabrics: use spot remover (Method 1).

*Creosote (see **Tar**)*

*Crude oil (see **Tar**)*

Curry
Soften with glycerine solution (Method 1), then use biological-detergent solution or upholstery/carpet shampoo (Method 3).

Deodorant
Soak in white-vinegar or ammonia solution (Method 3). If necessary use methylated spirit (Method 1).

*Dog mess (see **Vomit**)*

*Duplicating ink (see **Ink**)*

Dyes
Washable fabrics: Soak in biological-detergent solution (Method 3), then bleach if necessary, or use proprietary color remover.
Nonwashable fabrics: use methylated spirit plus ammonia (Method 1).

Egg
Use cold salt water (Method 3); hot water will set the stain. Use biological-detergent solution or upholstery/carpet shampoo (Method 3) and spot remover (Method 1) if necessary.

*Face cream (see **Foundation cream** or **Grease**)*

*Fats (see **Grease**)*

*Feces (see **Vomit**)*

*Felt-tip pen (see **Ink**)*

Fish slime
Use salt-water solution (Method 3).

*Flowers (see **Grass**)*

Foundation cream
Remove deposit.
Washable fabrics: soak in ammonia solution (Method 3). If the stain has dried, remove excess, loosen it with glycerine solution, then rinse and wash.
Nonwashable fabrics: use spot remover (Method 1) or absorbent powder (Method 2).

Fruit and fruit juice
Cotton or linen: cover stain with salt and then use boiling water (Method 4).
Other fabrics: use borax solution or upholstery/carpet shampoo (Method 3). Loosen dried stains with glycerine solution; rinse and dry before cleaning.

*Glue (see **Adhesives**)*

Grass
Use eucalyptus oil or glycerine or methylated spirit (Method 1).

Gravy
Use spot remover (Method 1). If gravy is browning only, no grease, use biological detergent solution (Method 3).

Grease
Remove deposit and use salt, cornflour or another absorbent powder (Method 2). Brush off when grease is absorbed. Repeat. Or use blotting paper and a warm iron (see Candle wax). If necessary, use spot remover (Method 1).

*Hairspray (see **Nail polish**)*

*Hair cream/oil (see **Grease**)*

Honey
Use biological-detergent solution (Method 3) or spot remover (Method 1).

*Ice cream (see **Cream**)*

INK
There are proprietary ink solvents available, so try these first.

Ink *(ballpoint and felt-tip)*
Use methylated spirit (Method 1) or spot remover.

Ink *(Indian)*
Use cold water then soap-flake solution (Method 3). Then ammonia solution (Method 3).

Ink *(printing)*
Use turpentine (Method 1).

Ink *(washable)*
Most writing inks can be removed by sponging or soaking at once in cold water (Method 3). Then use biological-detergent solution (Method 3). If necessary, use spot-remover (Method 1). If yellow stains remain, see Rust.

Iodine *(tincture)*
Washable fabrics: sponge immediately with water, then detergent solution

(Method 3). If necessary, have dry-cleaned professionally.
Nonwashable fabrics: use alcohol (Method 1) or have dry-cleaned professionally.

Jam/Marmalade
Use liquid-detergent or biological-detergent or borax solution (Method 3). If necessary, use spot remover (Method 1).

Juice (see Fruit)

Lead pencil
Use a soft eraser. If necessary, use spot remover or methylated spirit (Method 1).

Leaf stains (see Grass)

Lemon juice
Use borax solution (Method 3).

LIPSTICK
Sponge with eucalyptus oil or glycerine. Rinse. Then use lighter fluid or spot remover (Method 1).

Lipstick (indelible)
Rub with lard then use spot remover (Method 1).

Liqueurs (see Alcohol)

Makeup (see Foundation cream, Lipstick and Mascara)

Margarine (see Cream)

Marmalade (see Jam)

Mascara
Use spot remover (Method 1).

Mayonnaise (see Cream)

Meat juices (see Blood)

MEDICINE

Medicine (iron-based, see Rust)

Medicine (syrup-based)
Use soap solution (Method 3).

Medicine (tar-based, see Tar)

Metal polish
Use white spirit or lighter fluid or spot remover (Method 1).

Mildew
Washable fabrics: cover with lemon or lime juice and salt and leave to dry in the sun. Or use biological-detergent solution (Method 3) and dry in the sun after rinsing.
Nonwashable fabrics: have professionally dry-cleaned.

Milk
Sponge or soak in cold water. If necessary use borax solution or upholstery/carpet shampoo (Method 3). For hot milk stains use spot remover (Method 1).

Motor oil (see Tar)

Mud
Remove deposit. Use mild detergent solution (Method 3). Brush off dried stains then use spot remover (Method 1) if necessary.
Carpets: vacuum when dry. Use carpet shampoo (Method 3). If necessary, use methylated spirit (Method 1) on remaining color.

Mustard
Washable fabrics: use detergent solution (Method 3).
Nonwashable fabrics: use spot remover or methylated spirit (Method 1). Soften dried stains with glycerine, then rinse and dry before using spot remover.

Nail polish
Remove deposit then use acetone, amyl acetate or nonoily nail-polish remover (Method 1). If necessary, use methylated spirit (Method 1).

Nicotine
Use eucalyptus oil or methylated spirit (Method 1). Or soak in biological-detergent solution (Method 3).

Oil
Use absorbent powder (Method 2) then spot remover (Method 1) if necessary. (For vehicle oils, see Tar.)

PAINT

Paint (cellulose)
Use acetone or amyl acetate (Method 1).

Paint (enamel and oil-based)
Use turpentine or paintbrush cleaner (Method 1).

Paint (water-based)
Sponge immediately with cold water. Dried stains are usually impossible to remove. Try methylated spirit (Method 1).

Paraffin (see Grease)

Pencil (see Lead pencil)

Perfume
Sponge with water at once, then wash. If stain is dried in or fabric is nonwashable, use glycerine solution and rinse. Launder if possible or take to dry-cleaner.

Perspiration
Sponge with biological-detergent solution (Method 3). If stains are dried in, use white-vinegar or ammonia solution (Method 3) or spot remover (Method 1).

Plasticine/Play-Doh
Remove deposit then use spot remover or lighter fluid (Method 1).

Raindrops (see Water)

Resins (see Tar)

Rust
There are proprietary rust removers available on the market.
Washable fabrics: rub with lemon or lime juice and salt, and dry in the sun.
Nonwashable fabrics: have professionally dry-cleaned.

Salad dressing (see Cream)

Sand
Brush or vacuum. Use biological-detergent solution (Method 3).

Sauces (see Catsup or Cream)

Scorch marks
If cloth fibers have been burned, scorch marks may be impossible to remove.
Washable fabrics: use borax, hydrogen-peroxide or ammonia solution (Method 3).
Nonwashable fabrics: rub with glycerine solution, then rinse. If necessary, sponge with borax solution (Method 3).
Carpets: trim burned fibers with scissors. Then use carpet shampoo to which you have added 1 teaspoon (5 ml) white vinegar (Method 3). Rinse, then blot. For extensive burns, and burns on synthetic-fiber carpets, consult professionals.

Shellac
Use spot remover or methylated spirit (Method 1).

Shoe polish
Scrape off deposit. Use spot remover or mineral spirits (Method 1). Soak washable fabrics in ammonia solution (Method 3) afterwards, if necessary.
Upholstery and carpets: first use proprietary shampoo (Method 3). Then try spot remover (Method 1).

Smoke (see Soot)

Soap
Rewash article and rinse thoroughly.

Soot
Vacuum deposit. Do not brush as the stain may be pushed in.
Washable fabrics: soak in biological-detergent solution (Method 3).
Nonwashable fabrics: use an absorbent powder (Method 2), then vacuum again. Then use a spot remover (Method 1). Have large stains professionally dry-cleaned.

Soup (see Catsup or Cream)

Spirits (see Alcohol)

Suntan lotion
Use biological-detergent solution (Method 3).

Sweat (see Perspiration)

Syrup (see Jam)

Tar
Remove deposit. Use eucalyptus oil, glycerine solution or spot remover (Method 1).

Tea
Use borax solution or upholstery/carpet shampoo (Method 3). Loosen dried stains with glycerine solution first. (See also Milk, if coffee or tea contained milk.)

Tobacco (see Grass or Nicotine)

Tomato (see Fruit juice)

Transfer pattern (see Carbon paper)

Treacle (see Jam)

Turmeric (see Curry)

Urine
Washable fabrics: soak in biological-detergent solution or diaper-sterilizing solution (Method 3).
Nonwashable fabrics: sponge with cold water, then white-vinegar solution (Method 3). Have dried stains professionally dry-cleaned.
Upholstery: blot, then use spot remover (Method 1). If possible, rinse under cold running water.
Carpets: flush with soda water or sponge with white-vinegar solution (Method 3). Blot. Shampoo with added disinfectant (Method 3).

Varnish (see Shellac. If cellulose or polyurethane, see Paint)

Vinegar
Soak or sponge in biological-detergent solution (Method 3). (If the color of the fabric has been affected, see Acids.)

Vomit
Washable fabrics: remove deposit, then rinse with cold running water. Soak in biological-detergent solution (Method 3).
Nonwashable fabrics: remove deposit.

Sponge with upholstery or carpet shampoo, borax solution or ammonia solution (Method 3).
Upholstery: remove deposit. Blot then use spot remover (Method 1). If possible, rinse under cold, running water.
Carpets: remove deposit. Flush with soda water. Blot. Sponge with borax solution (Method 4). Shampoo with added antiseptic.

Water
Wash washable items. Hold nonwashable items in the steam from a boiling kettle or have dry-cleaned.
Carpets: mop up immediately. Dry outside or artificially, raising the carpet from the floor. Call professional dry-cleaner if flooded.

Wax (see Candle wax)

Wax polish (see Grease)

Wine (see Alcohol)

Yogurt
Use biological-detergent solution (Method 3) or spot remover (Method 1).

HOME REPAIRS

Your Home Workshop

TOOL CHEST

Every home should contain at least the basis of a workshop and the necessary tools to handle simple household repairs. Time and worry, as well as expense, will be saved if the right tools are at hand to deal with emergencies.

It may be enough for you to keep a drawer full of tools, or fill that space under the stairs with your tool chest, but you could find you get so carried away that you end up occupying the entire garage.

You may be tempted to buy the entire tool chest shown here, but it is better to start in a modest way and gradually purchase additional tools as and when the need arises – and then only if you have the space for them. It is frustrating not having the right tools for the job and having to work within the limits of those tools you do have, but at first it is sensible to buy the most basic and versatile tools and add specialized tools only when you need them.

When you do buy, always buy the best quality tools you can afford as they will last longer and perform better. You may also find that you look after expensive tools more carefully and do not lose them as often as inexpensive ones. If you are going to use a certain tool only once then rent it. It not only saves money but also means that, by using someone else's tool first, you familiarize yourself with it and will know what to look out for should you decide to buy the same piece of equipment later.

What equipment?

To start with all you need are the tools suggested in the box opposite. Whether or not to buy more equipment depends on how serious a carpenter you plan to be, how much space you have and what type of work you are planning to undertake.

Right A well-organized workshop, with adequate storage, surfaces, lighting and chairs, means that you will have the tools you need at hand, and enough space to work as comfortably as possible.

A flat surface

For serious woodworkers, the most important thing is a workbench, or at least as good a work surface as possible, if you do not wish to go out and buy a workbench at once. A Workmate is a very satisfactory substitute, and two Workmates are even better for holding long pieces of work. Your bench should be about 3 ft (90 cm) high, or more or less to suit your size – be careful not to strain your back – and should have a sturdy flat surface and a sunken area in which tools can be put when not in use. If possible, it should be equipped with two vices, a series of bench stops to hold the work while planing and some bench hooks to help when sawing.

It may be worth having several clamps, but they are not essential. Sliding wooden clamps to hold wood together while gluing it are useful for furniture repairs, especially as they do not leave dents in the wood, which metal clamps can do. Particularly useful are bar clamps, which are particularly long clamps.

Measuring

In addition to your steel tape, a folding rule (3 ft or 1 m) is best for small measurements. A combination square that measures both 90° and 45° is another useful measure. An adjustable bevel – an adjustable "square" that can be used for copying existing angles onto your piece of wood – is essential for any angled work.

Buy a short spirit level, about $2\frac{1}{2}$ ft (80 cm). That way it can fit into alcoves and awkward spaces and you can always hold it above a long piece of wood for a longer wall. Check for accuracy by turning the level around. If the bubble returns to the same place, the spirit level is accurate.

Marking

Scribes, a marking knife and a hard (2H) pencil are all used for marking wood once it is measured. Scribes are usually used for metal but are extremely accurate and easier to use than marking knives, which can slip. Pencils should be sharpened to a point shaped like a chisel: they last longer and are more

---

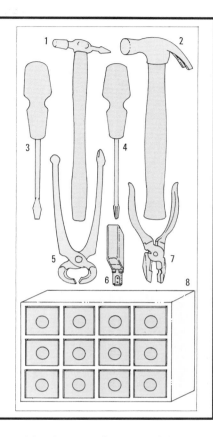

VERY FIRST TOOL CHEST

Before you buy a complete home workshop, see whether you enjoy doing-it-yourself. Below is a shortlist of very basic equipment that you will need:

- 16 oz (450 g) clawhammer (hold it near the base for maximum effect) (2)
- Small cross peen hammer (1)
- Small and medium flat-head screwdrivers for general use (never use them for opening cans of paint (3)
- Crosshead screwdrivers (again, the more the better) (4)
- Pincers (for pulling nails out of wood) (5)
- Pliers (for general work). Buy them with wire cutters at the side (7)
- Assortment of nails, screws, plastic wallplugs, picture hooks, etc. (Unless buying very unusual types, buy screws by the box of 100)
- Little chest of drawers in which to keep nails, screws, etc (8)
- 10 ft (3 m) steel tape measure with both imperial and metric measurements (6)

---

accurate. A bradawl can also be used for marking wood, although its main use is for starting small screws.

Chisels

If you can only afford one, a $\frac{1}{2}$ in (12 mm) wood chisel is the one to buy. Otherwise, buy chisels as and when you need them. Plastic-handled chisels are sturdier than wooden-handled ones, which need to be used with a mallet – or use a clawhammer and a wooden block.

Hammering

Two tools useful for smaller nails and panel pins are the cross peen (pin hammer) and the nail punch. The peen is used for hammering pins while they are held between the thumb and finger and the punch is used to hit nails once they are below the surface.

Sawing

There are many different saws that can be bought, but the most useful all-round saw is known as the crosscut or

combination panel saw, which has 10 teeth to 1 in (2.5 cm) and will do most work reasonably efficiently. If you can, buy a saw with a wooden handle (it is the most comfortable to use); a silver steel blade is the best. A coping saw is also useful for cutting awkward shapes.

Drilling

If you are considering buying an electric drill, remember that you can also add sawing and sanding attachments so that this tool has more than one use. A hand drill may also be useful, especially for drilling holes in wood-paneled walls. A hand brace is not essential unless you are drilling a lot of larger holes.

Planing

Wood is smoothed and reduced to size with a plane. There are several different types of plane for different purposes, but the versatile "jack plane" is the best all-round tool for planing, shaping, sizing and smoothing.

MAINTENANCE

Keep equipment in good working order

It is essential to keep tools sharp and properly set – often they will be even better than new if well cared for. Having sharp tools means they will perform better and the work will be easier. Indeed, you may have to sharpen tools when you first get them, especially if they are secondhand.

Sharpen wood chisels regularly and do not use them on other materials. Wood planes need regular adjustment and sharpening. Only when they are correctly set do they work well. Chisels, planes and other blades are usually sharpened with an oilstone.

Saw blades are sharpened with a file – a boring, though not difficult, task. It is easier to take your saws to a good local tool shop to do the job for you.

As well as sharpening, blades may need regrinding from time to time to remove nicks and other damage or simply to resquare them. This can be professionally carried out at a tool shop.

Always work on a flat, steady surface when sharpening tools. Do not remove more metal than is necessary to obtain the correct cutting angle.

When working

Do not force tools to do jobs they seem to be resisting. Either they may not be sharp enough or you may be using the wrong piece of equipment – or possibly the right piece of equipment in the wrong way. Even an electric drill should be treated with respect. It is easy to overload and damage the motor of a small electric drill, especially when using a circular-saw attachment; so if the motor loses speed or the motor pitch lowers, stop what you are doing and let the motor recover properly.

Another reason a piece of equipment might be struggling with its job is that there is an obstacle in the way. Take care to remove all nails when working on old wood: they can damage tools such as saws and chisels.

Avoid using tools for jobs they were not intended to do, as tools are fragile and can easily be damaged by the wrong use. For the same reason, do not lend tools or machinery to friends, no matter how difficult you may find it to say "no"; your tools are for your use only.

After use

Rub tools after use with an oily rag to clean them. The best oil for the purpose is sewing-machine oil.

Keep tools carefully stored and protect their cutting edges with plastic edging. Take care of measuring tools too. Tools should always be kept in a dry place and, if you are not going to use them for some time, it is a good idea to cover the metal parts with a light oil.

TAKING SAFETY PRECAUTIONS

When using power tools, always make sure the cord is safely behind you. Allow only the minimum amount of cord necessary to come over your shoulder or it could be sawed in two by mistake.

Before drilling into walls or floors, make sure there are no electric wires or pipes in the way.

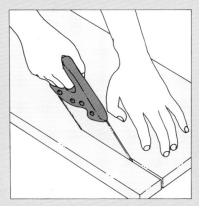

When cutting with anything sharp, from a saw to an adjustable knife or chisel, keep your fingers well out of the way of the blade. Always cut away from you: place your fingers behind the saw or knife, rather than in front, in case the tool slips, and hold the chisel so that it will not be pushed toward you.

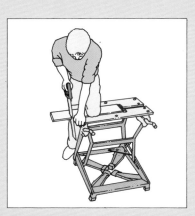

Work at the correct level for your body so that your back takes as little strain as possible. When sawing, keep your workbench low so your knee can rest on the wood; when planing, raise the workbench so you do not have to bend too far. With hammering, take fewer, harder hits, holding the hammer at its base, so you get a decent swing.

HOW TO STORE TOOLS

Your first job may be to build your own tool chest. This design allows room for more tools than shown here. Pegboard walls are useful because they allow tools to be moved easily to a new place when you add to your collection.

Do not throw tools together haphazardly because it will be difficult to find what you need when you want it. Also if tools are kept too close together they can damage each other.

The storage system you choose should enable equipment to hang or lie in such a way that tools are not damaged. For example, a plane should always lie on its side when it is not in use to protect the blade; paintbrushes should hang so that their bristles stay in shape, and no tools should be stored in a bathroom, laundry room or damp cellar where the condensation or damp will rust them.

A handy storage idea is to nail the lids of screw-top jars filled with nails, screws, etc to the undersides of shelves.

Care of tools
Check that all tools are in perfect condition. Sharp tools should be kept sharp. This means you are less likely to struggle with them and they are less likely to slip. Make sure hammer-heads are securely fixed onto their handles: it can be dangerous if the head suddenly flies off as you are using it.

Hang your tools from hooks, away from children.

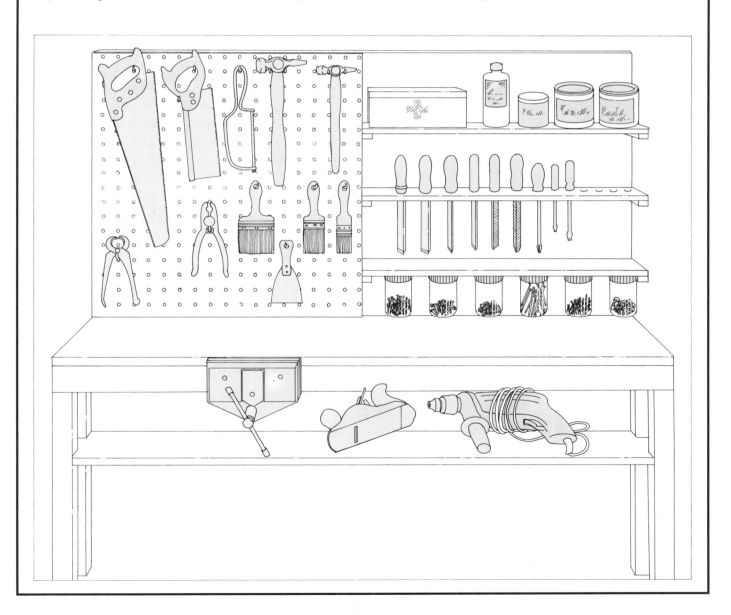

Energy Saving
THROUGHOUT THE HOME

If you are consciously saving energy, you should be able to answer "yes" to all, or at least most, of the questions below. If you have answered "no", then think about why and do something about it. Be sensible: there is no need to make drastic temperature reductions when there are old people or babies about, or when you are ill. There is also no need to turn off all the lights when you are out: a dark house may encourage burglars. Be aware of energy and you will notice how easy it is to save it.

The outside
Have you insulated your attic and temporarily blocked off unused chimneys? Have you got cavity walls and, if so, are they insulated? Are your radiators or electric heaters on inside rather than outside walls? If you live in a very windy site, have you planted a hedge or some trees that will act as a windbreak?

Windows
Have you installed double-glazing, either fitted or secondary? If not, have you put weather stripping around windows in all rooms apart from the kitchen and bathrooms? Do you use heavy interlined curtains or shutters? Have you put a valance at the tops of your windows? Do you close curtains or shutters at night and open them during the day? Are you blocking any under-window radiators with long curtains? Have you large skylights that are letting out the heat?

The front door
Have you put a flap or box behind your mail slot to stop drafts? Have you covered a very drafty front door with a thick curtain? Have you thought of building an internal lobby or a porch?

Floors
Have you covered all solid concrete floors? Have all your carpets got underlay? Have you filled up all the gaps between floorboards and baseboards? Have you nailed quadrant molding around really drafty baseboards?

Water
Have you insulated your water heater? Is the thermostat set for no higher than 30°F (55°C)? Are the cold-water tank and all the water pipes in the attic insulated? Have you reduced the water used by your toilet?

Lighting
Have you turned off any light that is not at this moment in use? Do you usually turn off any lights not in use? Are you using bright lights where essential and low-wattage bulbs elsewhere? Are you using dimmer switches?

Living-room
Have you made sure your living-room temperature is no higher than 68°F (20°C)? Are the television, stereo system and other electrical appliances turned off when they are not in use?

Garden/yard
Does your pet-flap automatically shut firmly behind your pet? Are you collecting rainwater with which to water your garden in the summer? Have you covered your soil with compost or bark to reduce evaporation?

Doors
Have you put automatic door closers on any doors that you use a lot? Do you close doors of unused rooms? Do you limit full heating to one or two rooms whenever possible?

Heating
Have you had your furnace and/or boiler serviced this year? Have you replaced old and worn heaters with more efficient new ones? Do your heating and hot-water systems have time- and temperature-control thermostats attached to them?

You
Have you put on another layer of clothing rather than turn up the heating? Are you trying to use less heat all the time? Are you using hand- rather than power-tools as often as possible? Are you walking, cycling or using public transportation whenever possible?

INSULATION

Insulating your home will help keep your heating costs down; it will also help keep the house cool in summer.

Water heaters

A 3 in (8 cm) thick insulating cover placed around the heater can cut heat loss by 75 percent.

Heater covers can be bought ready-made. You must measure the diameter and the vertical height of your tank from the bottom to the top of the dome so that you can buy the correct size of cover.

Attics

As much as 25 percent of your heat may be lost through your roof. If you have a flat roof, you could attempt to fit a false ceiling under your existing one or you can have it expertly insulated. Lining your ceilings with cork or wooden tongue-and-groove planks will help keep heat in.

Insulating materials

Attic insulation consists of filling the spaces between your ceiling joists with a thickness of at least 3 in (8 cm), prefer-

ably 4 in (10 cm), of insulating material. This can be either glass- or mineral-fiber matting or a similar material. Alternatively, a loose-fill material (such as mineral wool, vermiculite or glass or cellulose fiber) can be poured between the joists.

Tanks and pipes

When you insulate the attic, it gets colder, therefore any tanks and pipes in the attic will be more liable to freeze in cold weather, so these must also be insulated.

Tanks need at least 1 in (2.5 cm) of insulation, which can be either sheets of expanded polystyrene (styrofoam), fiberglass rolls, or a loose fill, which will need to be contained in a box. Unless water pipes are under the attic insulation or within the tank casing, they should all be insulated.

INSULATING THE ATTIC

As long as your attic has no awkward corners or obstructions, and there are regular spaces between the joists, you can use fiberglass batts. This comes in a roll and is simply unrolled and laid between the joists. You should also insulate overflow and hot-water pipes, and taps and joints (inset). For this, you can use rolls of fiberglass, foam, felt or

a similar material, or preformed molded insulation. Do not forget to insulate the trap door as well and make sure it has a draft-proof seal, and cover the sides and lid of the water tank. Do not, however, insulate under the tank as the warmth from below should be allowed to rise to prevent the water in the tank freezing in winter.

ATTIC SAFETY

- If there is any old asbestos in your attic, you will have to ask a specialist firm to remove it
- Always use proper insulating materials; old rags and newspapers are a fire hazard and attract insects
- Do not stand on the "ceiling" between the joists: it will not carry your weight. Instead lay a plank on top of the joists and stand on that
- Make sure there is always enough ventilation in your attic, otherwise condensation can occur and slowly damage the timber. Leave room for air to enter under the eaves
- Attic insulation made of fibers can irritate skin and lungs. Do not open the package until you are in the attic and wear rubber or gardening gloves, thick shoes and socks and a dust mask. It may help to wear goggles or glasses as strands of fiberglass can irritate your eyes. Once the job is over, rinse hands before washing them

BLEEDING RADIATORS

Trapped air will reduce the efficiency of any radiator. You can tell if there is any air trapped when the radiator feels hot at the bottom and much cooler at the top. As air rises in the heating system you will find that any radiators on the top floor of your house will have to be "bled" more often than any lower down. It is a good idea to check periodically if radiators need bleeding, especially after they have been turned off for a while, say, after the summer.

On most radiators all you need to

"bleed" them (clear the airlock) is a square-ended hollow key, which will open the vent valve. If you have lost your key and need a replacement, take an impression of the vent valve with a bar of wet soap and buy another the same size. Simply insert the key and slowly turn it anti-clockwise until you hear the hiss of escaping air. The moment the hissing stops and hot, dirty water starts flowing out around your key, shut the valve again. Always hold a jar or large rag under the valve to collect the water. If necessary, repeat the process later.

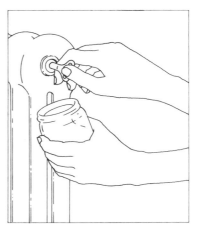

DRAFT-PROOFING

In an uninsulated house, drafts through windows, doors, unused fireplaces, gaps between floors and baseboards, ill-fitting doors and windows and ceiling hatches can account for as much as 15 percent of your heat escaping. All this can be avoided by using proper draft-proofing.

Ventilation

It is important not to overdo draft-proofing. Both you and your home need some fresh air, especially if you are to avoid damp. If you have a forced-air furnace, boilers, real fires, gas or oil heaters, fresh air is essential. And to avoid condensation there must be adequate ventilation in rooms in which moisture is produced, such as the kitchen. An exhaust fan will help, but opening a window is best.

Windows

There are many ways to draft-proof a window, from the very cheap and simple right through to double-glazing, but draft-proofing is much easier if your windows are hinged or pivot rather than sliding or sash.

There are various types of strip that can be stuck around the edges of windows to stop drafts coming in. Masking tape is the cheapest to use but not the most visually pleasing. Do not use other adhesive tapes as they leave a mark when removed. You can buy adhesive foam strips, which are cheap but, like masking tape, need to be replaced every year. Metal and plastic strips are more expensive, but last longer. Make sure that windows can still be securely closed after draft-proofing.

Doors

For draft-proofing the doorframe (two sides and the bottom – leave the top free for ventilation) you can use

adhesive plastic foam strip, which is cheap and easy to use but will probably need to be replaced annually. Plastic or metal strips can be glued or nailed to the inside of the doorframe and are not noticeable when properly fitted.

The gap between the bottom of the door and the floor is probably the largest and may be the problem to solve first.

Above A heavy curtain over the front door will help minimize cruel drafts during winter.

There are various types of aluminum strips fitted with plastic or rubber strips or brushes, which attach to the door, the floor or to both. There are also automatic draft-excluders that lift up when the door opens.

You can make your own seals with carpet or display felt. There are also less high-tech solutions, such as the very simple stuffed fabric draft-excluder or the thick curtain that can be hung from the top of your door (do not hang it from the doorframe or you will not be able to open the door). Draft-proof mail slots and pet-flaps too for additional warmth.

Fireplaces

Unused chimneys and flues can be sealed to cut off escaping heat. If you block up a fireplace opening, fit a ventilated cap on top of the chimney stack and a ventilation grille in the chimney-breast or flue, to prevent condensation. Or block off the chimney at the top to prevent down-drafts. Do not block up a flue permanently: few things are cosier than an open fire, provided your flue is in good repair.

Floors and baseboards

Heat can also escape through floors. You can lose up to 15 percent of your home heat under-foot. Gaps in floorboards and baseboards are the main causes of heat loss through wooden floors. A large, and costly, project may be to lift all the floorboards and put fiberglass or a similar matting material underneath them to act as insulation. On a smaller scale, you can fill the gaps between floorboards with plastic wood or papier-mâché (see page 87). Wooden strips nailed down between the edge of the baseboard and the floorboards will also help remove drafts.

Carpets

Using wall-to-wall carpets, ideally with felt or rubber underlay, will reduce heat loss, particularly with a concrete or tiled floor. Again, make sure you do not stop under-floor ventilation, which is necessary to protect the floor timbers from dampness and rot. Never block up any airbricks in external walls whether they are over- or under-floor: they are there to provide ventilation.

Double-glazing

If a room is well heated all day and if it has a large window, you may consider double-glazing, especially if you wish to cut down on noise as well: but as glazing is expensive, it may be worth doing only if your existing window is in bad condition and needs replacing anyway.

There are two main ways of double-glazing: secondary glazing and sealed unit glazing. Secondary glazing involves leaving your existing window *in situ* and adding a second window that opens independently. The advantages of secondary glazing are that you can keep any period windows and window-frames while removing any drafts from existing ill-fitting windows. Secondary glazing can be sliding or hinged and can match your existing windows exactly so that it is discreet and barely noticeable; usually, however, secondary glazing is made of metal or plastic.

Sealed unit glazing involves a window consisting of two sheets of glass accurately spaced apart in the factory and looking very similar to one pane of glass. The advantage of this type of glazing is its convenience, because it means you have only one window to open and close.

A third, and the cheapest, form of double-glazing is simply to cover your window with plastic sheeting for the winter. Attach the sheeting with double-sided adhesive tape or drawing pins and do not despair if some of your view is lost. Plexiglass panels are sturdier, reusable and easier to see through. Once again, you will not be able to open your window and you will also need to find somewhere to store the panels in the summer, when not using them.

For ideal heat insulation, the air space between the two panes of glass should be no more than $\frac{3}{4}$ in (2 cm) wide. For sound insulation an air gap must be at least 4 in (10 cm) wide and a heavier grade glass must be used. You will have to decide which of the two is your greater priority. If you are in any doubt, consult a double-glazing specialist. Always make sure double-glazed windows are easy to open or it could be dangerous if there is a fire.

RADIATORS

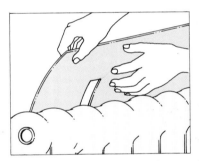

If radiators are placed on external walls, especially in old houses where the wall is not well insulated, there is a large amount of direct heat loss. One way of reducing this is to fix a sheet of reflective material, such as cooking foil or aluminum sheet, to the wall behind the radiator. You may be able to buy ready-made sheets; otherwise back the foil with cardboard and attach that to the wall, making sure that there is still enough space left behind the radiator for air to circulate.

If the radiator is under a window, you can place a shelf above it, again allowing enough room between the radiator and the shelf for air to circulate. Some modern radiators are designed to circulate the hot air around the room, so do not need a shelf or reflective backing sheet. Check with the manufacturer or supplier if your radiators do this.

REHANGING

Most drafts in a house are caused by badly fitting doors and windows. Wet weather causes wood to swell and stick, and windows and doors may need re-planing in order to open and close properly. They will also then need repainting, so remember to plane down enough wood to allow for the thickness of at least three coats of paint. Equally, the weather could have caused window- and doorframes to have warped or shrunk; again these will have to be seen to. There are several reasons why a door or window may need to be rehung; so check carefully before you start work.

Above A well-hung door will fit tightly, keeping out drafts, and will open and close smoothly. If you want to keep the natural wood finish on an external door, it will have to be sealed or varnished to prevent rain and damp from warping it.

DOORS

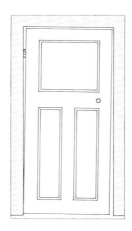

Loose top hinge
If the top hinge is worn, it needs to be replaced. If the screws are loose, remove them, fill the holes with a wood or fiber plug and then replace the screws. If the door has sagged at the hinges, it may be that both hinges have to be removed and the holes filled.

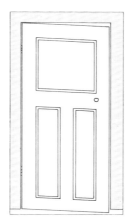

Badly fitting hinges
A gap on the hinge side of the door may occur for a number of reasons. The hinges may not be recessed to fit flush with both the door and the frame. In this case, remove the door, recess the hinges and rehang. A simpler problem to remedy is screws that have not been fully screwed in.

Doorframe distortion
If settlement of your home has caused the doorframe to distort, leaving a gap at the top, and the bottom of the door scraping the floor, it should be mended. Before rehanging, cut the top of the door to match the angle of the doorframe and add a new piece of wood to the bottom of the door.

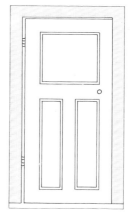

The opposite problem could have occurred and hinges could be too recessed, causing a gap at the opening side of the door. The gap may also be caused because the door has shrunk. You will need to undo the top hinge and place a piece of card between it and the doorframe and then refit the hinge. Then do the same to the bottom hinge.

REGLAZING

Pick a warm day for reglazing windows as glass is more brittle and will break more easily when it is cold.

Measuring up

First buy your glass. If you want to match existing glass, take a broken piece with you when you buy your new pane. Be as accurate as you can when measuring up. If the pane is too small, it will drop out, and if it is too big, it will not fit in — or only so tightly that expansion and contraction are not allowed for. Include the thickness of the putty in your measurements and then deduct $\frac{1}{4}$ in (5 mm) from this overall size.

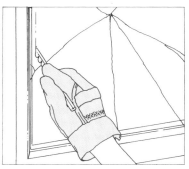

1 Put on a pair of thick gloves. Then, using a glass-cutter, score along the edge of the glass so that the pieces are easier to remove.

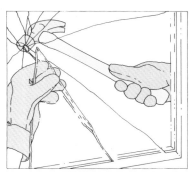

2 Using a hammer, remove the broken glass, disposing of it carefully.

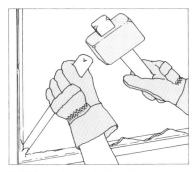

3 With an old wood chisel, tap away all the old putty until you are down to the bare frame. Be careful not to damage the wood.

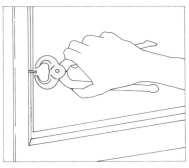

4 Remove all the old tacks with a pair of pincers; these will be different depending on whether the frame is wood or metal.

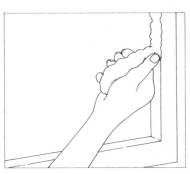

5 If necessary, paint the frame to prevent the putty falling out. Knead the putty and press it into the grooves along the back edge of the frame.

6 Rest the bottom of the glass on the bottom of the frame and gently press into position along all four sides (never push in the center of the pane).

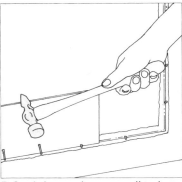

7 Gently hammer in some small tacks to keep the glass in place (if you put a small piece of card behind the tacks you will not damage the glass).

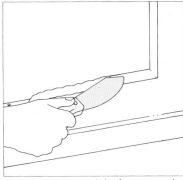

8 Apply putty around the frame, covering the tacks, and mold into a neat angle using a scraper blade. Leave for a week before painting.

Plumbing
YOUR RESPONSIBILITY

Although your home will probably already have water and electricity installed when you arrive, from then on it is your responsibility to use them correctly. Make sure you know how the controls work and find out where the supplies can be turned off in an emergency: if an emergency does arise, you may not have time to go searching for the controls. It is a good idea to label the main switches and stopcocks so they can be instantly recognized. Keep a list near the telephone of the names and numbers of local plumbers, electricians, etc, who provide emergency services, so that you can get in touch with them immediately should you need them.

Basic plumbing toolkit

Plumbing is often best left to the experts, but if you want to tackle any plumbing work yourself you will need a basic kit, which can be extended, depending on the jobs you want to do. Tools such as screwdrivers, hammers, measuring instruments and a plunger are general-purpose tools used in plumbing and that you will no doubt already have in your tool chest. Illustrated on the right are a few plumbing tools for more specialized jobs.

WHERE ARE THEY (AND CAN YOU USE THEM)?

- Water stopcock (near or just inside the boundary of your property)
- Mains stopcock (usually in the kitchen area or under the stairs)
- All other stopcocks in your home (and what they are for)
- Cold-water tank (and the stopcock that isolates it from the piping system)
- Furnace time-switch
- Boiler thermostat
- Room thermostat/s
- Tool box

PLUMBING EQUIPMENT

Gripping
The most important piece of equipment needed is an adjustable wrench (**6**) that will go from $\frac{1}{2}$ in (15 mm) to 1 in (2.5 cm), which means it can cope with all the nuts in the house. You will also need a pair of vice-grips (**7**) so that you can tighten the nuts (use the vice-grips to hold one nut still and the wrench to twist the other). If you are working with steel or galvanized pipes, you will need a small wrench (**3**). An adjustable basin wrench (**5**) is essential for tightening up nuts inside a sink – without one you can never reach the nuts that are leaking.

Fixing
When you do mechanical fittings, such as tightening the nut on a water pipe, you will need a small tub of nonhardening jointing compound (**1**) which will help seal pipes. You will also need a reel of PTFE (white Teflon) tape (**2**) to make up the gaps between metric and imperial fittings. Pass it between your fingers a few times to add static to the tape – that way it will stick better.

Cutting
If you already own a hacksaw you can use it for cutting all types of metal and plastic pipes. If you do not, buy pipe cutters (**4**).

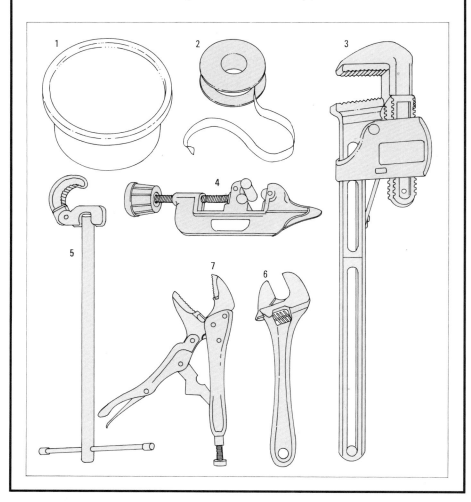

SAFETY WITH WATER

The most damage water can do in a home is to destroy it – it will probably leave you intact, unless it combines with electricity (see Electrics, page 76) when it can be fatal. The one time you must be careful with water and human lives is with children. Never leave a child alone with water and certainly never let a child bathe alone. Do not leave the room even to answer the front-door bell – children can drown in as little as 2 in (5 cm) of water.

Flooding

There are safeguards you can take to keep water under control. The most obvious is not leaving the room to make a telephone call when running a bath. Another is to stop flushing a blocked toilet, otherwise you may cause a flood. And remember to remove the sink plug if your washing machine empties its water into the sink.

Taking precautions

Any electrical appliance that uses water (dishwasher, washing machine, etc) should ideally be situated in the bottom floor of your home. If this is not possible, it is worth considering placing the appliance in a specially made metal box with an overflow pipe – just in case it does flood.

An overflowing toilet on a top floor can cause a great deal of damage, especially if your tank overflow pipe is blocked. So check it regularly to ensure it is not. Unfreezing a frozen pipe in the attic too quickly can also cause a flood if ice has cracked the pipe. If there is a flood in your home you must act fast as water is very heavy and can quite rapidly cause ceilings to collapse.

Above right To prevent accidental flooding, always keep a sink unplugged, particularly if the pipe from your washing machine empties into it.

BURST PIPE OR TANK

- Stop the water by turning it off at the supply valve
- Then, if necessary, turn on all the taps. This will drain your water tank
- Call your plumber or an emergency plumbing service as soon as you can. Even if you can turn the water off yourself, you may not be able to solve the problem without professional help
- Turn off your electricity at the fuse box if there is any danger of water interfering with your electrical circuits
- If there is a bulge in the ceiling in which water is collecting, pierce it with a sharp instrument, such as a pencil or screwdriver, and try and collect the water in a bucket. Otherwise the ceiling may collapse
- Do as much repair work as you can. Mop up water with towels and newspapers and lift up carpets to help them dry

UNBLOCKING

Avoiding blockages

All baths, basins and sinks should have a grid over the waste outlet to stop solids from blocking the trap or waste pipe below. But even small solids, such as tea leaves, hairs, vegetable scrapings and greasy and fatty liquids, can pass the grid and trap and block the sink.

Do not empty tea leaves into the sink or toilet. Always run hot water with a little detergent after pouring hot fat

Above Baths, basins, bidets and toilets can all become blocked with continued use. Never flush insoluble materials down the toilet, and remove hair regularly from bath and basin grids.

down the sink to make sure it cannot solidify in the bend of the trap. Never put disposable diapers or sanitary pads down a toilet bowl. Regularly pour a handful of washing soda and some boiling water down your drains to clear them, and every now and again clean out your kitchen-sink trap. Not only will this help to prevent blockages, but it will also stop any unpleasant smells arising from trapped matter.

Making a sink plunger

It is useful to have a sink plunger, but you can always make one by covering the end of a broom handle or long stick with a thick sponge or cloth-pad, which should be firmly secured. Pumped firmly up and down over the plug-hole, this helps to shift blockages.

CLEARING AN AIRLOCK

If there is no water coming from your tap, or it is only dribbling out, you probably have air in your water system. The first thing you should do is check that the water level is high enough in the cold feed tank; if it is not, call your plumber. If it is, try to drive the air out simply by letting the tap run for a long time. Or try tapping gently along the pipe, taking special care around bends, with a hammer-head wrapped in a thick cloth, to try to knock the air out.

Usually the airlocked tap is a hot-water tap, often in the kitchen. Attach one end of a shower or garden hose to the affected tap and the other end of the

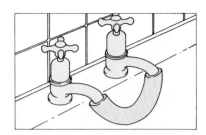

hose to the kitchen cold-water tap. Turn on first the affected hot-water and then the cold-water tap. The pressure coming from the cold-water tap in the kitchen should force the air out of the pipe and the hot tap should work again. This method will not, of course, work with mixer taps.

CLEARING A BLOCKED TOILET

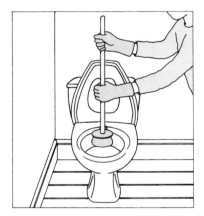

If a toilet bowl is blocked, do not keep flushing it or you may cause an overflow. Instead buy a plunger that looks like a long sink plunger, but has a metal plate above the rubber cup.

When unblocking a toilet you need to use a lot of energy because there is no flat surface in the base of the pan to help create an effective suction. The plunger can force only short, sharp rushes of water into the bend. Be careful not to damage the pan.

Once you have removed the blockage, flush to refill the trap. If it cannot be removed, call your plumber.

UNBLOCKING SINKS, BASINS AND BATHS

If your basin is blocked, you may have to dismantle the trap below it, but it is worth trying to clear it with a plunger.

Push a rag into the basin overflow so that air and water cannot escape as you are using the plunger.

Then, with a cup, remove some water so that there is only an inch or two in the basin, or run a little water into an empty basin. Remove the plug and put the plunger over the plug-hole and, leaving

the rubber cup stationary, move the plunger handle vigorously up and down for half a minute or so. If you have dislodged the blockage, the water will now drain out.

Turn on a tap and move the plunger up and down again. Remove the rag from the overflow and turn on the cold-water tap to refill the trap. For a double sink, push rags into both overflows and one plug-hole, to create an adequate vacuum.

BATHROOM MAINTENANCE

Simple repairs

As with everything, keeping your bathroom well maintained will save you money in the long run.

Damp

Try to minimize condensation: keep the shower doors closed whenever you are having a shower and open the windows a little during or after a very steamy bath. It helps lessen steam if you run the cold water into the bath first, followed by the hot. If all your family enjoy long, hot baths twice a day and do not want to keep the window open, install a window vent or exhaust fan in the bathroom.

It is important that water does not seep between a wall and the edges of a bath, shower or basin, where it could cause rotting. Most sealants come in colors to match basins and tiles or are transparent to match anything.

Toilet

If your toilet seat and cover are loose, these must be fixed, all the screws tightened and the washers replaced if they have disintegrated. Broken seats and covers should be replaced as they are very unhygienic. Measure the sizes of the holes in the pan and their distance apart when you go to buy a new unit.

Basin and bath

Older baths were often made of cast iron painted with enamel. These can be repainted if they become worn or chipped. If you have a modern cast-iron bath covered with vitreous enamel, do not try and re-enamel it yourself. Instead, ask your plumber.

Taps

If your tap drips you need to change the washer (see box). A dripping tap wastes water and, if it is a hot-water tap, it is wasting energy and your money as well (see below). Some modern taps do not need you to turn off the main water supply when repairing them, but always check before starting work.

SEALING GAPS

Gaps between a wall and the side of a bath, basin or sink can be filled with quadrant-shaped ceramic tiles to match an existing tiled wall or they can be filled with a rubber-based sealer. The sealer is easy to apply and, unlike plaster or putty, will remain elastic to allow for any further movement between the wall and the back of the fitting.

First you must clean the gap with a small nailbrush or toothbrush. Then wash along the gap with a hot detergent solution and leave to dry thoroughly. Cut the nozzle of your tube of sealer — remember that the lower the cut, the wider the strip of sealer. Hold the tube at an angle and work forwards, pushing

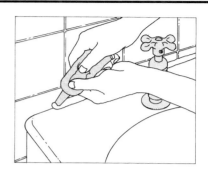

the tube, and squeezing sealer into the gap. You have five minutes to use a wet finger to press down any parts that are raised or bumpy, then you must leave it. After twenty-four hours you can trim off rough edges with a razor blade or sharp knife and use the basin again.

SAVING WATER

There are several easy ways in which to save water in your home.

- Have a shower rather than a bath. Turn off the water in the shower while shampooing and washing your hair, and in the basin while brushing your teeth
- Wash your hands in a sinkful of water rather than under running water
- Get rid of your hose: use a watering can to water your garden and a bucket to wash your car
- Check your appliances to see that they are working properly: faulty toilet cisterns and dripping taps waste water
- Make sure when buying a new washing machine that it has an economy cycle
- Wash only a full load at a time
- Choose a toilet that has both short and long flushes
- Put objects such as bricks, stones or a couple of weighted bottles (fill them with water) in your toilet cistern to reduce the amount of water it uses. (Be sure to check that none of these objects is touching any of the internal mechanism of the cistern)

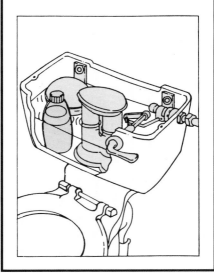

Left Bathrooms can be maintained with little effort: open windows when running a bath or shower, and keep the edges between a sink or bath and the wall well sealed and the tile grouting in good repair.

IF YOUR TAP DRIPS . . .

Find a screwdriver, wrench or adjustable wrench, small wrench, pliers, the correct size washer (buy several sizes if you are not sure which is the correct one) and a cloth. If your tap is a modern one with ceramic washers, your plumber will have to mend it.

Turn the water off at the supply valve and then turn on the tap and let all the water drain. Wait until there is no water coming out before starting work.

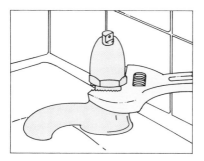

1 Remove the tap handle by pulling it off or unscrewing the retaining screw at the side. Pull the body off or up to expose a large hexagonal nut, which you should unscrew with your spanner.

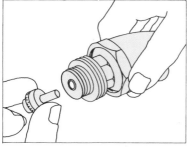

2 Then lift free the inside part of the tap (the headgear). You can now see the washer at the bottom, held by a small nut against a metal plate (the jumper plate).

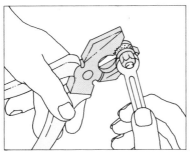

3 With your small wrench, undo the small nut, remove the old washer and clean up any messy bits.

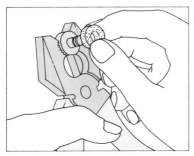

4 Now, fit the new washer with the maker's name facing downwards. Replace the nut, reassemble the tap and turn the water supply back on. Turn the tap on and off several times to check that it has stopped dripping.

Electrics

ELECTRICAL MAINTENANCE

Most electrical repairs should be carried out by a skilled electrician and carefully tested. Remember: *electricity can kill*, so be careful. In some countries it is illegal to install or to alter electrical systems without a professional qualification. Always check regulations before you attempt electrical work.

Working with electricity

The list below warns you about some of the perils of working with electricity.

General
- Always turn electricity off at the fuse box if you are working on fixed electrical equipment or where electric cables are sited
- Never touch electrical equipment with wet hands
- If water begins leaking into any electric fittings, turn off your power supply at once. Water conducts electricity and can cause fatal shocks
- Never use water to put out a fire in an electrical appliance unless you have turned the power off. Everything the water touches will become live
- If electrical fittings have got wet, do not turn the electricity back on until the wiring is absolutely dry or you will get an electric shock when you touch the switch

Above When extending the cord or speaker wires of a music center, use a cord connector rather than insulating tape, and run the cord along the edges of the room.

Appliances
- Make sure any electrical appliances you buy are approved and only buy the best quality
- Correct any faults in electrical appliances immediately
- Never cover or obstruct the air vents on electric heaters
- Unplug electrical appliances before cleaning or examining them
- Make sure each appliance is fitted with the correct fuse
- Have major appliances checked annually

Cords, plugs and sockets
- Never plug cords directly into a socket: always use a plug and make sure it is correctly wired
- Do not use wet or worn cords. Do not try to patch worn cords: have the entire cord replaced
- Never staple cords to a surface or let them run under floor coverings
- Make sure the cord comes from behind you and goes over your shoulder rather than lying in front of you when lawn-mowing, ironing, etc
- Replace cracked and chipped plugs and sockets immediately
- Install additional socket outlets rather than relying on adaptors or long cords
- Keep any outdoor socket outlets under cover or use a special waterproof box

Light fittings
- Do not exceed the maximum wattage recommended on fittings and lampshades
- Never run an electric appliance from a light fitting

Wiring
- Wire plugs correctly and never replace a cartridge fuse with fuse wire
- Always use ground wire with metal-cased equipment
- Have house wiring tested every five years; also check the ground system
- Have house wiring renewed every twenty-five years

BASIC ELECTRIC TOOL KIT

- Spare cartridge fuses for your fuse box and for your electrical appliances (**1**)
- Flashlight (**2**)
- Sharp knife with replaceable blades for stripping off insulation (**3**), or use a wire stripper (**8**)
- Card of assorted fuse wires (**4**)
- Screwdrivers with insulated handles and $\frac{1}{4}$ in (6 mm) and $\frac{1}{8}$ in (3 mm) tips (**5**)
- Screwdriver with neon tester for checking whether a terminal is live (**6**)
- Pliers or wire cutters with insulated handles for cutting cords and cables (**7, 9**)
- Selection of bulbs for your lamps
- Fire extinguishers

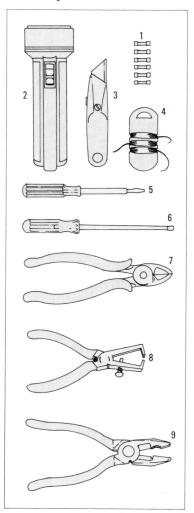

HOW TO WIRE AN ORDINARY PLUG

Various types of safety plug are now available, but all are wired as described below.

1 First gather together your appliance, cord and plug, a small screwdriver and a wire stripper and cutter or a sharp knife.

2 Remove the plug cover by loosening the main screw on the underside then remove one cord clamp screw and loosen the other.

3 Unscrew the three tiny screws from the terminals, but do not remove them or they may get lost.

4 Using the sharp knife, start at the bottom of the cord and carefully cut away about 2 in (5 cm) of the outer sheath, being careful not to cut into the three wires.

5 Fix the cord firmly under the screw. Each wire end should reach about $\frac{1}{2}$ in (13 mm) beyond its terminal.

6 Remember that the live wire is black; the neutral wire is white and the ground wire is a bare wire.

7 Using the wire strippers, remove the insulation from the three wire ends to expose $\frac{1}{4}$ in (6 mm) of wire for screw-hole terminals. Allow $\frac{1}{2}$ in (15 mm) for clamp-type terminals.

8 Twist the strands of wire together so no loose strands remain and either insert into the holes (screw-hole terminals) or loop clockwise round terminals (clamp-type). Tighten the three tiny terminal screws.

9 Replace plug cover, but do not force it; instead see why it is not closing properly. Tighten screw.

10 Shake plug. If anything rattles, undo it and start again.

How do fuses work?

A fuse is a safety device. It is designed as an intentional weak point in an electrical circuit. If something is overloading the circuit, the fuse will melt and break the connection to the appliance.

Breakers installed in electrical panels have largely replaced fuses in newer houses. When a circuit is overloaded the connection is broken and the power is cut. Power can be restored – after the cause of the overloading is identified and fixed – simply by resetting the appropriate switch in the breaker panel.

If you use too high-rating a fuse for its appliance, your fuse will no longer be a weak link; if the rating is too low, the fuse will blow at once. Read the appliance manufacturer's instructions.

If the new fuse blows the moment you have installed it then there is something wrong with the appliance. Unplug the appliance and call in your electrician.

If an appliance does not work . . .

If you think an appliance is broken, do not use it or you could damage it further. If the same fault recurs, reread the instruction manual to see what you are doing wrong or ask the manufacturer. But first check this list.

1 Make sure that the plug is properly pushed into the socket and that the socket is switched on.

2 Check that the appliance is switched on and that the controls are properly set.

3 Test that the socket is not broken by plugging into it an appliance you know to be working.

4 Make sure that the plug is correctly wired.

5 Check the main fuse box to see if a fuse has blown and, if necessary, replace it. Make sure there is not a power cut.

6 Do not use your appliance if it is broken or if the cord is worn.

Check your appliances

Vacuum cleaner
Do you need to empty or replace the dust bag? Is the nozzle clogged? Is the hose obstructed? Do you need to replace the filter? Has anything jammed the fan blades? Are the bristles too worn?

Washing machine
Is the water turned on? Are clothes loaded evenly? Is the door shut?

Dryer
Drying too slowly: is your load too heavy or clothes too wet? Is the filter full?
Running noisily: is the dryer resting unevenly on the floor? Is the belt loose?

Dishwasher
Cleans badly: are you stacking the dishes properly? Have you cleaned the filters? Is there enough salt/rinse aid, etc, in the machine? Have you been using too much detergent or have you changed brands recently? Are your detergent and water softener compatible?
Motor will not go: is the drain hose kinked? Is the impeller jammed with small pieces of food or broken glass?

Toaster
Have you removed the crumbs or are they jamming the mechanism?

Electric oven
Is the automatic control set at manual?

Refrigerator
Noisy: is the ground level?
Does not stay cold: have you changed the thermostat setting? Does the door seal need replacing? Have you put paper on the shelves, which has stopped the air circulating?
Food is freezing: have you changed the thermostat setting? Are the return air vents in the freezer compartment blocked?

Freezer
Did you leave the door open by mistake? Have you just introduced too much warm food into the freezer? Is your thermostat setting too high?

Decorating

PREPARATION

If your home needs only a fresh coat of paint, preparation work will be negligible. Your main concern will be to see that none of your furniture or fittings is marked or damaged in any other way during the course of redecoration. It may be a chore to move things out of the room or cover them with dustsheets, but it is necessary: even the most skilled decorator cannot avoid a few paint drips. You also want to be able to get on with the business of decorating without constantly having to worry about how clean a job you are doing.

Before you begin to paint, you should remove or cover all the furniture in the room; take down any curtains, lampshades, paintings, mirrors and anything else fixed to the wall; roll up and remove the carpet if you are worried about it, or simply cover the floor with dustsheets or newspapers.

If the surfaces to be repainted are in good condition, all you need do is dust or vacuum them, and wash them. For more fundamental decorating the preparation work can be rather a chore; yet it is essential. Every surface needs to be treated differently, depending on both the type of surface and the finish you want to achieve.

Another point to remember is to allow yourself sufficient time to complete the job in one go, and to pick a convenient time to do it, because the room you are working on will be out of use until you finish.

Tools of the trade

Whatever equipment you need for the job you should buy the best tools you can afford. If you look after them well, they will save you time and money. Always wash tools thoroughly after use with the appropriate solvent. Something to remember is that if you store them carefully they will last. For both painting and wallpapering – and possibly also for tiling – you may need a ladder (or two with a plank resting between them) to stand on.

PAINTING

The reason for buying good-quality equipment is because you do not want your paintbrush bristles to molt or your roller to get stiff. Three brushes – a 3 in (7.5 cm), a 2 in (5 cm) and a 1 in (2.5 cm) (**5**) – should be enough, unless you want to paint behind radiators, in which case a radiator brush (**6**) will be useful. For painting windowframes, you may prefer using a cutting-in brush (**7**) (with a 45°

angle tip); but whereas the cutting-in brush is not essential, a steady hand is.

If you are painting large areas, a tray and roller (**1**) with two different covers (**2**) (mohair for gloss paint and lambswool for emulsion and textured surfaces) are a must for speed. And before you start work, collect a few empty wide-necked glass jars (**4**) and some newspapers and rags (**3**) for cleaning them afterwards.

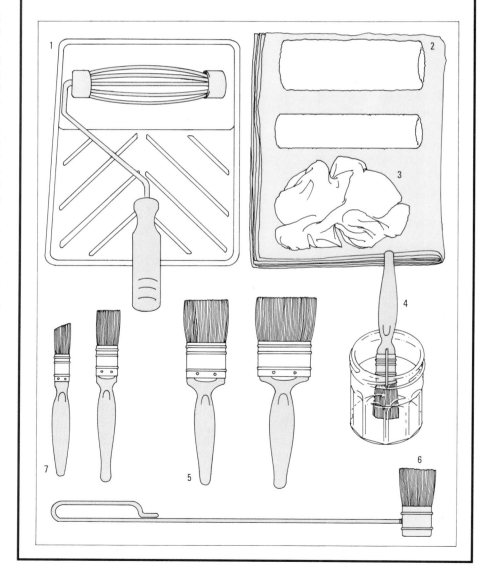

TILING

Fewer tools are necessary for tiling. For measuring, a tape (**4**), pencil (**8**) and spirit level (**5**) are essential. For cutting, you need two pieces of equipment: a scriber (**1**) with a tungsten carbide tip for scoring and then cutting tiles, and a pair of tile nippers or pincers (**2**) for cutting bits off them. A tile file or small carborundum stone (**9**) is then useful for smoothing the tile edges. A special notched spreader (**7**) or trowel (**3**) is used to ensure that the adhesive is evenly spread.

Once the tiles have stuck to the wall, a different spreader is used for applying grouting. The excess grout is then wiped off with an everyday household sponge (**6**).

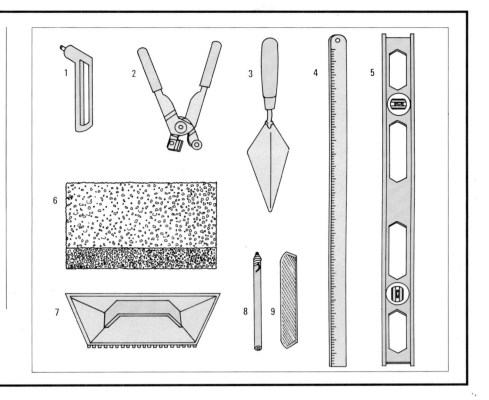

WALLPAPERING

For wallpapering you need a large, clean table to use as a flat surface for pasting. You will also need a steel tape (**5**), a plumb line (**6**) and a pencil (**8**) for measuring. Some specialist cutting instruments, such as a pair of wallpapering scissors (**9**) and a trimming knife (**2**), are essential. You should also have a bucket (**4**) in which to put the glue and a pasting brush (**3**) to apply it with. If you are using pre-pasted wallpapers, you will need a water trough. Finally, for smoothing on the paper you will need a paper-hanging brush (**7**) and a seam roller (**1**) for making sure the edges stay stuck – do not use it on textured wallpaper.

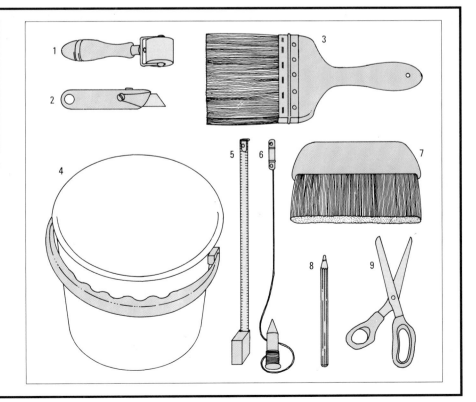

PAINTING

Painting hints

Colors always appear lighter on the color chart than they do when your entire room is painted in them, so always buy the smallest can of paint first and try it out. Once you have decided you like it, buy enough paint to cover all your surfaces, plus a little extra for retouching. There may be slight color differences between batches.

Before starting to paint, read the instructions on the can and make sure the paint is appropriate for the surface you intend to use it on. If you are using old paint, always remove any skin that has formed; do not stir it in. Never overload tools with paint: you only need to dip one-third of your brush into the paint. Always brush out each application before adding another.

Always paint working away from any natural light so that you can see what you are doing. If possible, make sure the light comes from the left if you are right-handed and from the right if you are left-handed. Paint the ceiling with your back to the light. Begin at the corner nearest to the window and paint in bands parallel to the window across the room. If you are painting doors, clean out the keyholes first or dirt will be picked up by the brush.

Painting a room

The order of painting should be first the ceiling, then the walls, and afterwards the windowframes and doors. Next paint any moldings and picture rails and finish with the baseboards.

Above Contrasting pastel colors on doors and walls can look very effective, and add interest to an otherwise stark room. Don't be afraid to try out a range of colors — you might be pleasantly surprised with the results.

Right White doors and windowframes against creamy-yellow or robin's-egg blue walls create a light, airy appearance, making a small room feel larger. These pale tones can be offset beautifully with a few dark accents, such as deep blue or fuchsia pink.

HOME REPAIRS

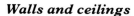

Walls and ceilings

Paint the edges and corners of walls and ceilings with a brush first and then paint the middle with a roller. Do not break in the middle of painting a wall, especially if you are using oil-based paints: you will be able to see "stop and start" edges. Stop only when you reach the corner. Cover the floor with drop cloths. When painting the baseboards shield the floor with sticky tape or a stiff sheet of board. This will also prevent the brush from picking up dirt off the floor.

Doors, windows and baseboards

These are normally painted with oil-based (gloss) paint. They should have two undercoats and a top coat and be lightly sanded down between each coat, leaving the paint to dry thoroughly before applying the next coat. If the finished result looks patchy when dry,

apply a second or even a third coat. Do not brush out gloss paint too thinly and always finish painting with light, upward strokes. Keep checking the paint after you have applied it; you may be able to brush out any runs while still wet. If you cannot complete oil-based paintwork in a day, wash brushes and keep in mineral spirits overnight.

After use

Clean equipment thoroughly: use turpentine or a commercial brush cleaner for oil-based paints and cold water for water-based paints. Rinse well and store brushes and rollers horizontally or hang them up. Hammer the tops on paint cans and then tip them upside-down to form an airtight seal. Pour a thin layer of mineral spirits on the top of gloss paint to stop a skin forming. Fill a small bottle with the paint you have used and keep it for touch-ups.

HOW MUCH PAINT?

Type	500 ml can	1 l can	2½ l can	5 l can
Undercoat	5–6	11	28	55
Gloss & eggshell	6–7	12–14	30–35	60–70
Vinyl matt & vinyl silk	6–8	11–15	28–38	55–75
Weatherproof	—	—	12–15	25–50

Figures show the number of square meters covered by one can of paint. Quantities vary depending on the surface painted. On a smooth surface paint will go further than on a textured one.

"GREEN" PAINTWORK

Since it makes sense to use as few chemicals in your home as possible, if you can avoid gloss paints – and therefore mineral spirits and turpentine – do so. Although the lead content of gloss paint is now being phased out, water-based paints are preferable and equipment can be cleaned with water.

If you want to leave wood unpainted, simply seal it with beeswax. Do not use a heat gun to strip it as not only will it

damage the wood, but it will also release gas fumes. Paint-strippers should also be avoided as they contain toxic chemicals that also damage the surface of the wood. Instead, sandpaper by hand.

Make quite sure that any paint used for children's furniture, such as the bed or chest of drawers, is lead-free. If any of your child's equipment is second-hand you should strip the bits he or she is likely to "chew" and repaint them with lead-free paint. If you are using spray paint, use CFC-free aerosols.

REPAINTING PROBLEM AREAS

Always make sure the paint you use is from the same batch as the paint you are matching. You can repaint small patches, but it may take a little time and patience to blend them into the rest of the wall surface.

Water-based paint

Wash the wall first with detergent solution, then rinse and dry. If paint has flaked, remove it with a stripping knife and gently sand the edges of the damaged area. If the flaking is extensive, apply a coat of stabilizing primer to the wall before repainting.

Before repainting, mix the new paint with a very little dust from your vacuum cleaner so that the color appears duller: the longer the paint has been on your wall, the more dust you will need to add to the new paint. When you have applied the paint you can then blur the edges of the patch by dabbing them gently with damp cotton batting while the paint is still wet, to blend it in.

Oil-based paint

First wash the painted surface with a sugar-soap solution (from a hardware shop), then rinse and dry thoroughly. Gently rub any scratches or chips on the old paintwork with fine sandpaper until the surface is smooth and then repaint. If the surface is badly chipped you may want to remove the old paint entirely. Use a heat gun with the greatest care and never on glazing bars on doors or windows or the glass will crack.

Once on a surface, oil-based paints quickly lose their gloss and discolor. To patch-paint, remove some of the gloss from new paint by thinning with mineral spirits. You can also try to match the color by adding a little yellow paint to your new color. Otherwise, paint the new section, finishing on an up-stroke, and then dip some cotton batting in a little mineral spirits, squeeze out excess liquid and then dab it around the borders to help soften the new, hard edge.

WALLPAPERING

Buy all the wallpaper you need at the same time, making sure that all the rolls carry the same batch number and look the same color. If you are using a pattern with a large repeat, you may need to allow for more paper. Store the rolls flat until you are ready to use them. Clear your walls of obstacles, if possible removing radiators, electric plates or switches, picture hooks, wall lights, etc. If necessary, hang lining paper first, using it horizontally and never overlapping the joins. Leave it to dry for at least twenty-four hours before papering the final layer. Before papering make sure that all paintwork in the room has been completed.

Planning your work

If your paper is plain, or has a small pattern, start papering near a corner on the window wall and work round the room to the door in both directions. If your paper has a large pattern, center it in a prominent place, such as over the fireplace, and work outwards in both directions. Hang all ceiling paper parallel to the main window in the room, starting at the window and working away from it.

Cutting

Always cut several lengths of paper at once, having made sure that the design matches. After cutting, number the strips on the back so that you know in which order to hang them. Always work from two or three rolls at the same time to reduce wastage. If the wallpaper has a large pattern, cut it so that the main pattern unit appears at the top of the wall after trimming. On each length allow an extra 2 in (5 cm) at both the top and bottom to help with positioning and trimming. This extra is also useful in the event that you have not measured the length accurately.

Pasting

If you are using wallpaper that hasn't been pre-pasted, make sure you are using the correct glue and following the manufacturer's instructions. Always paste from the center of the paper out to the edges, trying to avoid the glue seeping from underneath the paper onto the right side. Make sure each length is evenly soaked with glue and for the same amount of time. Then fold the paper, so that there is a large fold at the top and a smaller one at the bottom, with the pasted surfaces together. Remove any glue from the table with a sponge and some cold water before you paste the next sheet of wallpaper on it.

Hanging the paper

When you reach the wall, hold the top end of the paper by the corners and let the paper unfold. If you are using very long lengths of paper, ask someone to hold the paper so that it does not tear. Make sure the first length is straight by using a plumb bob. When the paper is in place, brush it out from the center, smoothing out any creases or air bubbles. If wrinkles appear, gently peel the paper back then brush it down again firmly; small wrinkles may disappear on drying. Air bubbles can be removed by pricking them with the point of a sharp knife and brushing the paper out flat.

If a bit of paper is not sticking, paste it again, then press hard. Keep a sponge or cloth handy to wipe off excess paste. To neaten the ceiling line, or trim round a doorway, use the point of your closed scissors to score the line you wish to cut; then pull away the paper and cut the required shape.

Corners

Never hang a length of paper so that more than $\frac{1}{2}$ in (13 mm) goes round to the adjoining wall. Cut it before hanging and brush it well into the corner. Once you have turned a corner, establish another vertical on the adjacent wall with your plumb bob.

Blistered wallpaper

If your paper blisters there are two possible courses of action. The simplest solution is to inject some wallpaper paste into each blister; this leaves only a

---

HOW MUCH WALLPAPER?

Walls
Measure the height of your room from the baseboard to the ceiling; then measure the perimeter of your room, including doors and windows. Figures show the rolls of wallpaper required.

Ceilings
Calculate the area in square meters and then divide by 5.

Distance around the room	Height from baseboard			
	7 ft 6 in (2.2 m)	8 ft 9 in (2.5 m)	9 ft 6 in (2.8 m)	10 ft 6 in (3.1 m)
32 ft (10 m)	4	5	5	5
40 ft (12 m)	5	6	6	7
48 ft (15 m)	6	7	7	8
56 ft (17 m)	7	8	9	10
64 ft (19 m)	8	9	10	11
74 ft (22 m)	9	10	11	12
80 ft (24 m)	11	13	14	16

pin-prick. You do this by filling a syringe with wallpaper paste and injecting a small amount into the center of each blister. Leave the paper for five minutes to give it time to absorb the paste and then gently flatten the blister to the wall with your fingers. Go over the blister with a roller until it is completely flat.

The other solution is to cut the blister and paste the paper again, which leaves larger cut-marks. You do this by cutting vertically and horizontally across the blister with a sharp knife, cutting slightly beyond the edge of each blister. You then pull back the corners of the blister and, using a small paintbrush, paste the wallpaper and leave it for a minute or two to soak. Then push the flaps back against the wall and flatten the area lightly with a seam roller.

Peeling wallpaper

If your paste was diluted too much or spread too thinly, your wallpaper may start to peel off or wrinkle. If this happens, lift the peeled section and apply a multi-purpose adhesive or a newly mixed, slightly thicker, solution of wallpaper paste. Roll back the paper lightly and smoothly.

PATCHING TORN WALLPAPER

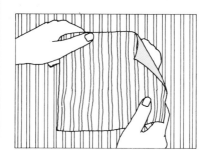

1 Tear off any loose or damaged paper, leaving only paper that is firmly fixed to the wall. Cut a piece of new paper about 3 in (7 cm) larger than the hole. Make sure the pattern on the new paper matches that of the surrounding paper.

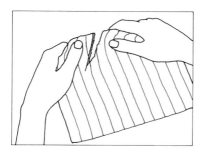

2 Then tear around the edges of the entire new piece so they become ragged. Carefully peel away the back of the paper so that the edges are about half the thickness of the rest of the patch. Check that you have not torn away too much paper.

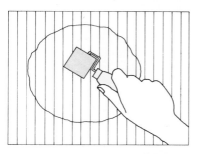

3 Paste the patch and leave it to dry for a few minutes, then stick it on the wall matching pattern to pattern. Leave for a minute and then roll the new piece lightly from center to edges.

VINYL AND BURLAP WALLPAPER

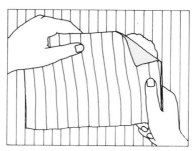

1 Some wall-coverings (vinyl, burlap, grasscloth etc) cannot be torn by hand. Cut a patch of new paper that is about 2 in (5 cm) larger than the hole. Take a piece of masking tape and rub it with your fingers to remove some of the stickiness. Then use it to stick the new piece of wallpaper over the damaged area, making sure the pattern matches.

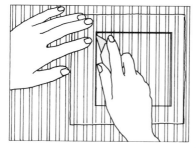

2 With a sharp knife cut through both layers of wallpaper in the shape of a square. Remove the new wallpaper piece and throw away the border and masking tape. Then peel away the old wallpaper within the cut marks.

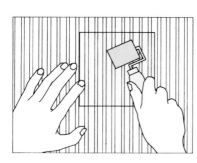

3 Paste the new paper and place it in the patch. Press lightly with a roller.

TILING

A word of warning: tiling is a fairly skilled job. You may find it easier – and cheaper in the long run – to ask a professional tiler to do it for you.

Tiling hints

Make sure you buy enough tiles so that you have a few left over: it can be very difficult to match tiles in color, thickness and design when some of your original ones have cracked and need replacing. Tiles that have built-in spacer lugs on their edges to insure accurate spacing are easier to lay – otherwise use matchsticks between the tiles to insure even spacing. If you want to use tiles around your fireplace or near a wood-burning stove, make sure they are heat-resistant.

Different tiles

Tiles come in three different types: those with four square edges (the standard tile); those with one rounded edge (for neat finishes around the perimeter of tiled areas) and those with two rounded edges (to finish off corners). You can also buy special tiles with built-in soap dishes, toilet-roll holders etc. Before you buy, work out how many of each type you need.

Adhesives

Make sure that you buy the right adhesive, for both the tiles and the surface you want to fix them to. Use water-resistant adhesive for tiles in shower cubicles and around basins and sinks, and heat-resistant adhesive for heat-resistant tiles. You must also buy water-resistant grout for use around sinks, basins, etc. Self-adhesive tiles are easier and cleaner to lay. For larger areas you can also buy sheets of tiles, which are quicker to lay than individual tiles.

Top Varying the sizes and pattern of tiles produces an unusual, attractive effect.

Right Tiles laid around a sink create a water-resistant, easily cleanable surface.

Preparation and planning

You can tile over old tiles, provided they are clean and as long as any cracked and loose tiles have been repaired or replaced. Other surfaces must be even and nonabsorbent as well as clean. Do not tile over wallpaper as the weight of the tiles will soon remove the paper. New plaster should be primed to make sure it does not absorb moisture from the tile adhesive.

Plan your layout so that cut tiles appear in the corners at the back of the room – not in the middle of the wall – and at the back of window and bath ledges, and not at the front.

Cutting tiles

To ensure a straight cut, first score the line on the glazed surface of the tile using a metal rule (straightedge) to cut against and a tile cutter to make the line. Place two matchsticks tip to tip on a table and lay the tile on top of them so that they are underneath the intended break. You will need to separate the matches so that they stick out on either side of the tile. Then press down gently on either side of the tile and the tile will snap in two.

If you need to cut out a shape from a tile, it is easiest first to make a cardboard template of the shape and then to mark and score the glazed surface with a tile cutter before nibbling out the required shape with pincers. Smooth the rough edge of a cut tile with a suitable file or a small carborundum stone. Work downwards, away from the glaze.

Sticking

If your space is confined, spread the adhesive directly onto the back of each tile. Otherwise always spread adhesive directly onto the wall. Cover about 1 square yd (1 square m) at a time and then comb the adhesive with the notched spreader, pressing hard on the wall. Then start laying the tiles, working in horizontal rows. Do not use a notched spreader on water-resistant adhesives. Always tile the main central area first before tiling the edges.

REGROUTING CERAMIC TILES

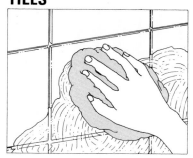

To apply clean grouting, remove as much of the original grouting as you can with a sharp-pointed scraper, taking care not to damage the tiles. Mix up the grouting cement in a bowl to the consistency of thick cream. Then, with a clean rag, rub the grouting over the tiles, pressing it well in. Use a damp sponge to wipe excess grouting from the face of the tiles and, before the grouting sets hard, smooth the joints with a rounded point, such as on a tongue depressor.

REPLACING A BROKEN TILE

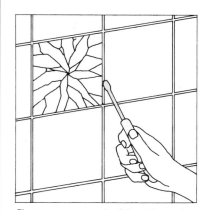 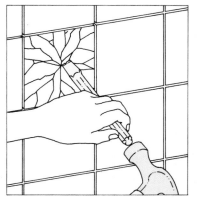

First remove as much of the old grouting as you can from around the damaged tile, using a sharp-pointed scraper. Then chip away the damaged tile with a hammer or mallet and chisel, working from the center to the edges of the tile. Scrape out the old adhesive, then glue a new tile in the same place; the glue can be spread onto the tile if it is easier. Be ready to prise the tile out again with a knife or chisel if the level is wrong. When several tiles need to be replaced, use spacers, as you would if laying new tiles. When the glue is dry, remove the spacers and grout the joints.

TILING LEDGES

To tile a window recess or the ledge around a bath, lay the tiles on the horizontal surface before you tile the sides. Place the whole tiles at the front and the cut tiles at the back.

Flooring

WOOD

With a wooden floor, you will be able to hear whether or not the boards are nailed down properly to the joists just by walking around; and you will easily spot any gaps between planks or rotten floorboards that should be replaced. Use wooden strips to cover gaps between the floor and baseboard or squeeze some transparent rubber sealant along the gap.

If your wooden floor is very uneven, it is best to level it with a floor-sanding machine. If you live in a very old house, however, it is better to leave your floor slightly crooked as each sanding shaves off a little bit more of the thickness of the boards.

If floorboards creak, it is because somewhere wood is rubbing against wood. Shake talcum powder or French chalk into the gaps; it will act as a lubricant and may stop the creaking. Otherwise you can nail boards down. If stairs creak, try the above or screw metal repair plates or shelf brackets underneath each step.

Opposite A wooden floor can be an attractive feature in a living room, providing a cleaner, more spacious look than fitted carpets, and creating the perfect background for a fine rug.

How to finish your wood floor

There are three ways of dealing with a timber floor. You can use a spirit-based wax polish, which is hard work but will look more and more beautiful as the years go by. You can use an oil-resin seal, which can be retouched annually. Or you can apply a hard polyurethane seal, which should be sanded off and replaced every three to four years.

Wax-polish finishes are very slippery and not suitable for kitchens. If you want to remove a wax finish from your wooden floor, rub the floor with mineral spirits or a liquid wax cleaner, using either a soft cloth or wire wool and rubbing in the direction of the grain.

If your wooden floor is sealed it will also be improved by polishing. Apply a little wax emulsion polish two or three times a year and shine before the polish dries. Do not use this polish unless your wooden floor has been sealed as it will damage any unsealed wood.

You can also paint a wooden floor, as you would do woodwork, with primer, two coats of undercoat and then one of topcoat. If you are using water-based paint, top this with at least three coats of varnish. If you are using oil-based paint, there is no need for varnish.

NAILING DOWN LOOSE BOARDS

First try hammering in the existing brads (special floorboard nails). If the boards are still loose, buy some more brads at least $\frac{3}{4}$ in (2 cm) longer than the thickness of the floorboards. Find the floor joists (they run at right angles to the floorboards and their positions can be seen from the nail locations) and make sure there are no pipes or electric cords or wires between the floorboards and the joins before banging the brads in. You may need to lift up a floorboard to check.

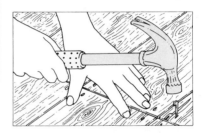

Position each new brad about $\frac{1}{2}$ in (1 cm) along the joist from an existing brad. Hammer the brads in well and then use a nail punch to knock the nail-heads below the surface.

FILLING GAPS BETWEEN THE FLOORBOARDS

Fill wide (over $\frac{1}{4}$ in [6 mm]) gaps between floorboards with made-to-measure tapered wooden strips. Cut strips to fit, glue their sides and then hammer them into the gaps. Once they are dry, carefully plane the strips so that they are level with the floor. Otherwise you could take up all the boards and relay them.

Fill small gaps between floorboards with plastic wood (add a small amount of stain to match the color of the wood) or transparent rubber sealant or papier-mâché. Make papier-mâché by tearing soft, white, unprinted paper into postage stamp-size pieces and mixing it

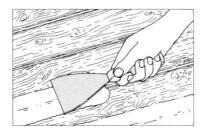

first with a little boiling water and then with a thick wallpaper paste – always use too much, rather than too little paste to make sure the papier-mâché will not shrink. Keep the mixture fairly dry

and very thick and use a scraper to push it into the gaps. If necessary, dye the paper with a proprietary liquid dye to match the floor color before applying. Sand after two to three days.

CARPETS

Carpet care

It is possible to clean a carpet yourself with a carpet shampoo as long as you follow the instructions and do not over-wet the carpet. Woolen or wool-mix carpets should not be cleaned too often as it is impossible to remove all the detergent, and the texture and color of the carpet will eventually suffer.

Machines can often be rented from supermarkets, dry-cleaners or convenience stores. Used with the proprietary cleaners that are sold with the machines, they do an adequate job, but are likely to be hard on the carpet.

Shampooing
If you want to shampoo your carpet, use a dry foam carpet shampoo, which will mean your carpet will not get too wet. Beware of carpet shampoos that contain bleaches and other alkalis that could damage your carpet. Once your carpet has been shampooed, you could have it professionally protected with a soil retardant – it will be much easier to keep clean thereafter.

Stain removal
Treat any stain as quickly as you can. First remove any solid deposit and blot up any excess liquid and then flood the stain with cold water, using a cloth or soda water, and blot immediately. Try not to get the carpet too wet. Never use salt or other absorbent materials on a carpet as they are difficult to remove. After treating the stain, shampoo the whole carpet.

Dyeing
If your carpet has faded or is very soiled you can have it dyed, but only if there is still a lot of wear left in it. Carpet dyeing is a long job, best left to the professionals. But if you do it yourself, there are various points to bear in mind. First of all, think about the effects of the original carpet color on the dye color. A yellow carpet dyed red, for example, will result in an orange carpet; if you dye a yellow carpet blue, the result will be green and so on. It is impossible to dye a carpet a lighter color than the one it already is.

Moving stair carpets
If your stair carpet is velvet pile, it is usually inadvisable to move it – unless you move it regularly or it is very badly soiled. The stripes created by the worn and flattened pile being bent around the steps are unattractive and will remain for a long time after the carpet has been moved. If the carpet is very soiled, however, this may be the preferable alternative. A hardier carpet, such as a hard-twist pile, will not have been as affected by the pile having been bent, so it should be all right to move.

Above The cleaning of Oriental rugs needs to be approached with care. Valuable rugs need professional treatment, less valuable ones can be gently cleaned at home.

Cleaning special rugs

Antique and Oriental rugs
Carpet-sweep rather than vacuum-clean them. Seek professional advice both on cleaning and on stain removal. If the rug is not valuable, take it to the garden, rub some damp tea leaves in and then shake them out and vacuum the carpet. This should remove the dust and brighten the colors. Or just wash rugs gently with warm soapy water, rinse, raise them off the ground and leave them to dry in the sun.

Cotton and rag rugs
These should be vacuumed as often as fitted carpets. If they are washable, then wash them. Otherwise shampoo them every now and again.

Felt carpets
Felt carpets are really only suitable for areas of light wear as they get easily stained and flattened. Carpet-sweep them regularly and shampoo them carefully, without overwetting them. Seek professional advice on removing stains.

Numdah rugs
These hand-embroidered rugs made of matted goat's hair should not be washed or shaken. Carpet-sweep and dry-clean if necessary.

Shaggy and fur rugs
Shake these outdoors as often as you can and beat them occasionally, but do not hang them over a line. Instead lay them on a sheet and beat them gently with a rattan beater. Vacuum only if you have a vacuum cleaner with variable speed settings and use the slowest speed. Otherwise you can turn them over and vacuum the backs. When necessary, have them professionally cleaned.

Sheepskin and goatskin rugs
Carpet-sweep or vacuum daily. Unless washable, shampoo them occasionally without wetting their backs. Seek professional advice on stain removal.

PATCHING A FOAM-BACKED CARPET

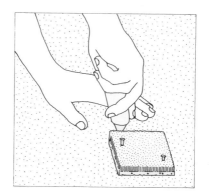

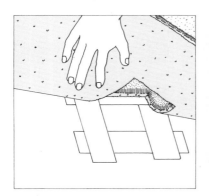

If your carpet is foam-backed, do not turn it over, but cut out the damaged area from the front. Pin the new patch on top of the damaged area with a couple of carpet tacks and then use the new patch as a template to cut out the damaged carpet.

Make sure the pile of the patch matches that of the sound carpet and that the cuts are clean and straight. Pull out the tacks, lift off the patch and remove the damaged square of carpet.

Turn back the carpet and stick strips of adhesive tape along the edges of the hole, overlapping the hole by at least $\frac{1}{2}$ in (1 cm) at each edge. Then turn back the carpet and press in the patch, making sure it is well stuck to the tape.

PATCHING BROADLOOM

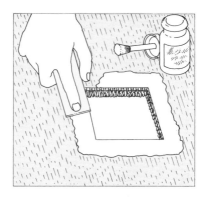

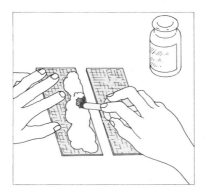

You can easily patch a small area of broadloom (non foam-backed carpet) up to 9 in (23 cm) square. Lift the carpet from the floor and from the back cut out a small square around the damaged area. To cut out the square, use a sharp knife and place a piece of wood underneath so that you do not cut through anything else. Then apply a 1 in (2.5 cm) border of latex adhesive around the sides of the square. Cut two (or more if necessary)

strips of burlap tape long enough to overlap the square by 1 in (2.5 cm) on all four sides and stick them to the back of the carpet over the hole.

Lay the square over a remnant of carpet (or use a piece of carpet that is permanently covered by furniture), matching the pattern if there is one.

Then use the square as a template to cut out a patch. Make sure the direction of the pile matches that of the surrounding carpet. Cover the back and edges (not the tufts) of the patch with adhesive and then stick it into the existing carpet from the right side. Make sure the edges are firmly stuck down.

OTHER FLOORS

Hard and semi-hard flooring

Most floors just need to be regularly swept and washed to keep them clean. They may need sealing or special attention if they get heavy use. Kitchen floors get the hardest use – from shoes, grit, chairs being pulled in and out, heat, dropped food, insects and damp. Shiny floors are more resistant to dirt, but may be dangerously slippery. Hard floors, made of stone, brick and tiles, last longer than soft or semi-soft floors; some surfaces, such as marble, may last a long time but will stain easily. If floors of such materials as marble and cork become soiled, seek professional advice as to whether the top layer can be removed to restore the original color.

Right Bricks make ideal hard floors – they wear well and last a long time. They can be sealed but this tends to make them more slippery.

Above Marble floors look beautiful and are hard-wearing, but they stain quite easily.

REPLACING A DAMAGED CLAY OR QUARRY TILE

Before you try removing the damaged tile, make sure that you can buy a replacement tile that is the same color,

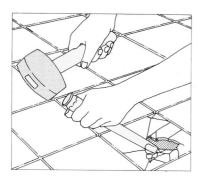

size and thickness. Then tap the damaged tile with a hammer until it is all cracked and, working from the center outwards, chip the tile out with a small chisel, with which you can then smooth the concrete underneath. Clean the floor and make sure the new tile fits. It should

be a little lower than the rest of the floor.

Remove the tile and spread on adhesive or a mixture of 1 part cement to

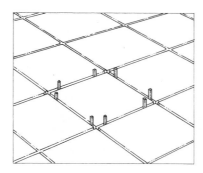

3 parts sand and a little water. Press the tile in position, making sure there is an even space all round — use matchsticks if there are no spacer lugs on the tile. Remove any surface adhesive with a trowel. Leave for one day and then remove the matchsticks and grout using the above sand-and-cement mixture. Remove surplus grout with a damp sponge. Do not walk on for four days.

REPLACING A VINYL TILE

Chisel out the old tile then scrape the surface thoroughly. Do not dig into the backing. Clean well, then glue the floor using a serrated spreader. Heat the new tile a little, ease it into the four corners first, then press down from the center outwards to get rid of any air bubbles. Remove excess adhesive with a damp cloth. Seal to match the floor.

TO STOP MATS SLIPPING

To stop small rush and coconut mats from curling and slipping, stitch a piece of linoleum under each end, the full width of the mat and from 6 to 12 in (15–30 cm) long. Bore holes in the linoleum and stitch with string.

REPAIRING SHEET VINYL AND LINOLEUM

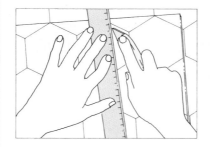

Lay the offcut over the torn piece of floor covering and move it around until the pattern matches. Cut through both pieces of flooring using a sharp knife and a metal rule, to make sure that both the patch and the torn piece are the same size. Remove the torn piece with a scraper, cover the new piece with adhesive and stick it into the hole, making sure it is firmly in place.

BINDING RUGS AND RUNNERS

Most rugs and runners will eventually fray, but this is especially true of woven carpets, rugs, sisal, cord and coconut matting. The simplest (and quickest) way of preventing this is to glue a strip of binding to the edges of the mat. A more lasting way is to sew on the binding or to use a combination of the two. The best binding is burlap in a color matching or contrasting with the rug.

First trim the edges of the rug with either a sharp pair of scissors or a sharp knife and a metal ruler (place a piece of wood underneath the rug so that you do not cut the floor). Make sure the cut is straight, or the binding will be uneven.

Then cut a piece of 3 in (7·5 cm) burlap binding tape to the same length as the rug and glue half the width of the tape with a rubber contact adhesive. Apply the same adhesive to a strip 1½ in (4 cm) wide along the top edge of the rug. When both the tape and the rug are nearly dry, stick them together. They should stick at once.

Turn the rug round and do the same thing again with the other half of the tape and the top (formerly bottom) edge of the rug. Make sure that the glue has stuck properly along the entire length of the rug. Wipe off any surplus.

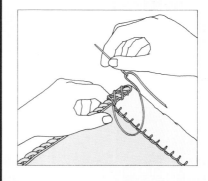

Otherwise use the same tape, only this time stitch the tape to the rug, using a thick carpet needle and a waxed thread the same color as the tape. Use a tight overstitching at the ends and a running or blanket stitch along the sides.

Furniture & Furnishings
FURNITURE

Antique furniture

Before you start cleaning wooden furniture, make sure you have identified the surface correctly and never try to clean valuable antique wood, especially not with modern furniture polishes. If your antique furniture does get greasy, rub it with a chamois leather and a little 1-to-8 white-vinegar-and-water solution. Dry and buff, then polish as usual with beeswax. Antique wood will warp and crack if left in a hot, sunny, centrally heated room. Keep blinds closed and use humidifiers, or simply leave bowls of water around the room.

French-polished furniture

Many antiques, as well as good-quality modern reproduction furniture, have French-polish finishes. If damaged, such as by white heat marks, the entire surface may need replacing and should be done professionally. Never stand hot or wet things directly on a French-polished surface and wipe up spilled alcohol immediately. French polishing just needs to be regularly dusted. Any small stains can be removed by gently rubbing with a 1-to-8 solution of white-vinegar and water, using a chamois leather. Dry well and polish afterwards with furniture cream or wax polish. If the surface is scratched, you can try rubbing with furniture renovator or DIY French polish in the direction of the grain, following instructions.

Modern furniture

Because wood is a porous material, most modern wooden furniture is factory-treated to protect it against dirt and moisture. Modern finishes are often hard-wearing lacquers that need little cleaning and should be treated as you would a plastic, rather than a wooden surface. Remove scratches by rubbing with liquid metal polish and never use abrasives. Some modern wooden furni-ture is given a wax or French-polish finish, though this is rare; others are given oil finishes or even painted. Treat painted wooden furniture as you would any painted wooden surfaces.

Oil-finished and wax-polished furniture

Wax polish and oil finishes need regular polishing or oiling to keep them clean and to help protect their surfaces. Never use oiled or treated dusters on furniture with waxed surfaces and never use wax on oiled surfaces.

Teak and afrormosia

Never use ordinary furniture polish or wax polishes on these woods. Instead, rub with teak oil or cream two or three times a year. Rub heat marks with a soft cloth dipped in turpentine, then buff up with an equal-parts solution of linseed oil and mineral spiritis.

Untreated wood

Unsealed or unpolished wood, such as old pine tables, can be scrubbed with water and detergent after use. Make sure you dry it thoroughly. Rub hardwood countertops and cutting boards along the grain with linseed oil or teak oil twice a year. Never soak cutting boards or wooden salad bowls in water. Wooden salad bowls are best just wiped with paper towels after use and left until the next salad is prepared.

Garden furniture, usually cedar or hardwoods, should be treated with exterior-grade wood preservative. Any marks can be removed by rubbing along the grain with steel wool. You can seal these woods with a varnish used for boats, although prolonged exposure outdoors may mean that you have to revarnish from time to time.

POLISHING BRASS HANDLES

If wax-polished wooden furniture has brass handles, polish the handles at the same time as you are polishing the wood and with the same wax furniture polish. A proprietary brass cleaner can leave white marks on the surrounding wood that would have to be professionally removed. If you want shiny handles, carefully remove them to clean and then replace them.

Stain removal from wood

A simple dusting and an occasional use of the appropriate polish should suffice on most types of wood. If you do have stains to remove, wipe them up (then see below). Never attempt to remove a stain from any piece you think may be valuable; have it professionally restored. Always test cleaning agents first on an inconspicuous part of wooden furniture.

Alcohol
Mop up quickly, then rub the wood with the palm of your hand to add some of your natural oil back into the wood. Then mop with a little teak oil, furniture polish or some linseed oil, depending on the wood. If the stain is still there, rub with a paste of vegetable oil mixed with cigarette ash. Remove the paste and rewax.

Blood
Sandpaper the natural wood surface and swab carefully with hydrogen peroxide. Rinse afterwards. Blood is unlikely to stain a treated surface.

Candle wax/fats/grease/oils
Remove by rubbing with lighter fuel.

Cigarette burns/white heat marks
Remove the finish with methylated spirit. When dry, recolor the wood with a proprietary wood stain, wax crayons or shoe polish (see Scratches,

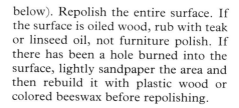
below). Repolish the entire surface. If the surface is oiled wood, rub with teak or linseed oil, not furniture polish. If there has been a hole burned into the surface, lightly sandpaper the area and then rebuild it with plastic wood or colored beeswax before repolishing.

Dents

Fill the hole with a wet rag and leave for a few hours. Or cover the dent with a damp cotton cloth and heat it with the tip of a warm iron until it steams. When the wood has dried, rewax or polish the surface.

Glue

Remove glue by rubbing with cold cream, peanut butter or salad oil.

Ink

Soak up excess fluid with a damp cloth and then dab the stain with lemon juice. Repeat until the stain has been bleached out thoroughly.

Paper

If paper has stuck onto your wooden surface, cover it with salad oil, leave it for two hours and then remove it.

Scratches

Rub scratches with wax crayons/shoe polish/eyebrow pencil or any waxy substance you can think of – as long as you match the color. For ebony, use black; for mahogany, use dark brown; and for oak and pine, use white or pale brown. For walnut, rub with the meat of a fresh walnut. For red mahogany, paint iodine onto the scratch with a fine brush and rewax the surface once dry. For maple, dilute the iodine with alcohol and rewax once dry.

Water marks, white

Rub in the direction of the grain with fine steel wool dipped in vegetable oil or use a paste of oil and cigarette ash and then buff with a damp cloth. Or apply an equal solution of linseed oil and turpentine. Leave for two hours and then remove with vinegar.

Right The mellow wood of this dining suite is the result of regular attention and care.

POWDER-POST BEETLE

Always check newly acquired pieces of wooden furniture for pinhead-size holes. You may find you are bringing home powder-post beetle, which will enjoy exploring your other pieces of furniture. Inspect the holes: if they show clean wood inside with sharp edges, the insect may no longer be there; if wood-dust is found under the piece, it will have to be treated. In the case of a valuable piece or an antique, consult a specialist firm.

If the piece is not valuable and you wish to treat it yourself, drop a proprietary wood-boring insect killer fluid into any holes made by the insect, making sure you drop it directly into the holes rather than onto the surrounding surface, possibly by using a syringe. Then press beeswax into the holes with a special applicator or a warm spoon handle. Smooth and repolish.

On nonaffected or treated pieces of furniture, occasionally use furniture cream on any unpolished undersides you can reach, both to preserve the wood and discourage powder-post beetle.

VENEER, GILT & LEATHER

Veneer

Veneer is the term used when a thin layer of quality wood, such as mahogany or walnut, is glued to the surface of coarser wood to add an elegance and richness to the piece of furniture. You should treat veneer according to the type of wood used. If the veneer surface is damaged, then it is difficult to repair, especially if the piece is valuable, and you should seek the advice of a professional restorer.

Mop up any spills on veneer immediately to prevent them marking the surface and check regularly to see the veneer is not blistering. Be careful if there are any pieces missing from your veneered or inlaid surface because the area next to the hole is often loose and will easily come away. Make sure your duster has not got any loose threads that could get caught on the veneer.

If a veneered or inlaid surface has a grease, fat or oil stain, cover the stain thickly with talcum powder and place a few paper tissues on top. Heat the paper with a hot non-steam iron, being careful not to burn it. The grease should be absorbed by the powder.

Gilt

Gilding is gold leaf rubbed onto a surface, such as wood, metal or plaster. It will last for years and not tarnish, providing the surface is not rubbed and does not come into contact with water. Gilded furniture just needs to be very gently dusted, but only if the gilt is not flaking. Always seek professional advice on restoring. If the gilt is intact, but dirty, clean it by dabbing the surface gently with a cut raw onion or with a soft cloth that has been dipped in warm turpentine or mineral spirits. Both turpentine and mineral spirits are highly inflammable, so warm it by standing the bottle in hot water, not over an open flame.

If you want to retouch gilt, do not use gold paint as it is a totally different substance, but try wax gilt, which comes in many tones of gold. Test it first on an unseen surface.

Leather

Leather can keep supple and beautiful for years – it can even improve with age, provided it is treated every month or so. Before treating leather you must test it for color fastness. In an unseen place, wipe the leather gently with a damp, soapy cloth. If no color is removed, wipe on a mixture of 3 parts to 2 parts castor oil and rubbing alcohol. Leave for twenty-four hours, then wipe with castor oil. If the leather has become stiff and thick, rub in saddle soap or leather conditioner with a sponge or soft brush, working the lather in well. Do this every day until the leather becomes supple.

To prevent cracking, rub dark leather on desks once or twice a year with warm castor oil, and white leather with white petroleum jelly, applying it with your fingertips and removing it with a soft cloth. Or you can rub it regularly with a mixture of equal measures of vinegar and methylated spirit mixed with double measures of both linseed oil and turpentine. Shake well before use and apply the mixture sparingly with a soft rag and then polish.

Removing stains

Remove stains from leather carefully with a little mineral spirit, being sure not to rub too hard or to use too much. Test it first in case the color of the leather is removed as well. If large areas of leather need to be brightened, rub with leather polish in a matching color. If a small area of color has been rubbed off or scratched, retouch it by stippling leather stain in the correct color with the tip of a fine watercolor brush. Do not use any color on the surrounding area; retouch only the worn spot.

Finishing touches

Always finish leather work by polishing with a proprietary wax dressing or cream on a soft cloth. Treat the leather about once a month like this. Dust or

Above Real leather furniture is expensive to buy but, with the correct care, it will last and keep looking good for years.

Opposite The high gloss on beautiful veneered furniture like this can be maintained by polishing in the usual way, according to the wood used.

vacuum leather upholstery regularly. Never use detergent, gasoline or ammonia on leather. Never rinse leather after washing with soap. If leather is badly damaged, do not attempt to treat it yourself, but seek professional advice.

Chamois-leather upholstery should be washed using warm soapy water and rinsed with warm water to which you have added a dash of olive oil. Leave it to dry naturally.

Leather desktops

Wash with soapsuds keeping the leather as dry as possible. If necessary, rub with leather conditioner or leather restorer to keep the leather supple, but be very careful not to touch any surrounding wood or embossed gilding.

Fake-leather upholstery

Fake leather should never be cleaned with wax or cream polish as it will not absorb it. Sticky marks can be removed with a mild detergent (not soap) solution and polished with a soft cloth.

RESTORING BUBBLED VENEER

Never buy a cheap antique with a bubbled or blistered veneer, thinking you are getting a bargain. Large areas of blistered veneer on valuable antiques cannot be repaired at home but must be treated by a professional restorer.

If you want to try to remove a small bubble, neatly cut the bubble across the top along the line of the wood grain with a sharp knife. Then gently squeeze a little glue into the cut. Press the veneer back into place and cover with several layers of blotting or brown paper or a folded sheet and iron for a few minutes with a hot, dry iron. Leave a heavy weight on the repaired veneer until the adhesive has set. Or simply glue the loose veneer and tape or clamp it back in position until the glue has set. Protect the veneer from the clamp by laying a thick paper pad on the patch and attaching the clamp to that.

UPHOLSTERY

If all your upholstery needs is a good cleaning, then make sure you follow manufacturers' care instructions. Use a clean cloth and do not overwet the fabric. Use a proprietary dry-foam upholstery shampoo or soapsuds. Test it on an unseen part of the chair first and do not let anyone sit on the cleaned chair until it is completely dry. Do not use household detergent. If your upholstery is velvet or velveteen, tapestry or other delicate material or water-repellent, have it professionally dry-cleaned. Horsehair upholstery should be brushed regularly and grease stains removed with spot remover.

Loose covers are much easier to keep clean. Follow the manufacturer's care label and iron them on the wrong side so that the fabric does not become shiny. Replace loose covers when they are still a little damp so they dry to the shape of the chair.

Old upholstered furniture

The most common problems with padded armchairs are broken springs and torn or ripped fabric. You can replace springs and webbing (although it may be easier to have this done professionally) and you can stitch fabric almost invisibly if you are careful. You can also take safeguards by using arm covers.

Below A dowdy but comfortable chair can be transformed by upholstering it with modern, fresh fabrics. Loose covers are preferable because they can be washed easily.

REPLACING CHAIR AND SOFA BUTTONS

There are two methods of replacing a button on the back of a chair, depending on whether the button is decorative or a double-button that holds both cover and filling in place. For both you need a piece of mattress twine and a mattress needle long enough to go through the upholstery and you must know how to tie a slip-knot.

For a double-button, push the thread through the back hook of the front button, then thread both ends of the thread through the needle. Push both threads through the chair from the front,

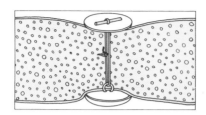

using the old hole (for strength, bring the needle through at a slightly different place at the back). Thread on a flat button at the back and attach it with a slip-knot. Tighten or loosen it until it looks right and then lock the knot and push into the thickness of the upholstery.

ATTACHING DECORATIVE BUTTONS

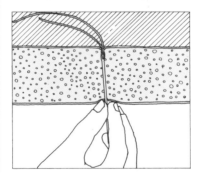

For a decorative button, push the needle deep into the upholstery (but do not come out at the back). Push the needle

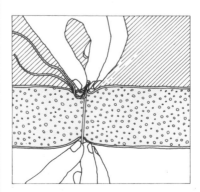

head out about $\frac{1}{4}$ in (6 mm) away from the first thread, so there are two threads hanging out of the front of the chair-back. Cut these so they are each about

6 in (15 cm) long and thread the button to one of them.

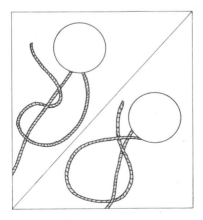

Tie a slip-knot with both tails, push the button into the chair and tie a half-hitch knot. Pull tight. Wind the threads round the button and bury in the sofa.

CHAIR ARMS

Mending a tear

Trim any loose threads on the tear but do not make the tear any larger. Cut a piece of fabric a little longer and 1 in (2.5 cm) wider on either side than the tear. The fabric does not have to match that of your armchair, but it should be strong.

Push the patch through the tear, and place it under the tear, making sure that the tear is centered on the patch and that the patch is flat. Gently pull back the tear and use a knife to apply the appropriate adhesive to the underside of the ripped fabric of the armchair and the top of the new patch.

Wait until the glue is tacky and then press down, first on one side of the tear and then the other, pulling the sides of the tear as close together as possible. If the tear pulls open again, repeat the exercise and use some stitches to help hold the tear together.

Make some arm covers in a matching fabric to cover the patches or to prevent tears occurring in the first place.

PICTURES & PICTURE FRAMES

Looking after pictures

Ideally pictures, especially if valuable, should be hung away from light, heat, drafts and damp. They should not be placed above radiators or next to standard or table lamps. Even picture lights are bad for valuable paintings, which can be adversely affected by both the heat and the light.

Heavy frames should be hung on two double hooks and be supported underneath to prevent the frame coming apart under the weight. If you fix a wooden batten to the wall for the picture to rest on it will help carry the weight. Always make sure picture hooks are large enough – use a double hook if you are in any doubt at all.

Use picture wire to hang your paintings and prints: it is neat, lightweight and will not disintegrate over time. String or thread, on the other hand, may eventually rot or fray.

Make sure that you do not hang a painting where you could pierce an electric wire; if you are unsure about where exactly these run, avoid hanging your pictures anywhere near wall lights.

Oil paintings

Unless you know your oil painting has no value or you painted it yourself and could paint another like it should something go wrong, it should be cleaned by an expert. At most, you can wipe it very gently with a damp cloth to remove any dust or simply brush it with an absolutely clean, soft paintbrush.

If your oil painting is of no value, you can try cleaning it with a little turpentine or mineral spirits. Use cotton wool and change the pieces constantly so that the cotton wool remains clean.

You can patch a hole or a rip in an oil painting by sticking a piece of unprimed canvas to the back with melted beeswax.

Pictures can be scattered individually throughout the rooms of a house or some of them grouped together, as here, to make a collective impact.

Lay the oil painting face down on a thick pile of greaseproof paper and dip the canvas patch into the melted wax before applying it directly to the back of the picture. Smooth it down gently with a palette knife. If you press too hard you may crack the paint on the other side.

Prints and watercolors

Works of art on paper should always be kept under glass and behind a frame to prevent them getting dirty. Even clip-on frames do not provide adequate protection from dust. Keep the glass clean by regularly wiping it with a little warm water and cotton batting, taking care not to let any water seep under the edges of the frame. Never attempt to clean or patch an antique or valuable print or watercolor.

Removing stains
Never put water anywhere near your watercolor picture, or you may ruin it. If a print is very stained it may be best to put it in a new mount, because you could lose a lot of its character by cleaning it. If you do decide to clean it, dusting the print with some fresh white breadcrumbs – without the crust – will help remove surface grime. Rubbing it very gently with a soft, white eraser will

also help – be careful not to rub away the paper itself, or the pencil marks if the print turns out to be a drawing.

Old rust-like stains on prints can be bleached away by immersing the print in a bleach solution using 5 ml of chloromine T to 1 pint ($\frac{1}{2}$l) water. Do not attempt to do this yourself if your print is valuable. Test it first to make sure the ink is colorfast; many Oriental prints are not. Rinse the print well afterwards in clean water and dry it by placing it flat between two thick wads of blotting paper and a sheet of board, both top and bottom. Then keep the print tightly clamped until it is dry.

Remove grease from both prints and watercolors by dabbing very gently with a piece of cotton batting that has been dampened with a little acetone. When the acetone has loosened the grease, cover the whole of the stained area with blotting paper and press it gently with a warm iron. You may need to use several pieces of blotting paper to remove the grease completely.

Mending tears
Mend a small tear or hole in your print by gluing a good-quality artist's paper over the back of the hole. Then use a very fine brush to touch up any colors that are missing from the print, matching shades as closely as possible.

MENDING PICTURE FRAMES

Old frames are worth restoring and you can tackle simple repairs yourself, although if the frame is valuable the work should be left to an expert.

The first thing to break with frames is usually the corners. If your frame is falling apart, take it to pieces, removing all the pins and scrape off the old glue. Sand the faces of the corners until you have removed all the varnish and/or paint. Put adhesive on both faces and bond together using a corner clamp – or find another way of clamping the corners until the adhesive works. Then drive in panel pins or wooden pegs across the join through its thickest part.

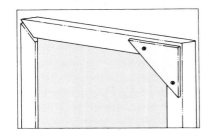

You can simply strengthen the corners of a picture frame without taking the whole frame to pieces. To do this, screw diagonal or triangular corner plates of plywood or metal to the back of the frame. Another way of strengthening the frame is to drill diagonally across the corners of the frame and glue in wooden dowels (plugs).

ORNAMENTS

Care of ornaments

Cleaning rare and valuable objects or jewelry should be done only by professionals. Some ornaments wear graciously and should not be cleaned, but just dusted occasionally.

Take care even when lifting ornaments. For example, a valuable statue should not be picked up by its head or hand, but should be supported at its thickest point, often the base, by both your hands. Often handles of heavy vases or rims of large bowls are not strong enough to support the entire object, so think before you lift.

When hand-washing fragile, hand-painted ornaments, use a plastic bowl in case they slip out of your hand and warm, not hot water, with a little mild detergent. Put only one object in the bowl at any one time and do not use abrasives but clean crevices with an old toothbrush used gently. Rinse in warm, clear water and dry carefully or drain on a soft towel or a pile of paper towels.

Special cases

Alabaster

Alabaster is absorbent and will be stained by water. It should be wiped gently with mineral spirits, gasoline or paint solvent. To remove stains, rub the alabaster with a piece of cloth moistened with turpentine and dipped in powdered pumice-stone. Polish well with a little beeswax dissolved in turpentine or with a wax furniture polish.

Bone, horn, ivory and tortoiseshell

Bone, horn, ivory and tortoiseshell are likely to become dirty and greasy quickly. To clean them, rub gently with a little methylated spirit on a clean soft cloth. Polish spots with whiting and methylated spirit.

If you want to, you can lighten the color of ivory and bone by bleaching Make a paste of whiting and hydrogen

peroxide, cover the piece and then let it dry in the sun. Remove the paste with a damp cloth and buff with a soft cloth. Or rub the object gently with fine abrasive powder on a dampened cloth.

Tortoiseshell can simply be kept clean by rubbing it gently with a cloth dipped in a little olive oil.

China (from porcelain to earthenware)

All china not labeled as suitable for a dishwasher should be washed by hand in warm water with mild detergent. Use a plastic bowl in your sink if you have a tendency to let soapy items slip out from between your fingers. Never use strong abrasives on china or you will damage the glaze. Most domestic stains can be removed from china by rubbing with moistened household salt or bicarbonate of soda. Coarse china is porous and stains easily, for example, tea and coffee stains in mugs. Clean them by soaking in bleach occasionally.

Glass

Glass can be machine-washed unless old, delicate or painted. Always support the bowl of a glass while cleaning or drying it, by placing your fingers either side of the stem and cupping your hand under the bowl. Always rinse glass well in warm water and dry it carefully with a linen glass cloth. Until drying, leave the glass upright and filled with hot water. Pouring out the water at the last minute

will make the glass easier to dry. Never drain glasses by standing them on their rims. Polish decorative glass with an impregnated silver wadding.

If glasses have stuck together, put cold water in the inner glass and hold the outer one in warm water. If a stopper is jammed in a decanter, apply a mixture of 2 parts mineral spirit, 1 part glycerine and 1 part salt to the join between the bottle and the stopper. Leave it for a day, then carefully tap the stopper and see if it will come out. If it has broken inside the neck, expand the neck by running hot water over it.

Glass vases and jars

To clean badly stained glass vases, jars, decanters, etc, fill with a solution of warm water and biological detergent or a solution of $\frac{1}{4}$ pint (150 ml) vinegar and 1 tablespoon (15 ml) cooking salt. You could also use some hot soapy water and a little clean silver sand or fill the vessel with water and a denture-cleaning tablet. Leave overnight and occasionally shake gently.

To remove lime deposits, use a proprietary stain-removing tablet in water or soak the glass in rainwater for a week and then scrub with a toothbrush.

Above Treat delicate china like this with respect and wash in the dishwasher only if safe to do so.

Right Keep glass vases sparkling clean by washing in hot soapy water.

MENDING BROKEN CHINA

It is best to mend breakages as soon as possible or you are bound to lose some of the pieces.

Make sure the pieces fit together and that their edges are clean. If they are not, wash them in a mild detergent solution and leave them to dry. Rub off old glue with acetone, using a silk cloth. Once the edges are clean, do not touch them or they will get greasy and the adhesive will not stick.

Make sure you have the correct adhesive and use it only after reading the manufacturer's instructions.

Fill a box with sand and place the object in it with the hole at the top. Glue the edges of two pieces and stick them together. Remove surplus adhesive at once or when it is rubbery, according to the manufacturer's instructions. You can use a wide brown-paper gummed strip to help stick the joins. As the paper dries, it shrinks and pulls the pieces together. Fix the strip at right angles to the join.

Allow each piece to set a little before sticking the next piece to it. To help the adhesive stick, keep the glued china warm with a fan heater or hair-dryer. Once all the pieces are stuck, leave the mended object for a few days to set before moving it.

Be careful about using cups and teapots with mended handles: the handles can drop off again and the hot tea may scald you.

METALS

Metal care

All metals are susceptible to rust and being worn away by corrosion. Modern metals are often coated with paint or enamel finishes, but if these are chipped the metal underneath becomes quickly vulnerable. Never use harsh abrasives on metals and never leave them in prolonged contact with acids (such as lemons and tomatoes). On unprotected metals, tarnish can be removed with a proprietary abrasive polish.

Always identify the metal you wish to clean before you start cleaning it. Soft-metal polishes, such as silver polish, will not shine hard metals, but hard-metal polishes, such as brass polish, could damage soft metals. If your metal piece is antique or valuable, seek professional advice when cleaning it.

Special cases

Aluminum (pots and pans, kettles, teapots, baking tins)
Never use washing soda on aluminum and do not put it in the dishwasher. Instead hand-wash with hot water and mild detergent and rub with soap-filled steel-wool pads in one direction only. Always rinse and dry well. Discolored pans benefit from having lemon rinds or vinegar and water boiled up for a few minutes in them. Do not put a hot aluminum pan directly into water as it could buckle.

Anodized aluminum (trays, light fittings, saucepan lids, trolleys)
Anodized aluminum has had its natural coating thickened, and the surface has become harder, which should prevent corrosion. All it needs is to be wiped with a damp cloth and thoroughly dried. To give the item extra shine, use a liquid wax polish.

Brass (fire tools, door handles, saucepans, kettles, ornaments)
Wash kettles and saucepans with hot

detergent solution; soaking will remove stubborn food stains. Dry thoroughly and remove light stains with lemon juice or a paste of vinegar, salt and flour. Polish ornaments regularly with brass metal polish. If not lacquered or constantly cleaned, brass eventually develops a green incrustation known as verdigris, which can be cleaned with a strong ammonia solution. Lacquered brass should just be rubbed with a soft duster.

Britannia metal (see Pewter)

Bronze (ornaments)
Bronze normally just needs to be rubbed with a soft duster, using a brush, if necessary, for the ornamental parts. If very dirty, wash items in hot vinegar, then rinse, dry and buff thoroughly, or simply rub well with a few drops of oil and then remove with a soft duster. Brush off green verdigris with a stiff, not a wire, brush and then swab item with a 1-to-9 acetic acid and water solution. Rinse, dry and buff. If lacquered bronze is peeling, relacquer.

Cast iron (saucepans and pots)
Always dry carefully to avoid rust and coat with vegetable oil. Store cast iron in a dry place, and do not store pans with their lids on or they will rust. Do not run cold water into a hot cast-iron pan or it will crack. For cast iron coated with enamel, see below. If coated with a non-stick surface, do not use abrasives or metal cooking implements. Simply wash after use in a hot soap solution.

Chrome and chromium plating (metal furniture, taps, electrical appliances, etc)
If very dirty, wash with warm soap solution; otherwise just dust regularly with a soft duster. Use a chrome cleaner for mild corrosion. Do not use washing soda, salt or harsh abrasives on chrome.

Copper (saucepans, kettles, ornaments)
Copper must be kept clean to avoid verdigris, which is poisonous. Wash regularly in a hot detergent solution, and clean stains with lemon juice or a paste of equal parts of vinegar, salt and flour. Copper can form poisonous salts with acids from foods, so make sure any copper saucepans are lined with tin. If your copper pan has developed verdigris, make sure it is not used for cooking as it is poisonous.

Polish ornaments with copper cleaner and remove green verdigris by swabbing with a soap solution to which you have added a few drops of ammonia.

Enamel, porcelain enamel (saucepans, ovens, sinks, baths, etc)
Most stains can be removed by simply soaking the item in hot detergent solution. Use moistened bicarbonate of soda or a proprietary cleaner for cleaning dirty ovens. Never use harsh abrasives, which can ruin the coating.

Gold and platinum (jewelry)
Do not clean gold-plated items too often. Gold and platinum just need

Opposite A gleaming display of objects made from different metals.

Above left Lacquered brass needs only a light rub; unlacquered brass needs polishing.

Above right Pewter and Britannia metal do not have the high shine of metals like brass.

rubbing with a duster or chamois leather and occasionally washing in a warm, mild detergent solution, rinsing and drying with a chamois. Use a silver metal polish on tarnished low-carat gold. Take high-carat gold to be professionally cleaned. Store gold in tissue paper or a chamois leather to protect it.

Iron and steel, not *tinned, enameled or stainless* (gates, *pots and pans, fire irons*)

Wash unprotected iron and steel with an abrasive powder and keep them clean and dry. If possible, apply a layer of grease, such as lanolin, to prevent rust. Remove rust with paraffin-moistened steel wool or a proprietary cleaner. If painted or galvanized, wash with hot detergent solution and dry well. Varnished iron should just be buffed.

Lead (ornaments)

Scrub general stains with turpentine or an abrasive powder. Remove white deposits by boiling in several changes of water then place in a 1-to-9 vinegar and water solution and rinse in water containing a little bicarbonate of soda. Rinse in distilled water.

Pewter and Britannia metal, modern pewter (tankards, ornaments)

Dust pewter regularly and wash with soap solution or rub clean with a cabbage leaf. Remove grease stains by rubbing with methylated spirit, then rinse and dry. Clean Britannia metal with a proprietary polish.

Silver and silver plate (jewelry, cutlery, ornaments)

Any food containing acid, such as vinegar and lemon juice, can mark silver, so wash the silver as quickly as possible after use, rinse and dry. Egg can tarnish silver too (rub with salt before washing).

Do not use abrasives, wire or steel wool or bleach or silver, and do not wrap silver in newspaper. Use and wash silver regularly so that you will not have to polish it as often. Store silver in special bags or rolls of cloth which are available from jewelers and department stores, or wrap in tissue paper and put in polythene bags.

Clean silver teapots by filling the teapot with boiling water plus 1 tablespoon (15 ml) washing soda and some foil. Leave for one hour and then rinse well. For regular cleaning, wash silver and then clean with a proprietary silver cleaner, well away from a stainless-steel sink, which can be damaged by silver cleaner. Wash again after cleaning and dry thoroughly.

Very tarnished silver (not if bone-handled or with inset stones) can be placed in an old aluminum saucepan half-filled with hot water. Bring to the boil, add a little washing soda (1 part washing soda to 20 parts water) and then immerse the silver. After a minute or two of simmering, when you see the tarnish has gone, remove the silver and wash it in a warm soap solution. Rinse and dry thoroughly and then polish as usual.

Stainless steel (cutlery, pots and pans, teapots)

Do not wash a stainless-steel frying pan with either soap or detergent to dissolve the grease. Instead, wash with clear, hot water and allow the grease to build up. Rub the inside lightly with lard before storing. Other stainless-steel items should be washed with hot detergent suds, rinsed and dried. If pitmarks are caused by salt and acids in foods, remove them with fine soap-filled steel wool or a proprietary cleaner. Burn marks cannot be removed from stainless steel. Clean teapots by filling with boiling water plus 1 tablespoon (15 ml) washing soda; rinse well after an hour.

Tinware (baking tins, saucepan linings)

Wash after use in hot detergent suds, rinse and dry thoroughly by putting it in a cooling oven. Store in a dry place. Boil badly discolored baking tins in washing soda and water. Remove rust marks by rubbing with cooking oil or with a raw potato dipped in mild abrasive powder, wash and dry.

103

THE SAFE HOME

General Principles
YOUR RESPONSIBILITY

Your home is probably somewhere you feel quite safe, and yet many serious accidents take place in homes: every day people fall, drown, suffocate, choke, are electrocuted and poisoned. By thinking ahead you can do much to prevent these accidents happening: making your home safe is your responsibility.

Keeping yourself and your family safe is a task that is becoming increasingly important, and more worrying. It used to be almost enough to keep a cat to devour the odd mouse, to shut the front door at night and to make sure your open fire was not burning too fiercely before you went to bed. Today safety in the home covers everything from security to pollution, as each new "convenience" appliance brings its own risks. These risks can be reduced if they are recognized in the first place. How best to deal with them is discussed below.

The risks

Fire
The risk of fire has been with us since time immemorial, only there are now more ways of both causing fires and extinguishing them. Obvious causes of fires in the home are cigarettes, lighters, candles, matches, unattended irons and frying pans. There are many steps you can take to reduce the risk of a fire starting in your home; there are also ways of containing it once it does start. Make yourself familiar with all of these (see pages 134–7).

Water
The combination of water and electricity can be fatal, so be very careful – especially if you have a flood in your home. Water can be very destructive, so use it thoughtfully: keep an eye on a running tap and place washing machines and dishwashers in places where they will cause the least damage if they do flood. Be sure that you know how to turn your water off at the supply valve and always call a plumber if you are in any doubt about your water system.

Gas and electricity
The danger from gas is explosion; from electricity, fire. Make sure you know how both systems work in your home and how to turn them off at the main supply in a hurry. Check individual appliances regularly or have them serviced by an expert when necessary. Use appliances correctly too, following manufacturers' instructions.

Falls
Many people fall at home, especially the very old and very young. You can safeguard against certain falls by making sure you use nonslip polish on shiny floors, that your rugs have special nonslip underfelt placed under them and that all steps or changes of level are well lit. If your home has uneven floors, frayed carpets or loose floor tiles it is up to you to mend them.

Other accidents
Medicines, drugs, cleaning fluids, paints, weedkillers and sharp implements, etc, need to be locked away or put out of reach of children. Food needs to be handled with care to prevent poisoning and stored so as to protect it from being contaminated, or simply aging. Flammable fluids must be kept safely according to relevant regulations and all storage must be uncluttered and easy to reach when needed.

Building and decorating
There are now safety regulations that apply to almost all aspects of a building. There are fire-retardant specifications for internal walls, doors, paints, etc, to help prevent a fire spreading; there are specifications for bathroom and toilet positioning to ensure hygiene; and there are flame-retardant covers and fillings for upholstered furniture as well as flame-resistant fabrics that can be used for clothing. Most appliances also have to comply with stringent safety regulations; so avoid buying electrical goods in flea markets and make sure new goods meet the standards set by the relevant body.

Damp
The main danger from the weather is damp, which can get into your home from the top, bottom or sides. In damp conditions, timber is exposed to attack by mold and fungi, such as wet and dry rot, and your walls are exposed to rising damp. Dampness may need expert attention or you may be able to deal with it yourself. What you can do is keep your home dry and well ventilated and keep a constant check that water is not penetrating your home through the roof, the walls or the floor.

Pests
Many pests are health hazards, and it is important to keep them at bay. There are specialist firms that will remove them from your home by fumigation or use of insecticides and poisons, but you can try to prevent pest infestations in the first place by keeping a clean home.

Clear out any birds nesting in your roof or eaves and give cats flea collars to wear. Keep other flying pests out with mesh screens over open windows and doors and always keep your kitchen and cupboard floors and surfaces spotlessly clean. Never leave food out unprotected, empty your compost bin regularly and keep rubbish in closed bags or cans. If you suspect rodents, keep food in mouse-proof containers and any holes in baseboards securely filled.

Poisons
Many of the household products we have been taking for granted and freely using around the home have recently been shown to be hazardous either to our health or to the environment. For example, aerosol containers, used for everything from shaving foam to whipped cream, contain CFCs, which are now known to be destroying the ozone layer. Stop buying household products in aerosol containers or buy only non-CFC brands. Many lumber treatments, insect killers, do-it-yourself materials and household cleaners are also known to be toxic. If possible, use a "green" alternative.

Look after yourself

Avoid all unnecessary risks: know your limitations and ask for professional help in tackling tasks if you feel they may be beyond your capability. Never undertake work alone, especially if it could be dangerous – such as working on ladders, working with electricity, etc. Learn basic first aid from a recognized authority and keep a well-stocked first-aid kit. Look after tools and equipment and use them only in a safe environment. Plan ahead and give yourself plenty of space. Accidents happen when you least expect them.

A kitchen should be kept as uncluttered as possible. The floor and the work surfaces must be easy to keep clean; never leave any food out uncovered. Use saucepans on the back burners and always turn pan handles inwards. Avoid trailing cords on kettles and other electrical appliances.

Room by Room

KITCHENS

On guard

Because so much time is spent in the kitchen, it is important that you are aware of the many potential hazards.

Plan your kitchen so that it is as safe as possible; for example, don't hang implements that you will need to reach at the back of the stove if this will involve you stretching over the stovetop to get at them. Always use electrical equipment that meets stringent safety standards; choose a food processor or a coffee grinder that will not operate unless the lid is fixed securely.

Accidents can happen within seconds: the important thing is to keep your head. Have a fire blanket handy in a kitchen, and fit a smoke alarm near the door of, or just outside, the kitchen – not anywhere near the stove or it will cause continual false alarms. Listed below are some of the things that you should be alert to.

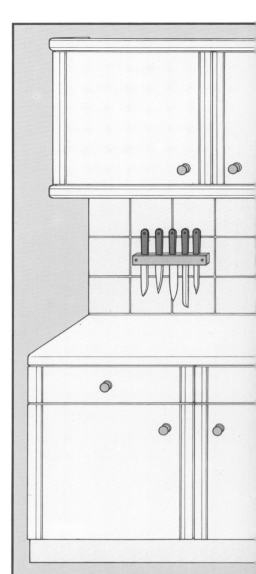

CHILDREN IN THE KITCHEN

If your child spends a lot of time in the kitchen, it is worth putting him in a playpen until he can walk. After that, allocate a special part of the kitchen for him to play in and use a safety gate so that he cannot stray. Once he does, it is a good idea to fix child-proof locks on all doors, cupboards, fridges, freezers, dishwashers, etc; also remove all fragile and dangerous objects from low-level drawers. Garbage pails should be high enough not to become toys, but if your garbage pail proves irresistible to your child, why not let him have it as a toy and buy another one for your own use.

Try to make the cooking area out of bounds. Otherwise, place saucepan handles, cords of electric appliances, hot food and drinks and sharp knives safely out of a child's reach. Sockets should be at worktop height and you should either put a guard around the top of your stove or oven or try to cook on the back burners with pan handles turned inwards. Never leave full saucepans, teapots or cups on a kitchen table within reach of your child and avoid using tablecloths until your child has passed the age when he might be tempted to pull them off.

GOLDEN RULES

- Never leave deep-frying pans unattended. Fat ignites spontaneously when it reaches 400°F (204°C) and is the cause of most fires in the kitchen. Remove the pan from the heat if the fat begins to smoke. Smother pan fires with a damp cloth or fire blanket, not with water
- Keep a fire blanket near the stovetop, but not where you would have to reach over the stove to get it, and position a fire extinguisher within easy reach

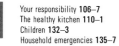
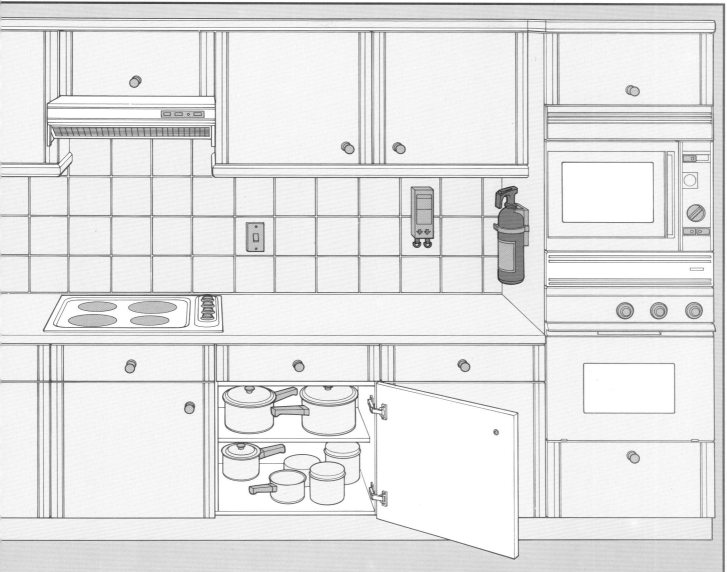

- Make sure the pilot lights on your gas stove are always lit, especially after cleaning the top of the stove or spilling liquids
- Do not pry open can lids with your fingers. Always wipe the top of can lids first in case they fall in the can
- Do not polish your kitchen floor too highly or it can cause a fall. Wipe up spills, especially greasy ones, at once
- Buy an oven with an insulated door: ordinary doors can become very hot. Never dry cloths over a stove

- The sharper a knife is, the safer it is. Keep your knives sharp and never leave them lying on a worktop if there are children about
- Make sure poisons, disinfectants and household chemicals are locked up
- If cupboards are too high, they can be a hazard. Lower them so that you can reach them easily, and place heavy items at waist height – if they are too low you could hurt your back
- Change or replace the grease-collecting filter in your range hood regularly or it may catch fire

- Do not put electrical equipment in water or you could electrocute yourself. Never touch any switch or electrical appliance with wet hands. Always unplug appliances after use and before cleaning them with a damp cloth. All electrical kitchen equipment is potentially dangerous

Keep dangerous kitchen items well away from children: sharp knives out of reach at the back of the countertop, household chemicals locked away. Use low-level cupboards only for safe and unbreakable equipment.

THE HEALTHY KITCHEN

Safety in the kitchen means more than simply taking the common-sense precautions outlined on pages 108–9. It also means recognizing the ecological and health hazards in the kitchen and being aware of how to safeguard against them or even avoid them.

Saving resources

In planning your kitchen, it is now important to think not only about the most efficient use of space, but also about how to save energy and avoid pollution. Many of the everyday appliances in our kitchens are heavy consumers of energy and some even pollute the atmosphere. Fridges and freezers, for example, give off CFCs, which are known to damage the ozone layer. It may be some time before you will be able to buy a safe alternative, but you can make sure that you use a fridge or freezer efficiently. Never buy one that is too big for your needs, keep it as full as possible and defrost it regularly.

Stoves and ovens – whether they are fueled by gas or electricity – are the biggest users of energy in the kitchen. Plan your cooking so as not to waste energy. Always cook more than one dish at a time in your oven, use stacked steamers to cook all the vegetables at the same time, but using only one saucepan, put lids on saucepans, use the right size pans for the source of heat and do not overcook food. Before using any electrical equipment, each time you reach for a switch ask yourself: do I really need to turn this on or could I just as easily do this by hand?

Water consumption
Saving water also takes a little forethought. Use a bowl in your sink rather than leaving the tap running and boil only as much water in your electric kettle as you think you will need. Do not turn the dishwasher on until you have a full load; use economy settings where possible and get an expert to service the machine regularly.

Waste disposal

The kitchen generates more waste than any other room in the home. Take steps to cut down on waste and recycle or reuse whatever you can. Avoid buying overpackaged goods. Choose fresh food that is sold loose, returnable glass bottles rather than plastic ones and aluminum cans that can be recycled. If you have to buy packaged goods, choose those wrapped in cardboard, greaseproof paper or cellophane, which is biodegradable. Keep any leftover food and organic matter for garden compost; sort other types of waste into separate bins (one for glass, another for paper, etc) for various methods of disposal, depending on the local services available to you.

Toxic and nonbiodegradable cleaning products that get washed down the sink pollute the water. Always read the labels to check the contents of any product you use and try to buy nontoxic alternatives where possible.

MICROWAVE OVENS

Microwave ovens accelerate cooking times and therefore can save energy – and cost less to run. On the other hand, they encourage the use of convenience foods, which means that there are more packaging materials to throw away. There are also ongoing debates about their safety: some brands have been found not to heat food through to the right temperatures at which food-poisoning bugs are killed.

Check that the microwave you buy meets the relevant safety standards and always follow the manufacturer's safety instructions when using it.

Microwave ovens can leak radiation so make sure the door-seal is kept clean and in good condition. If the door is broken, do not operate the oven or try to repair it yourself. Microwave ovens should always be repaired and regularly serviced by an expert.

Below A kitchen with few appliances consumes little energy and reduces the potential for environmental damage.

Your responsibility 106–7
Kitchens 108–9
Kitchen storage 112–3
Chilled kitchen storage 114–5

Kitchen 158–9

THE SAFE HOME

HOW MUCH ELECTRICITY DO YOU USE

The items below are the most energy consuming in the home. The figures relate to continuous use at full capacity, and do not take account of variations in power during operation. For example, once a dishwasher has heated up the water, it will operate at a lower power during subsequent cycles.

Appliance	Average wattage (1,000 watts used for 1 hour = 1 kWh)
Barbecue	1,350
Convection heater	500–2,000
Deep fryer	1,500
Dishwasher	1,300
Fan heater	500–2,000
Grill	1,300
Iron	1,000
Kettle	1,500
Oven & Stove	12,500
Toaster oven	1,100
Toaster	1,150
Dryer	5,000
Washing machine	500
Wok	1,150

In comparison, a clock, clock radio, standard lamp, radio, home security and fire alarm all use under 20 watts.

If possible use mains electricity rather than battery power. Most batteries contain hazardous materials which corrode, and, when disposed of, can lead to air pollution problems.

Right Clean work surfaces and chopping boards mean that you can prepare food on them as hygienically as possible.

Preparing food

The day-to-day preparation of food in your kitchen calls for strict hygiene to safeguard you and your family against food poisoning. Bacteria, which cause most cases of food poisoning, will multiply on food, given the right conditions. To prevent this, it is essential to keep your hands and all equipment and surfaces spotlessly clean. Never use a knife or any blade with which you have cut raw meat or fish to cut anything else afterwards – wash it the moment you have used it. Scrub chopping boards and marble tops clean between uses. Always keep cooked and raw food separate. Food that is left out should be covered. Remember that bacteria breed in warm temperatures, so cool food down as quickly as possible after cooking (not in the fridge or freezer or it could warm up other foods).

Most bacteria are killed by very high temperatures, so always make sure that food is cooked right through. Take special care to thaw frozen fish and poultry thoroughly before cooking – the bacteria will have stopped multiplying in the freezer, but they may still be present and will die only if exposed to very great heat. Be careful when using a microwave oven, as microwaves do not always heat food to temperatures at which food poisoning bacteria are killed. Pressure cookers, on the other hand, are useful because they cook at very high temperatures.

Checking labels

If you or anyone in your family suffers from allergies, you should be careful about the food you buy. Certain food additives can cause allergic reactions in some people. Always check the ingredients listed on labels of food and drink sold in supermarkets and try to choose "wholefoods" or "organic" foods rather than those produced with the help of artificial fertilizers, pesticides, preservatives or additives.

Safe materials

Some of the materials used in your kitchen may also be hazardous to your health. For example, aluminum pans and some nonstick coatings are now thought to contaminate food and increase the risk of certain diseases. Copper pans sometimes accumulate a poisonous deposit of verdigris if not cleaned properly. Certain plastics used in laminated surfaces, food containers and clingfilm give off harmful gas. Where possible, use stainless steel, cast-iron, toughened glass or enamel.

THE "GREEN" KITCHEN

- Keep a "green" compost bin for any vegetable peelings, uncooked leftover food and eggshells. If you have not got a garden, give it regularly to someone who has
- To save water, use a plastic dishwashing bowl in your sink
- If thermos flasks have coffee- or tea-stained interiors, put some crushed eggshells inside together with a little hot water and shake well. Then wash. Never immerse a thermos flask in water

KITCHEN STORAGE

All food spoils eventually, but there are ways of storing that will preserve it longer. If food is sold sealed, do not transfer it to another container unless you are ready to eat it and always look at date stamps on any food you buy and plan to keep. Be organized: after each shopping trip, put new food at the back of your shelves, moving older food to the front so that you will use it first.

Your kitchen, larder, refrigerator and freezer should be kept clean, and kitchen and larder surfaces should be dry. Keep rapidly perishable items in a refrigerator or freezer and other goods in a cool, dry larder, pantry or cellar. Do not store soaps and detergents, even in closed boxes, in the same cupboard as food or the smell will pervade the food.

Insects

It is essential to keep insects away from food. As many insect repellents contain poisons that can harm you too, use herbal insect repellents and put metal gauze screens on your windows to exclude flies and other insects.

Cover food containers with a sieve, fabric mesh or a sheet of greaseproof paper or foil. Plastic wrap may contain a carcinogenic plasticizer, which, if warm, can be absorbed by foods, especially fatty ones such as cheese. It is better not to let plastic wrap touch food. Never leave food uncovered in the kitchen and clean your compost container and/or garbage pail regularly, or they will both attract insects.

Containers

Storage jars should always be airtight as the shelf life of many products depends on the exclusion of air. You can buy special sealed glass storage jars; otherwise the best containers are made of ceramic or stainless steel. Nonglazed porous surfaces can contain mold and bacteria in the cracks, which can contaminate food and are best avoided.

Storage rules

Biscuits, crackers, etc
Once open, store in a metal box or tightly closed jar. Do not store with cakes or they will become soggy.

Bread
Keep in the bread bin, which should be as airtight as possible. Remove moldy bread at once.

Cake
Store in a metal cake tin – keep a piece of apple or slice of bread in the tin to help it last longer. Do not store with biscuits.

Canned foods
Canned food keeps longer because the air has been kept out, so beware of cans with dents (especially on the seam), rusty cans, cans with a rounded end and cans that smell odd. Keep cans in a cool, dry place. Once open, remove the contents and eat within a few days.

Coffee (beans or ground)
Once the bag is open, roll up the top and keep it in an airtight container. If you want to keep coffee for a long time, you can freeze it.

Coffee (instant)
Always replace the lid.

Eggs
Keep in a cool place. Do not wash them or you will remove the protective film from their shells.

Flour
Store in container with a lid – not in a plastic bag. Cornflour should also be kept in an airtight jar.

Herbs
Keep dried herbs in dark, airtight containers in a cool place.

Jams, honey, marmalade
Use quickly once opened. Store in a cool larder (or the refrigerator).

Nuts
Loose nuts should not be stored in a larder as they can go rancid (instead, keep them in the freezer).

Oil
Store in a cool, dark larder (or in the refrigerator).

Pasta, pulses, rice
Store in an airtight container.

Potatoes, root vegetables
Keep in the dark in a cool larder, pantry (or the refrigerator).

Sugar
Keep in an airtight container with a piece of bread.

Tea
Store in an airtight container.

Vegetables (fresh)
Make sure that cool air is circulating around them.

THE LARDER

We all think of a larder as a luxury and not a necessity. Yet the correct storage of food is so important that ideally a larder should be incorporated into every home. A larder should be a chilly cell with thick walls and cold surfaces. It should be situated next to the kitchen and attached to the coolest wall of your house. Floors should be made from cold bricks, walls lined with glazed tiles and shelves made of marble, slate or stone. Hooks for hanging salamis or onions are also practical. The door to the kitchen should be well insulated to keep the warmth of the kitchen out and the top window and lower airhole should be fly-proofed.

Many raw foods such as apples and potatoes keep longer in a cool larder than in a vegetable basket in a warm kitchen, and cheeses and butter store better in a larder than in a fridge.

Top Clear storage jars come in a range of interesting shapes and have the further advantage of making their contents easy to identify.

Above Baskets serve as good containers for fruit and vegetables because air circulates freely through the weave. Store them away from direct light.

CHILLED KITCHEN STORAGE

REFRIGERATOR CONTENTS

- Store all meat and fish at the top
- Take meat out of any plastic container, wrap it loosely so it can breathe and place it on a rack over a clean plate
- Cooked meats should be kept covered
- Never let raw meat or fish drip onto or touch other food in the refrigerator: bacteria spread easily from raw to cooked foods

- Fish and cheese should be wrapped in aluminum foil to stop the smell from contaminating other foods
- Vegetables can be kept in the vegetable drawer of your refrigerator; remove them from plastic bags or they will decay quickly
- The contents of cans, once they are opened, should be transferred to other containers.

Refrigerator

A refrigerator is designed to store perishable foods at the standard temperature of 35° to 40°F (2° to 7°C). To ensure safety, always follow the manufacturer's instructions for use.

Do not overload the refrigerator with food as this prevents the cold air from circulating. Always cover food to stop smells penetrating other foods. Defrost regularly and clean the interior with moistened bicarbonate of soda. Remember to inspect the refrigerator often for forgotten foods. Never force the refrigerator door shut or you could damage the door-seal or door.

Putting hot food into the refrigerator causes condensation and warms up other foods. First let food cool down in the larder if you have one.

Freezer

A freezer stores food at a standard temperature of 0°F (−18°C). To make sure it stays this cold, keep it at least two-thirds full and tightly packed and open the door as little as possible. Freeze only foods that are fresh, cold and in perfect condition. Never refreeze anything once it has been defrosted or you could poison yourself – bread and cakes are the only exception. If you do not want to eat thawed food immediately, cook it and then refreeze it.

Frozen food should be clearly marked, stating contents and date frozen. Wrap food to be frozen in waterproof and airtight packaging. Follow the manufacturer's instructions, and those on bought frozen food, on the length of time you can keep food frozen. As a general rule, aim to clear out the contents of your freezer every four months.

Defrost the freezer regularly once the layer of ice is about $\frac{1}{2}$ in (1 cm) thick and wipe the inside clean with moistened bicarbonate of soda.

Right All food can be stored in the freezer or refrigerator as long as it is fresh.

FREEZER CONTENTS

- Separate pieces of meat and fish with two sheets of greaseproof paper so that you can remove them singly
- Make sure poultry and rolled joints are fully thawed before cooking, preferably in the refrigerator or microwave, rather than in a warm room. Unthawed areas of meat may not get hot enough during cooking to kill food-poisoning bacteria
- Be careful of freezing fish and shellfish – it has often been frozen already. Only fish caught that day should be frozen. Fish should be thawed slowly in the refrigerator, then cooked as soon as possible

- Fresh vegetables should be blanched, then rinsed in very cold water and well drained before freezing. Blanching kills any bacteria that may cause loss of flavor and color
- Mushrooms should be sautéed in butter before freezing or frozen raw; potatoes should be cooked almost completely before freezing
- Once frozen, celery, bananas, tomatoes, lettuce, cucumber, radishes, endive and chicory cannot be eaten raw but can be used for cooking
- Soft fruit can be frozen whole or puréed. Freeze hard fruit whole, sliced

or puréed. Frozen ice cream only lasts for up to two months
- Soft cheeses and double cream freeze well; fresh milk, yogurt, sour cream, cream cheese, single cream and hard cheese do not
- Do not freeze eggs in their shells; either they must be lightly whisked or the eggs and whites frozen individually. Hard-boiled eggs cannot be frozen
- Wrap bread, cakes and pastries in foil or plastic bags before freezing. Sandwiches freeze well, except those filled with egg, banana, tomato, cucumber or lettuce

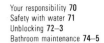
BATHROOMS

If your bathroom is big enough, it is perfectly possible to create a comfortable, appealing room with a feminine look by using appropriate furniture and fabrics. Traditional soft furnishings will offset the starkness of modern sanitary fittings.

The bathroom should be a sanctuary where you just have to shut the door to escape from the rest of the world. It also needs to be totally hygienic and free of dirt and germs, as well as completely safe for young and old alike. To enjoy peace of mind in a bathroom you need also to be aware of what the dangers are and what could go wrong.

SAFETY MEASURES

Most toilet bowl cleaners are poisonous and should be used with care. Never be tempted to use two different toilet bowl cleaners together: they can give off toxic fumes or even cause an explosion. Store all toilet cleaners and brushes safely away from children.

That the germs of legionnaires' disease have been discovered trapped in shower heads shows how important it is to unscrew them and clean the rose.

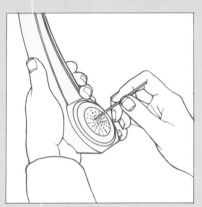

Push a needle or other fine point into the holes to unclog them.

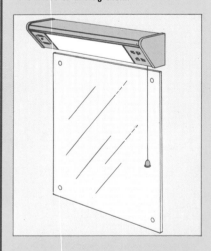

Make sure the bathroom is well lit. Shaving lights should shine on your face and not on the mirror. If you use an electric shaver, install a properly insulated shaver outlet.

The hazards

Children

Children must be constantly supervised in the bathroom. Make sure they cannot lock themselves in, and fit all bathroom and toilet door locks above child height. Never leave one or more small children alone in the bath, not even while you answer the telephone.

Keep cleaning equipment, including toilet brushes, medicines and pills safely locked away. Razor blades, both in use and discarded, must also be removed: never throw disposable razors in the wastebasket in case your child forages in it.

Every day, clean your toilet and keep the lid closed or young children will regard it as one of their favorite toys, not only to wash their hands in but also as a receptacle for their toys.

Water: flooding

There is an obvious danger from water in a bathroom. Guard against the possibility of a flood starting, not just from your forgetting to turn off the taps when running a bath or basin full of water, but also from a defective overflow pipe on your toilet.

For safety reasons, there are some manufacturers who will not service washing machines or dryers that are installed in bathrooms. Check first with the relevant manufacturer and if you do install laundry equipment in your bathroom, make sure you leave a space of at least 6 ft (1.8 m) between them and your bath or shower. Place the machine in a special tank with an overflow in case it breaks down and floods.

Water: scalding

To avoid the danger of scalding, particularly in the very young and very old, always test the water in a bath or shower before using it. Set the thermostat so that water in the hot tap is never more than 130°F (54°C).

Running cold water into your bath before hot not only prevents scalding but also helps reduce the amount of steam in the bathroom.

Water: condensation

Condensation can lead to problems of damp. Having an enclosed shower minimizes steam, as does painting your bathroom walls with a water-based, rather than an oil-based paint. Open the window for a while when the bathroom is very steamy and do not block permanent exhaust vents.

Electricity

Bringing electrical appliances, such as hair-dryers, into the bathroom can kill. Remove all nonsafety sockets and electric switches from the bathroom: install lights that can be switched on only from outside or pull switches for lights and heaters. Use only special safety sockets for electric shavers.

Wall-mount any electric heaters and keep them well away from the bath. Never bring a free-standing heater of any kind into the bathroom where it might be kicked, tripped over, or cause any other accident.

Other electric appliances that run on alternating current such as radios should be kept on shelves well away from the sink and tub.

Accidents

Wet, slippery surfaces can cause falls. Use nonslip mats in the bath and keep the floor as dry as possible. Cover glass shower doors with safety film so that, if they accidentally break, they will at least not splinter.

Make sure any gas water heater has a special sealed flue and have it serviced annually. Check frequently that the pilot light is still lit.

SAFETY IN THE BATHROOM

- Fix a handrail to the wall beside the bath.
- Put a nonslip mat in the bath for added safety.
- Use water-based paint on the walls and, if possible, install an enclosed shower to minimize condensation.
- Fit a strong light over the mirror.
- Ensure there is proper ventilation.
- If you have small children, make sure the toilet seat lid is kept down.
- Never leave razors lying around.
- Keep disinfectants, cleaning materials and medicines properly secure and out of the reach of children.

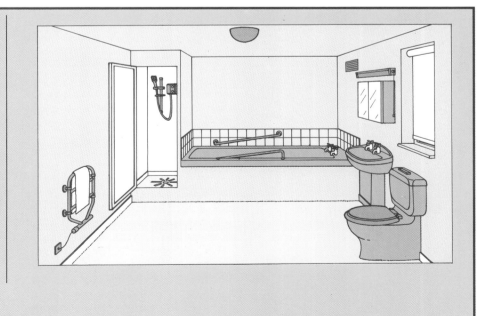

PLANNING YOUR BATHROOM

Water and energy are precious resources and we should be careful not to waste them. In planning your bathroom and how you use it, take into account how best to conserve both water and energy. Remember that washbasins and bidets are much more economical with water than baths and are often all you need for a good clean.

The shower

Showers are more conservation-minded than baths, as well as being more purifying to wash in. Because of the easy temperature control, they can also be stimulating for the body. A shower in which you change the temperature rapidly from hot to cold and back again is particularly invigorating. Finish on a cold shower to close the pores of your skin.

To enjoy the full benefits of a shower, you need good water pressure. If the shower is at the top of the house or where the pressure is low you may have to consider putting in a power shower to deal with this problem.

HOW MUCH WATER DO YOU USE?

Use	Average water consumption
Toilet	3 gallons (11 liters) a flush
Bath	29 gallons (110 liters)
Shower	9–11 gallons (34–43 liters)
Washing machine	36 gallons (135 liters) a wash
Dishwasher	11–17 gallons (43–65 liters) a wash
Garden sprinkler	2.2 gallons (10 liters) a minute

If you are interested in finding out more about how much water you use, you can install a water meter. You can use it either for your own personal interest or to check your water rates if they seem particularly high in relation to the amount of water you use.

The toilet

Your toilet is the biggest water user in your home. You can now buy a dual flush toilet, which has a short flush, using only 2.1 gallons (10 liters) per flush or half the amount of the standard toilet. Manufacturers are experimenting with shorter flushes, but until they come up with something, place a brick or water-filled bottle in your tank to displace some of the water and give your toilet a smaller flush. Just be careful the object does not interfere with any of the workings of your tank.

Your toilet also uses energy. Each time you flush, your local pumping station switches on its pumps to keep the pressure in the system. You may also be using additional energy if your toilet is directly attached to a pump. There is not much you can do to save energy – except use the toilet less!

THE BATHROOM CABINET

- There are now many cosmetics and toiletries that are "cruelty-free" (not tested on animals); buy these products whenever possible
- Try to buy products with the minimum of packaging and that the manufacturers will refill. Any plastic packaging should be biodegradable
- Look for products made from natural ingredients and that contain no animal products. Many bath-foaming products contain the allergen formaldehyde
- Aerosols should be labeled "ozone friendly" or "CFC-free". If possible, ban all nonessential aerosols from your home as the cans are not recyclable
- Toilet deodorants should be avoided altogether. Many contain a chemical that is a potential water pollutant
- Buy toilet paper containing recycled fiber, or choose uncolored rather than colored paper as colored paper is less biodegradable

The bath

The shape of the bath used in the West has evolved from oval tubs and chair and hip baths. It is designed for lying full length, has a large surface area (which means the water cools rapidly) and is very wasteful on water. In the East, soaking baths are shorter, occasionally wider and much deeper, with inside steps which both help you to get in and out and act as seats.

In general, a bath uses over 250 percent more water than a shower, with corner baths using the most water.

Left If you have the space, the most luxurious alternative is to have a separate shower fitted.

Right If space is limited, you can still have a shower as part of the tap attachment on your bath.

BEDROOM & NURSERIES

On average, you spend one-third of your time in bed – and far longer when you are a child or ill – so the atmosphere in your bedroom should be peaceful, harmonious and, of course, safe.

Taking precautions

Fire
Never smoke in bed. It is just too dangerous a risk to take. Have a battery-operated smoke alarm installed inside, or just outside, your and your child's bedrooms; check that you can hear it wherever you are in your home.

Before going to sleep, turn off any bedside lamps, electric heaters and televisions. Never drape scarves over lamps to dim them or you could cause a fire. If you like having a light on in the night, buy a night-light or leave the corridor light on or replace your bedside light bulb with one of a weaker wattage.

Medicines
Never take medicine in the dark, just in case you have picked up the wrong bottle or remembered the instructions incorrectly. Keep all medicines, including birth-control pills, hidden away if you have children.

Below Bedrooms should be airy, peaceful places where you can sleep in restful comfort. Apart from an adequate circulation of air, to keep the room from becoming stuffy, a supportive mattress is necessary for a good night's sleep.

THE RIGHT TEMPERATURE

Bedrooms are often too dry, hot and stuffy. The ideal temperature is quite cool – between 55° and 60°F (13° and 15°C) – a little higher for children and the elderly. A hot-water bottle or an electric blanket in your bed (never both at the same time) before bedtime makes the bed itself inviting. Before going to bed, always turn off the electric under-blanket. If you need heat during the night, buy an electric overblanket or use a hot-water bottle (see also page 131). Several layers of thin blankets on your bed will feel warmer than one thick one. Make sure that eiderdowns, duvets and quilts are not stuffed with polyurethane foam mixtures. All these should be made of fire-retardant materials.

General principles 106–7
Children 132–3
First aid 146–9

Making improvements 154–5
Bedrooms 162–3

THE SAFE HOME

SLEEP WELL

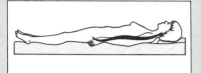
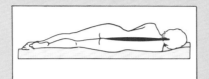

A simple test will tell you how good your mattress is for your sleeping posture. If you find it difficult to roll from side to side in bed, your mattress is too soft; and if you can slide your hand under the small of your back when lying flat, your mattress is too hard.

The right bed should support the spine and yet allow the hips and shoulders to lie naturally. The shape of your spine should be a shallow S-shape when you lie flat and and a straight line when you lie on your side. As a general rule, the heavier you are, the firmer a mattress you will need. One medium-thickness pillow should be enough to support the nape of your neck and position your head correctly while you are sleeping.

Children's bedrooms

Furniture and lamps

Check that your child cannot get locked in any wardrobes, closets or cupboards: all doors should be able to be opened from the inside.

Choose heavy, stable furniture that he cannot knock or pull over onto himself and do not let a child under five sleep on a top bunk in case he falls out. Replace all free-standing lamps with wall-mounted or ceiling lights that cannot be knocked over or cause a fire.

Materials

Make sure that all the paint used in your child's room is lead-free and nontoxic, especially that on your baby's cot. Why not buy a cot with a natural wood finish and simply polish it with beeswax? Natural-fiber bedding, such as untreated cotton flannelette sheets and cellular cotton blankets, are best for you and your child. Wash them before using for the first time.

In bed

Do not give a child a pillow in bed until he asks for one; he might be smothered. If you need to raise his head because he has a cold, put one under the mattress. Never let a cat or dog sleep with a baby in case it lies on his face, and never leave a baby alone in bed with a propped-up bottle or potato chips or nuts in case he chokes. In homes where you might not hear your baby scream, you should always have a baby alarm. There are several kinds available, one of the best being the sort that has a battery-powered intercom that you can carry with you from room to room.

Heaters

To make sure children do not burn their hands on radiators or heating registers, fit them with a thermostat so you can turn the temperature down. If you do not have central heating, use a convector heater in your child's room. They are safe to use although, like other heaters, they should never be put below curtains or used for drying clothes on.

Other dangers

During the day, keep safety plugs or night-lights in sockets so that your child cannot stick his fingers or anything else into the socket holes.

Place a safety gate outside your child's bedroom before he can walk so that he is used to it being there. There is nothing more dangerous than a toddler climbing out of his cot and being able to fall down stairs or explore the house while you are still asleep.

NURSERY SAFETY

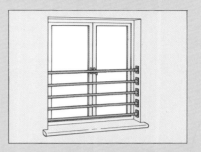

Windows on upper floors should be guarded with vertical bars that are easily removable in case of fire. If bars are not removable, they should be horizontal and only go halfway up the window. Any lower windows without bars must have safety catches. Never leave a bed or chair under a window – your child could climb onto it and then out of the open window.

Toys should be kept within your child's reach, or unseen in a closed cupboard, rather than on display on high shelves. It is tempting for your child to climb up to get them, which could cause an accident.

Check that toys meet national safety standards and look carefully at any toys your child is given before letting him play with them. Remove any toy with sharp edges and do not let a toddler walk with a pencil (or any other sharp implement) in his hand or mouth in case he falls. Give small children large, chunky toys; toys with small parts, or beads, marbles, etc, can be easily be put in their mouths and up their noses.

LIVING ROOMS & STUDIES

You should be able to relax in your living room without having to worry about safety. The main risk of injury is from fire (or the combination of fire and water); make sure double-glazed windows can be opened easily in case of a fire in your home.

The hazards

Fire
Guard both open fires and wall-mounted heaters well. In some countries it is illegal to leave a child under twelve alone in a room with an unguarded fire. If you have children, use a fireguard that is fixed to the wall on either side of the fire. If you sift ashes after a real fire, wear gloves and keep children out of the way.

Check for fire-retardant labels when buying furniture. Never buy polyurethane foam mixtures for cushions or upholstered furniture: if they catch fire, dangerous toxic fumes will be released within minutes. You can have polyurethane foam specially treated or covered with treated upholstery material, but the best thing to do is banish it entirely.

Wires and cables
Keep electric cords and telephone wires short so that they do not trip people up. If necessary, add extra outlets. It is dangerous to lay wires under carpets as faulty wiring may cause a fire.

Televisions
Never tamper with a television set yourself. Taking the back off one can be more dangerous than you thought: some of the 20,000 volts generated by a color television can remain in the set for a few days after it has been switched off. Professional repairers have special machines that discharge the volts. Do not place a vase of flowers or any water-holding container on top of a television: if it tips over it could cause an electrical fire. Always switch a television off at the socket after use: they have been known to cause a fire in an electrical storm.

Children

Coffee tables should be child-friendly with rounded corners and low enough for a child not to be able to crawl under. Glass table tops are dangerous to children, as are matches, pins, cigarettes, needles and other sharp or hot objects left lying on a table. Keep vases, delicate china, glass ornaments or any precious objects out of the way of children.

Make sure children cannot get into your drinks cupboard: even a little alcohol can be dangerous to a child.

Right In this comfortable living room, the coffee table is low with rounded corners to minimize painful knocks, delicate ornaments are kept out of the way and a fender guards the carpet (and the children).

Below Natural light floods this desktop, but there is an adjustable lamp to shine a direct beam onto the work should the day be cloudy, or if working at night.

WORKING POSITIONS

If you sit at a desk all day long, it is very important that you take care of your body. Eat well and move about and try to go for a walk at some time.

Notice how you are sitting, especially when typing or writing. Are you hunched over or cramped up? Are your shoulders tense or relaxed? It is most important that a chair gives your body proper support. Buy one on which the height and back angle can be adjusted to your own requirements.

If you can arrange to work in natural light, do so: it is better for your eyes. If you do close-up work, exercise your eyes by looking into the distance every now and again. If you work on a personal computer or a word processor, look away from the screen every twenty minutes for at least thirty seconds.

Some materials connected with the office, such as glue and fixatives, are health hazards and give off unnatural smells. Typewriter correction fluids also contain a chemical that damages the atmosphere. Always keep the window open if you have to use them and avoid glue in non-CFC aerosol cans.

Living rooms, halls & stairs **30—1**
Around the home **36—42**

Energy saving **62—9**
Decorating **78—85**
Flooring **86—91**

HALL & STAIRS

Planning ahead

Never forget that your hall and stairs are important as fire-escape routes and should be kept clear at all times. If possible, bicycles, carriages and strollers should not be stored in the hall, and all hall furniture should be small enough for you to be able to get past it easily. Fix the hall telephone to the wall to keep it out of both your and your child's way.

Above Hallways and stair landings should be kept as clear as possible of furniture, bicycles and strollers that might get in your way. If you are rushing to answer the door or leaving the house in an emergency, such obstructions will trip you up.

Your responsibility **106–7**
Old people **130–1**
Children **132–3**

Making improvements **154–5**
Style & color **166–7**
Furnishings **176–83**

THE SAFE HOME

TAKE NO CHANCES

Trailing dressing-gown and bathrobe hems, backless slippers and loose shoe soles can cause falls. Shorten hems and mend broken footwear and clothing. Do not wear smooth-soled slippers or heels that catch on thick pile carpet if you are unsure of your step.

Always keep one hand free to hold on to the handrail, especially if carrying a child, and always walk up and down stairs carefully. Even if there is someone at the front door, take your time. Do not rush down stairs; let visitors wait.

Toys and other objects left on the stairs can trip people up. Whenever you use the stairs, automatically pick up anything lying on them and carry it up, or down,

Right When carrying a child up the stairs always hold on to the handrail.

with you. Coats should be hung up and not draped over the banisters or the newelpost as they will eventually slip off. Install a coatrack or at least a few hooks by the front door for coats, hats and umbrellas.

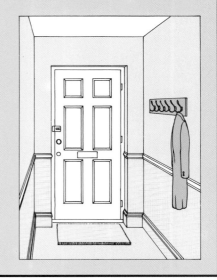

Steps and stairs

Lighting should be bright and evenly distributed, with no gloomy spots or shadows. Keep a light on at night if elderly people or young children will be using the stairs. To make life easier, install two-way light switches.

If your steps are steep, make sure your handrail is secure and at the correct height for everyone using the stairs. Do not use rope handrails. If someone has difficulty climbing the stairs, fix an extra handrail to the wall.

Lay the stair carpet so that it reaches well beyond the top step covering each landing and make sure it is tightly fitting and well fixed. Mend any loose, torn or frayed stair carpet and tighten stair rods as soon as they become loose. If linoleum is broken or floor tiles are lifting, they should be mended or replaced immediately as well.

If your steps, landings or corridor floors are polished, use nonslip polish on them and never place a loose rug at the bottom of the stairs as it can easily slip. If any hall rugs are worn or frayed,

mend them. The doormat too can be a danger hazard. Recess it into the floor so it cannot slide or be tripped over.

Safety gates

There is some controversy about the usefulness of safety gates. Children catch their fingers in the accordion-style gates, and adults may fall over them if they forget they're there. The gates can also lull parents into an unwarranted feeling of security. A child may discover how to open the gate when the parent least expects it. Nevertheless, you may decide that gates are needed.

If your child is an early walker, safety gates at both the top and the bottom of your stairs can save a few tumbles, but if your child is a late walker you should try and make do without them. It is much safer to teach a child how to climb up and down the stairs. Always supervise a small child on the stairs. Keep safety gates closed at night to stop your child exploring while you are asleep.

THE FRONT DOOR

The front door is your main line of defense against intruders. Make sure that both the door and the frame are strong and that the latch is not faulty. Check that the locks are secure and high enough so that your child cannot open it and let himself out. If your front door is glass-paneled so that anyone can see in, consider changing it to a more secure all-wood door.

Your mail slot should be large enough for your newspapers to be pushed through so that they don't have to pile up on the doorstep if you have gone away for the weekend and forgotten to cancel them. Make sure that there is a flap behind so that a burglar cannot look in and see whether you are at home.

A peephole will let you see who is outside before you decide whether you want to open the door – or a bolt on a chain will let you speak without fully opening the door. Otherwise simply stick your head out of the window and check.

Safety Outdoors

THE GARDEN

Paths

Make sure the garden path is in good condition with no loose or uneven stones on which people could trip. Your steps should be safe too. Always sweep leaves and moss from steps and paths or they become very slippery. If the access to your house is along a path or up or down steps, make sure it is well lit. If your house is set well back from the road, lay your front path with a noisy, crunchy substance like gravel, so that you can hear anyone coming down it.

Boundaries

Always check fences to see that there are no protruding nails or splinters. If your garden is on a main road, think about growing a thick hedge to protect your family from breathing in too many toxic exhaust fumes. Fit a child-proof catch to the garden gate and repair any holes in your fence or hedge.

Water

Ponds should be covered or enclosed if you have small children. A child can drown in 2 in (5 cm) of water. If your garden is on a river or stream, fence it off for the same reason. Do not leave buckets of water lying around either. Always supervise a child's water play, even in a paddling pool. If children cannot step out of a paddling pool on their own, they are too young to use it.

Animals

If possible, pet bowls should be kept outside. If they must be indoors, keep them out of a child's way.

Although compost heaps are excellent as they get rid of your organic waste and feed your garden with valuable nutrients, rotting animal matter and bones should not be put on as they may attract unwanted animals.

CONSERVATORY SAFETY

Many accidents in the home are caused by children running into glass. Make sure all glazed doors have toughened or laminated safety glass that will minimize injuries if broken, or consider using plastic glazing. A cheaper solution is to buy safety film, which you can fix to glass windows and doors. The film will hold pieces of broken glass in place and can prevent serious injuries.

Sticking cutout pictures on glass walls and doors at children's eye level so they can easily see that there is a barrier is a good temporary solution. The pictures can change as you get bored with them or the children cease to notice them. Once children are older the pictures can be removed altogether.

A shelf placed across the glazed wall of a conservatory gives the plants maximum light and acts as a deterrent for children.

Keep sandboxes covered when not in use as they become an attractive toilet for stray cats. Make sure children never play with the excrement of cats or dogs. Both cat and dog feces can spread many diseases, the most harmful of which is toxocara, which can affect the brain, the lungs and the eyes.

Fire

Never light a bonfire or barbecue using gasoline and supervise all fires carefully, especially with children about. A fire can easily get out of control and set light to an overhanging tree in your neighbor's garden, if not your own – keep a hose or a bucket of water handy. Do not choose a windy day to light a bonfire and keep it well away from your house. Do not burn household rubbish such as rubber, foam or ceiling tiles, which can give off toxic gases. Completely extinguish bonfires at night.

Tools

Always keep gardening equipment in good condition and put tools away after use. Keep them locked in a shed that is inaccessible to children. Ideally, install special exterior sockets and use a residual current circuit-breaker.

Never let a child push or drive a lawnmower or play near a lawnmower in use. Always keep the electric cable

NATURAL POISONS

Remove all poisonous plants and toadstools from your garden and all plants with tempting poisonous berries, such as yew, woody and black nightshade, holly and privet. Laburnum and lupin seeds are dangerous too. Teach children not to eat anything out of the garden, but if they have and are suffering, take them to hospital with a sample of the plant.

The tetanus bacterium lives in the soil and can easily enter the body through cuts and splinters. Make sure you and your child are immunized against tetanus.

Man-made poisons
Do not use enticing-looking slug or insect repellents in your garden if you have children and make sure that any chemicals you use will not poison your family or pets.

over your shoulder and away from the blade when using power hedge-trimmers or a lawnmower – use a brightly colored cable to avoid mowing over it. Never use electric lawnmowers when it is raining or when the grass is wet, and do not leave them or any other electrical equipment out in the rain. Never pull an electric lawnmower toward you and never pick it up when it is on. Do not leave any mower unattended when the motor is running.

Garden furniture

In the spring, check garden swings, climbing frames, deckchairs and other garden furniture to see if fittings have corroded or rotted during the winter months. Supervise younger children, especially when several are playing together. Make sure swings hanging from branches will hold your weight; if they do not, they probably are not safe for your child to use either.

One of the greatest pleasures of spring and summer is to sit outdoors on a sunny terrace or patio. But it is important to make sure that all garden furniture is sturdy and stable; wooden chairs and tables may start to rot, especially if left outside. Check all outdoor furniture each spring. Teach older children how to open and close folding garden chairs correctly.

TOOLSHEDS & GARAGES

Safety first

Your workshop should have generous storage space, plenty of socket outlets and a solid workbench, and be well lit. You should use it only when you are wide awake and sensibly clad. Floppy pullovers with long drooping sleeves can be dangerous or, at the very least, you can ruin them. Accidents can also easily happen if you are feeling drowsy. If you can, lock the door of your toolshed and keep young children out of it.

Tools

Always carry sharp tools with their points facing downwards, and teach older children to do the same. Lock your tools away after use and keep them in perfect condition. Use the right tool for the job and in the proper way. Keep both hands placed firmly behind any cutting edge and work away from the body with saws, chisels and knives.

Power tools

After use, unplug power tools and do not leave them where children can reach them. Remember to keep the cord behind you when using them and also to unplug them when you are changing parts and accessories. Do not lift tools by their cables; you could weaken the electrical connection. Always use properly insulated extension cables and make sure power tools are correctly wired and fused. Have all sockets professionally installed.

If you are using power tools outside, have special outdoor sockets fitted and use a residual current circuit-breaker. Make sure any extension leads used outdoors are in good condition. Water, for example on wet paths, and electricity are a lethal combination.

As soon as they are old enough, teach children the right way to use power tools, sharp blades and dangerous chemicals. Explain to them the importance of using them only when an adult is present.

THE "GREEN" TOOLSHED AND GARAGE

Pouring any synthetic goods made from petrochemicals down the sink or drain can contribute to the contamination of our drinking water. If you have a choice, use natural, nontoxic household products. If not, campaign for a hazardous-waste collection service to be started in your neighborhood.

Take used car oil, transmission fluid and batteries to a service station or reclamation center for recycling.

Keep thinners and turpentine in tightly closed jars. When the contaminants have settled, strain the thinner through muslin and reuse the liquid. Once the contaminants have solidified, dispose of the container with household waste.

Oil-based paints, paint strippers, wood stains, preservatives and polishes that you wish to dispose of should be taken to a hazardous-waste collection center if there is one near you.

Water-based paint containers can be disposed of with other household waste.

CAR SAFETY

Never leave the car engine running in the garage as exhaust fumes can be deadly in an enclosed space.

At once
- Make sure your car takes unleaded gasoline. Lead in the atmosphere is a danger to the health of the community, particularly children
- All passengers should wear seat belts, even in the rear of your car. It is now illegal for any child under the age of sixteen to travel in the back of a car without being strapped in
- Make sure your car is safe for children of any age to travel in. If you have not already done so, buy a car seat that conforms to safety standards for your child at once

Monthly
- Check the oil

- Check the water: open the radiator when the engine is cold
- Check all the tire pressures when the car is cold, including the spare tire
- Make sure tires have sufficient tread (there are legal requirements determining this)
- See that there is enough distilled water in the battery (this is more important in summer than in winter)
- Make sure all your lights work and replace any defective bulbs
- Check that there is water in your windshield-washer bottle

Regularly
- Service your car as recommended
- The moment you notice a fault, have it seen to

Yearly
- Check all the documentation is in order
- In the late autumn, make sure there is enough anti-freeze in the radiator

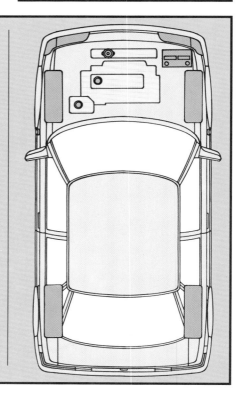

Poisons

Never leave chemicals or any other poisonous or corrosive substances lying around and never decant them into soft-drink bottles or any other container. No matter how safe it might seem at the time, you will invariably forget what is in the container or how to use it.

Make sure you have adequate storage for flammable fuels. Check regulations for storage, and never smoke where inflammable substances are stored. Get rid of any rubbish. Do not build up collections of oily rags, tin cans, old newspapers or anything else. All such collections stored in a toolshed, workshop, garage, or anywhere else, are potentially dangerous.

When using poisonous substances, be careful. Always read and follow any manufacturer's instructions. Do not smoke, make sure you have adequate ventilation and protect your hands, clothes and face. Even household adhesives can be potentially dangerous.

Ladders

Buy a sturdy but lightweight ladder with a handhold and use it instead of balancing on a fragile chair or a pile of boxes. Ladders must be kept in good condition and always placed on a flat surface. Do not overreach from a ladder and if you are at all unsure of its stability, ask someone to hold the bottom. Never use the ladder if you are alone at home, in case you fall. Keep ladders locked away from potential burglars.

BICYCLE SAFETY

- On both your and older children's bicycles, check steering and brakes frequently and have bicycles regularly serviced. Brakes should work effectively and brake cables should not be frayed
- Equip all bicycles with a bell or horn
- For night-time cycling, make sure bicycle lights work. Mount them as high as possible, and aim them at motorists' eyes
- Tires should have enough tread and be properly pumped up

- When cycling, wear a sensible crash helmet, bicycle clips and goggles or sunglasses. Wear fluorescent bands or jackets in the day and reflective ones at night.
- Plan your route before leaving home and know your highway traffic regulations. Always bear in mind the car driver's point of view
- Any child riding on your bicycle with you must not sit on the handlebars or crossbar, nor on the luggage rack behind you. He should sit on a special child safety seat, preferably one with a high back and an integral safety harness
- Children's tricycles and bicycles should be regularly checked and any loose screws, nuts and bolts tightened or replaced
- Fit a young child's first bicycle with stabilizers until he is fully confident

Special Considerations
OLD PEOPLE

About half the fatal accidents in the home happen to those over the age of sixty-five. With many elderly people the problem is how slowly and tactfully to change their lives. You should be able to make things easier for elderly relatives without them feeling that you think they are incapable of anything.

If you can, find out about installing a personal-alarm system, which could put both your and their minds at rest. That way, all they need do is press a button to get professional help, no matter how far away you are at the time. Make sure their home is as vandal-proof as possible and always do things before being asked – otherwise you could wait a long

time: most old people are rightly proud and loath to ask for help. A telecom and telephone in a convenient position means that they do not have to rush to answer the door.

The hazards

Cold
As you get older it becomes increasingly difficult to maintain a constant body temperature. At the same time you grow less sensitive to changes in external temperatures. The combination of these means that old people can often be

cold without feeling so. If their body temperature falls below 95° F (35° C), hypothermia sets in; if it is not treated at once, this can be fatal.

It is important that the home of any elderly person is kept above 61° F (16° C). If you find it is not, you must turn up the heating, make sure they have on enough thick clothes or light blankets and make warm drinks. Work out for them the most economical heating system and check the insulation in their home. Also make sure that their rooms are well ventilated and kept slightly moist, not damp, as the dry air caused by heating can make chest infections worse.

Never rely on the old saying they do not feel cold. If you notice that they are saying they feel warm in a bitterly cold room, they could already be suffering from hypothermia. Other danger signs are drowsiness, slurred speech and parts of their body normally kept covered, such as the stomach or armpits, being very cold. If in any doubt, move them immediately into warmer surroundings, wrap them in a light layer of blankets, give them a warm nourishing drink and call the doctor. Do not give them alcohol as it will further stimulate heat loss, and do not suddenly change their temperature by sitting them next to a fire or giving them a hot-water bottle.

Fires

All fires should be protected. They should not be able to be knocked over or fallen against. In the kitchen, make sure there are special safety gas or electric stove and oven controls with easy-to-manage knobs and with warning lights that show when appliances are on.

Falls

The elderly are often far more unsteady on their feet, so it is not surprising that falls are the most frequent accidents in the homes of the elderly. As elderly bones are more brittle than those of a younger person and take longer to mend, it is especially important to prevent falls. Floors must be kept in perfect condition with nothing left on them that could trip someone up. Plan the home of an elderly person so that there is as much storage space as possible within easy reach, involving as little bending or climbing as possible.

Check that rugs and stair carpets are not worn or torn and floor tiles are not peeling up. All carpets should have a nonslip backing and the floor underneath them should never be polished. There should be at least one firm handrail on the staircase. Seek professional advice on having handholds fitted around the bath and toilet.

Opposite A comfortable sitting room for an older person, with a chair drawn up by the fire, and a place for a favorite pet.

Medicines

Sleeping pills and strong medication should not be left beside an elderly person's bed. All medicines should be clearly labeled and you should never change their pills from one container to another. Make sure they can open any child-proof container on their own and read and understand the doctor's instructions on the label.

Kitchen equipment

Bear in mind that the old often have less reliable memories and slower reactions, which can be dangerous in the kitchen. Invest in automatic equipment, such as an electric kettle that turns itself off or a thermostatically controlled deep-frying pan that can never burn. However, never force them to change to equipment you enjoy using. If they feel happier with something they have had for years, and know how to use, check it is safe, have it serviced and let them carry on using it.

Remove any chipped or broken dishes and place a plastic bowl in the kitchen sink to avoid breakages. Make sure saucepan handles are firmly fixed and brightly colored so they are easy to find. Can openers should be easy to use and tap handles to turn on and off – find out about taps that can be operated with wrists and elbows.

Lighting

Make sure all rooms and corridors have night-lights and lights that are easy to turn on with two-way switches. Also lighting should be bright enough so that elderly persons do not have to strain their eyes, particularly when reading. Though less attractive, fluorescent lighting is often easier to see by than an ordinary tungsten bulb.

In the garden, too, it is important that paths and steps are well lit and paving stones level. The path should be kept clean and dry; fallen leaves and moss should be removed.

In bed

An electric overblanket that can be left on all night is safer than an underblanket. In cases of incontinence an electric underblanket should not be used, and the mattress should be covered with a waterproof rubber sheet to protect it.

A personal stereo is a useful friend for long, lonely nights. Listening to a concert or other people's problems on the radio brings a sense of contact with the outside world and can lessen feelings of loneliness. And soothing music is just the tonic for a restful night's sleep.

SAFETY WITH ELECTRIC BLANKETS

- Follow the manufacturer's instructions both for using and cleaning the blanket. Always have the blanket serviced regularly, approximately every two years
- Never plug an electric blanket into a light fixture in case it is switched on unintentionally, nor into an adaptor being used for another appliance
- Do not use an underblanket as an overblanket and vice versa
- If the blanket is wet, dry it out naturally before using it. Do not turn it on if it is wet
- Never use a hot-water bottle with an electric blanket in case it leaks

- Do not use an electric blanket folded or creased. Tie it securely to the mattress and, when not in use, leave it tied flat to a spare bed rather than rolled or folded
- Never stick pins into an electric blanket
- If there is any likelihood of incontinence, do not use the blanket
- Check frequently for frayed edges, loose connections at the plug and controls, fabric wear, scorch marks, damage to the flexible cord and displaced heating wires. Have any faults seen to at once by the manufacturer or an electrician

CHILDREN

Children are particularly vulnerable to accidents in the home, most of which can be avoided by careful planning. As a child develops, you will always have to be one step ahead to foresee the likely areas of danger. Don't be upset if you are constantly having to change your home to accommodate your growing child and his needs.

The hazards

Newborn

While your baby is immobile, there is little harm that he can do to himself, but you should always keep him in earshot in case he starts to make unfamiliar noises. Keep him warm: remember that young babies, whose sensitivity to temperature has not yet developed, are at risk of getting hypothermia. Make sure that their room, like that of the old, is kept above 61° F (16° C).

Thoroughly disinfect anything the baby comes into contact with, do not let your dog lick his face and do not put his Jolly Jumper or reclining chair on a high surface or it may tip off.

Toddlers

Once your baby can move independently, he will want to explore and you will need to make sure that the world in which you allow him to explore is safe. It is important to put all objects you do not want him to touch high up out of his way and to lock up anything that could possibly harm him.

Everything on his level should be made safe, including sockets, radiators and wastepaper baskets. Make sure floors and furniture are splinter-free and put safety catches on all low-level cupboards containing fragile or potentially dangerous objects.

Paint anything he might chew with lead-free paint, screw free-standing bookcases and cabinets to the wall so that he cannot pull them on top of himself and do not use dangling tablecloths that are tempting to pull. Never

Left As soon as they are mobile, babies are eager to explore. Until they have learned to cope with stairs safely on their own, a gate fitted at the top will protect them from falls — and will give you peace of mind!

Below Leaving a young baby in a playpen, with plenty of toys to keep him amused, will keep him out of harm's way. It will also make life a lot easier for you as you will be able to get on with ordinary chores without constantly having to watch him. Do have the playpen in the same room as you, however, so that you can keep an eye on him.

leave the room unattended when the iron is on or put hot drinks near the edge of a table where he can reach them.

It is simpler if you keep your child in a playpen until he can walk – if he has always been put in one he will not object to it. It is also sensible to put children into safety harnesses, in high chairs, strollers or carriages as soon as they can sit up. You should also put a child in reins when you go for walks so that you do not constantly have to shout "Stop! Come here!" or "No!" after him.

Equipment

Always buy equipment that has met approved safety standards and use it according to the manufacturer's instructions. Keep toys and bicycles clean, and check them regularly to see they have not become dangerous. Fit all windows above ground level with safety catches or detachable bars, and cover all full-size windows with safety film or replace them with ones made of safety glass. Do not leave chairs or beds under windows and never give children an electric blanket.

Above Never leave a child alone to play in front of the fireplace. Fit a fireguard around the fire, fixed to the wall on either side, so that your baby cannot move it.

CHILDREN ARE SENSIBLE

It is best to get children used to adult ways as soon as possible. If you decide not to put safety gates on the stairs, but teach your child to walk (or slide) up and down stairs as soon as he is able to, it may take more time at first but it could be rewarded in the long run. Similarly, teach them that the bath is slippery and they should take care rather than putting a nonslip bathmat in the bath.

On the whole, children know their physical limitations. Although you should always supervise them, especially when in the bath and on the monkey bars, they are usually not more adventurous than they know they can be. It is rare for a child to fall from a tree, slide or monkey bars unless he has been deliberately pushed by another child or put somewhere that he could never have got to on his own by an adult. If two or more children are playing together they should always be supervised: sand can be thrown in eyes, a toy car can be used as a club and a child can be pushed over in a wading pool.

SPECIAL HAZARDS

It is frightening for both a child and his keeper if he gets lost. Whether at the beach, in the park or in the shops, it is all too easy not to notice where your child has wandered off to – and he may not notice until he is quite lost that you are no longer in sight. Always keep an eye on children in public places.

Medicines look like sweets, only their effects can be deadly. Lock up all medicines and never use empty drink bottles for cleaning fluids or chemicals in case children think they are soft drinks.

Baby walkers may seem the ideal answer to keep your child amused while you get on with things, but they can be dangerous. Children have been known to fall down flights of stairs, into open fires and onto hard stone floors. Instead, be patient – in a few weeks they will be able to walk for themselves.

In the kitchen
- Make sure you turn all saucepan handles inwards and, where possible, use the back rings on the stove. Never let your child play with the knobs on the oven.
- Keep knives and other sharp kitchen tools out of your child's reach: use a knife block or magnetic rack high up on the wall.
- Never leave an iron where a child could pull it down.
- Do not have long, trailing cords on electrical equipment, which a child could reach: use curly cords instead.
- Always disconnect electrical appliances such as toasters and kettles when not in use.
- Keep doors of washing machines and dryers shut when not in use, so that your child cannot climb into them and get trapped.

In the living room
- Keep alcoholic drinks locked away.
- Keep cigarettes, matches and cigarette lighters out of children's reach.
- Secure trailing cords with cable clips.
- Conceal electric sockets behind furniture, or use socket covers.
- Make sure your child cannot reach the back of the television or video recorder: if fiddled with, they could give an electric shock.
- Never put hot drinks within children's reach, and never pass hot drinks over their heads.

In the nursery
- Do not use a pillow for a baby under one year old, or it could smother him.
- Never let your baby sleep with a ribbon or drawstring round his neck: there is the chance it could catch on something and strangle him.

PET SAFETY

Kittens will make affectionate and playful pets if your children follow basic rules of safety and kindness.

A family pet can be a great source of happiness and pleasure, and can help children to learn how to be responsible and caring. Pets make excellent companions for all ages, from children to the elderly. Dogs can help to keep your home safe as they may alert you to intruders and discourage burglars from breaking in.

Pet ownership brings with it a great deal of responsibility, which must be taken seriously; for this reason, it is not a good idea to give pets as gifts. Also, pets can cause accidents and spread diseases if they are not properly cared for. If you have children, teach them to respect animals and warn them that unfamiliar animals can bite and scratch, and must be approached with caution.

General principles

Dogs

- Dogs must be exercised every day (particularly large dogs) or they may become frustrated and could damage your home and garden.
- Dogs need love and affection and should not be ignored or left alone for long periods of time.
- Proper obedience training is essential for keeping your dog under control in public areas and at home.
- Wash food dishes every day and keep them separate from your own.

Cats

- Cats are very independent pets and are happiest if you give them some freedom.
- They will groom and clean their fur themselves.
- Cats require a litter tray or access to the outdoors. Be sure to change the litter every day to prevent the spread of disease and germs.

ANIMAL BITES

Dog or cat bites and scratches should be treated immediately. Wash the wound with clean water and apply an antiseptic cream. Seek medical attention if the bite is serious as your child may need an anti-tetanus shot. If you live in an area where rabies is a danger, try to find the owner of the dog and determine if it has been vaccinated against rabies. If not, you must contact your doctor immediately for rabies treatment, as it is a dangerous disease that can cause death.

Birds

- There are many different types and sizes of birds that make suitable pets – from budgies to parrots.
- Your bird's cage should be large enough for it to move around in and exercise its wings.
- Ensure that your bird has an ample supply of fresh water and bird seed in its cage. A piece of cuttlefish should be inserted through the cage wires so that the bird can keep its beak and claws in trim.

Other small animals

- Mice, hamsters, guinea pigs and gerbils make good pets for older children, and should be kept in a cage.
- Be sure the cage is cleaned weekly and that they have fresh water.
- Supplement their diets with some fresh lettuce or other greens every few days.

DISCOURAGE YOUR CHILD FROM:

- Stroking the animal's fur the wrong way, blowing on it or pulling its tail
- Bothering the animal when it is eating, sleeping or chewing on a bone
- Letting the dog lick his or her face
- Approaching a strange animal on the street or playing with stray cats

Household Emergencies

GAS

Gas is as safe as any other fuel, provided it is used properly. The danger from natural gas is not of poisoning but of explosion, asphyxiation or fire.

For your own safety, find out where the main gas tap is for your home (it is usually near the main gas meter) and how to turn it off. If the tap is difficult to reach, have it professionally moved to a more accessible site. Before you turn it off, turn off all appliance taps and pilot lights and when you turn it back on again, remember to relight all the pilot lights on all your appliances.

Safety

Have all gas appliances, including your water heater and furnace, serviced regularly – at least once a year – by a specialist. Never do any repair or main-tenance work on gas systems by yourself.

Make sure new gas appliances are officially approved by national safety standards and that any installation work needed is carried out by a specialist.

Many of the accidents caused by faulty appliances involve buying secondhand. If in doubt, do not buy.

In order to work safely and efficiently, all gas appliances need to breathe in fresh air and some appliances need a chimney or flue into which they can expel spent gases.

Gas flames should burn blue with a clearly defined paler blue cone in the center. If they are burning yellow, stop using the appliance and seek professional help immediately. Make sure the pilot lights do not go out and light them at once if they do.

ESCAPE ROUTES

It is important to work out escape routes from every room in your home, bearing in mind the young and the elderly in particular. The staircase may be the most obvious route, but what if you are cut off from it?

Research the different types of safety equipment available and imagine your family using them in an emergency.

Make sure you can easily get out of each window and door in your home. Check that safety bars, window locks or double-glazing have not made the windows impossible to open wide enough for you to squeeze out in a hurry. It is important that each room has its own emergency escape route, and that all members of the family are made aware of the various exit routes in the event of an emergency.

IF YOU SMELL GAS...

If you smell gas in the street, report it at once. If you smell gas in your home, do not try to mend the gas leak yourself. You could cause an explosion. Instead...

1 Turn off the whole supply at the main gas tap immediately.

2 Open all windows and doors to get rid of the gas.

3 Put out any cigarette and do not light a match or candle. Turn off any electric fire burning in the same room.

4 Do not turn on a light, or operate any other electrical switch (including a doorbell): the spark could ignite the gas. If it is dark, find a torch.

OR...
Check all the switches on your gas stove and see if a pilot light has accidentally gone out. If a pilot light is turned on, but has gone out, turn it off, then open the windows and wait until the gas smell has gone before relighting.

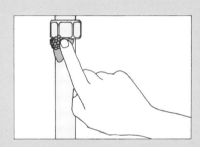

OR...
If you suspect a leaking joint, apply a little liquid detergent to the hole. If it bubbles, you have found the leak. Do not attempt to mend it yourself.

5 If you cannot solve the problem, seek professional help.

FIRE SAFETY

If you notice discoloration or staining on the wall next to your gas fire or water heater, or around the appliance casing itself, it may mean your chimney or flue have become blocked. An unusual smell may be the first clue you are given. In either case, stop using the appliance and seek professional help.

Check regularly that air holes or vents supplying the fresh air to your gas appliance are not blocked.

FIRE

No one expects a fire, but you should face up to the possibility of one so that you are prepared if it happens.

Ask yourself

Do all family members know what to do if there is a fire? Have you sat down together and worked out sensible escape routes from each room? Does even your youngest child know the number to dial in case of fire? Do you all know how to turn off the water, electricity and gas supply at the supply valves?

Have you got smoke detectors fitted around your home (apart from in the kitchen, in case they go off whenever you cook)? Have you made sure you can hear them clearly no matter where you are in your home? Have you bought enough fire extinguishers (at least one for each floor of your house) and does everyone know where they are?

Do you have a fire blanket mounted next to your stove? Are there special fire extinguishers for use on electric heaters, if you have them? Do you all know how to use them properly? Are your fire extinguishers in working order?

FITTING A SMOKE ALARM

Fit a smoke alarm just outside a kitchen: you do not want it set off each time you cook

Install a smoke alarm in a sitting room, but well away from the fire

Install a smoke alarm in the hall, near the bottom of the stairwell

Fit a smoke detector in or just outside a garage or workshop

FIRE EXTINGUISHERS

It is best to go for a multi-purpose extinguisher, unless you want one for a specific purpose. Always aim fire extinguishers at the base of the fire.

- Multi-purpose fire extinguishers can be used on any fire
- Water fire extinguishers are suitable for wood, paint or cloth fibers. They are not to be used on flammable liquids, such as burning oil, or on electrical fires
- Foam and dry-powder fire extinguishers can be used on flammable liquids (oils, fats, spirits, etc)
- Use carbon dioxide or vaporizing liquid fire extinguishers on electrical fires
- Maintain your fire extinguishers properly and have them recharged or replaced when necessary

TAKING ACTION

If a fire starts...

1 The most important thing is to evacuate everyone else from the building and then to make sure your escape route is assured.
2 Then call the fire department yourself; never rely on anybody else doing so.
3 Position somebody outside to signal to the fire department when it arrives.

4 If you must go back inside to find someone, cover your face with a wet cloth to protect your lungs and kneel down below the level of the smoke.

If it is a small fire...

1 Put the fire out by pouring water on upholstery, bedding, carpet, etc that is just beginning to smolder.
2 If the fire is already burning, quickly close the windows in the room and leave the room, closing the door behind you so that drafts cannot fan the fire.
3 Close the doors in every room of your home, even in rooms away from the fire, to help prevent the fire spreading – it can take a fire up to 30 minutes to burn through a door.
4 Call for the fire department and leave your home with your entire family.

If it is an electric fire...

Never pour water on the appliance in case you get an electric shock.
1 Turn off the electricity at the main switch and extinguish the fire with the appropriate fire extinguisher or smother the flames with a heavy rug or blanket.
2 If the fire is spreading see ''If a fire starts...'' above.

Right If the television catches fire, turn it off at the fuse box and drape a heavy cloth over the appliance to extinguish the flames.

If it is a fat fire...

Never pour water on a fat fire – it will spread the blaze.

1 Turn the heat off under the pan.

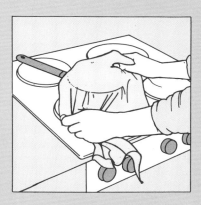

2 Cut the air off by smothering flames with a lid, large plate, tin tray, damp cloth, fire blanket or the appropriate fire extinguisher.

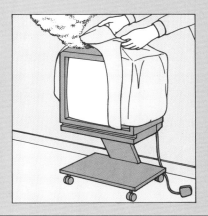

If you are cut off by the fire...

1 Close the door of the room you are in and also close any other opening to the rest of the building.

2 Seal any cracks around the bottom of the door with bedding, blankets or rugs.
3 Open the window and shout for help.
4 If you cannot lean out of the window, lie close to the floor until you hear the fire department arrive.
5 If you cannot wait for the fire department, make a rope by knotting together sheets, belts, etc. Tie one end to a heavy piece of furniture and throw the other end out of the window. Then climb down it or throw cushions or a mattress out of the window and drop down. This should be done only as a last resort and only from the second floor – no higher.

If clothing is on fire...

1 If your clothing catches fire, roll on the floor to extinguish the flames.
2 If someone else's clothing is on fire, lay them on the floor and wrap them in blankets, rugs or a thick coat to extinguish the flames, or throw a bucket of water over them.

Security
BURGLARY

Wherever you live, no matter what type of home you live in or how many valuables you have, being burgled is a shattering experience. The worth of the goods stolen is often irrelevant; what matters is the memories that have been taken and the shock and distress that have been caused.

Many breakins are the result of casual thieves (rather than experienced as well as highly skilled professional criminals) who could have been deterred by a locked window or a new lock. Simple precautions can act as deterrent to all but the most determined thieves. For advice on the best method of making your home secure, go to a locksmith or your insurance company.

Facing the facts

How attractive is your home to a burglar? Do you live in an inner-city area and therefore stand a higher chance of being burgled? Are you out at work all day? Do you have neighbors who might notice any suspicious movements? Do you have a neighborhood-watch scheme?

In fact, your neighbors may be your best defense against burglary. If you are on good terms with the people next door, then they will know who should be on your property and who should not. Those of us who prefer to lead private lives, having nothing to do with our neighbors, may pay a price in terms of security.

Remember that most burglaries take place during the day, rather than at night, and a burglar can be in and out of your home in a few minutes.

Making it hard for burglars

It is easy for burglars to tell if your home is empty during the day. Make it more difficult. Make sure your mail slot is large enough for all your newspapers to fit through and install a flap so the burglar cannot peep through and see that the house looks empty.

Buy a time-switch (or two) so that lights (and a radio) will come on in your home as soon as it begins to get dark. A dark house with the curtains open is an obvious sign that no one is at home. The light from the video digital display or your checkbook lying on the sofa next to the window are also signs that there is something to take. A spotlight fitted outside your home that comes on when there is someone in the garden could be enough to make a burglar think twice.

Being aware of the risks

Detached houses are more at risk than semi-detached or terraced properties, often because they are secluded and neighbors cannot see or hear burglars at work. Also at risk are houses and apartments near the ends of streets or backing onto alleyways, parks, fields or empty lots. Walls, fences and shrubs around the garden may give you greater privacy, but they give the burglar greater privacy as well. Patio doors give you a good view; they also give the burglar a good view (and entrance) in.

Women living on their own are often vulnerable. They should use their initials (and surname) only in the telephone directory and on the door bell – consider adding a false name as well so there appear to be several people living there. Take all necessary precautions.

Opening the door

Do not open the door to anyone you do not know unless you have checked his or her identification. There are many confidence tricksters, and elderly people are particularly vulnerable to them. Even children pretending to organize a party for the handicapped and women posing as social workers have fronted burglaries. The best protection is a door viewer and door chain or a telecom, which enables you to ask for further information and proof of identity before letting in a stranger. Make sure the area outside the front door is well lit at night.

Car thefts

Many thefts do not involve your home, but often just your car. Whenever you leave your car, always shut the windows, lock the trunk and all the doors and remove the radio/tape deck and any valuables that can be seen from the street. Remember also to remove the ignition key. Having an alarm fitted in your car is also a valuable deterrent.

NOT LETTING STRANGERS IN

If the person outside the door does not look familiar, but you are nervous about asking who they are and checking their credentials, the best thing is to make an excuse. It is also another way of implying that many more people live in the house than actually do – especially useful for single women.

If the caller insists on coming back you can always arrange to have a friend, or policeman, with you when they call. Try to ascertain when this will be.

"Sorry, you cannot come in ...

... I am a friend of the family, I do not live here."

... I am the cleaner/nanny. I cannot make any decisions for the family."

... I am the tenant, the landlord is out."

... I am just hanging the curtains. The family are coming back soon. Sorry I cannot help you."

... (stick your head out of the window) I am ill in bed. Please come back another time if it is important."

... Before you go, what did you say your name was and where are you from? I'll let him/them know."

ANYTHING OF VALUE?

In most cases a burglar entering a home does not know what he is going to steal. He just presumes that you will have something he wants. Even the contents of an average home freezer could be worth taking.

Never imagine that you have nothing of interest for a burglar; the items illustrated on the right are what most commonplace burglars are after.

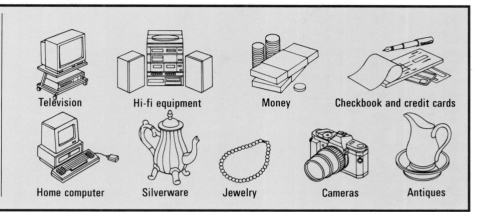

Television   Hi-fi equipment   Money   Checkbook and credit cards

Home computer   Silverware   Jewelry   Cameras   Antiques

HOW SECURE IS YOUR HOME?

- Are the external doors either fitted with a deadlock or, at top and bottom, with a key-operated security bolt?
- Are the windows and French and patio doors on the ground floor fitted with key-operated locks?
- Are the windows and skylights on the upper floors that overlook flat roofs and/or are adjacent to downpipes fitted with key-operated locks?
- Do you have a burglar alarm that you use at night and whenever your home is left unattended?
- Do you draw your curtains and leave a downstairs light on (in a room, not just in the hall) when you go out in the evening?
- Are your garage and shed doors and windows secure and all ladders locked away?
- If you live in an apartment, is the main entrance secure?
- Do you ask a neighbor to push mail and/or newspapers through the mail slot when you are away?
- Do you use lights on a timer switch when you are away?

OUTSIDE

A barking dog will probably scare off almost as many burglars as an alarm. A front door visible from the road is also safer than one sheltered from view by a thick hedge. An infrared light that turns itself on as anyone approaches will also give a burglar second thoughts. And a home with the doors bolted and windows shuttered is obviously harder to penetrate than one with the window left open so the cat can get in.

A thief may not, however, be put off by anything you do, but you may discourage the casual intruder. But no matter how effective your alarm system, you must remember to turn it on and to lock up your home carefully each time you go out. Even if you are just popping to the corner store or across the road for a chat, always lock up behind you.

DOOR LOCKS

The best protection for all doors are security deadbolts. The deadbolt action means the locks cannot be locked or unlocked without a key, so if the burglar is in your home and wishes to leave through the front door he cannot do so unless a key is to hand.

There are two types of security deadbolt: a mortice deadbolt, which is set into the door, and a deadbolt rim lock, which screws onto the door. If the door is thin, a rim lock is preferable as fitting a mortice could actually weaken the door.

Doors that are never used as the final exit can be more economically – but just as effectively – secured by key-operated security bolts fitted at top and bottom. Ordinary bolts, especially when used near glazed panels, mail slots, etc, can easily be overcome from the outside. They can, however, be utilized to good effect at night on fire-escape routes. Doors that open outwards have exposed hinges and it may be possible to remove the hinge pins from the outside. Therefore, fit hinge bolts top and bottom on all outward-opening doors.

Locks & burglar alarms

If the locks on your front door are inadequate, or not properly used, a thief can easily break in, and such ease of entry will arouse little suspicion. Most doors are fitted only with cylinder locks, which are easy to overcome and provide very little security. Keys demand looking after, even if your front door has a security lock – they will not be effective if in the wrong hands.

House keys should be kept on you and not under the doormat or hanging on a string behind the letterbox. They should never be kept in your handbag together with any form of identity. If your house keys are stolen, tell the police and change the locks. Even if the keys are returned, another set could always have already been cut. Always remember to change the locks when you move into a new home.

The most common alarm system for domestic use can have many different components such as door contacts, pressure mats, ultrasonic sound and infrared lights to detect the burglar. Most alarms have an audible warning device that sounds when the alarm is activated. The sound will probably cut out after about 20 minutes. Some models also use lights and some signal to a monitoring station that notifies the police. The police will require you to provide the names, addresses and telephone numbers of two key holders, possibly neighbors, who should be able to get to your home within 20 minutes. They should be able to deactivate the alarm and allow police access.

Your system should be capable of being switched on, both at night and when your home is left unattended. Sometimes an intrusion alarm may be required by your insurance company.

Above left Bars fitted to a window need not make your home look like a prison. A trellis like this one can add a new decorative element to a window, and internal wooden shutters are another attractive and unobtrusive security device.

Above All windows should be fitted with the appropriate security locks. To make sure that you have the right lock for each window, get specialist advice. You can then fit the locks yourself, or have this done by a professional locksmith.

WINDOW LOCKS

All windows accessible from the outside should have locks — even the smallest and narrowest of windows can be squeezed through by a child. There are various locks suitable for metal-framed, sash and other wood-framed windows, some of which lock the window and others the handle. Windows that are permanently closed should be screwed to their cases. On others, double-glazing and laminated glass act as deterrents.

Fit key-operated locks to all windows as it is then impossible for the thief to cut a small hole in the window and open the window by hand — unless he has a copy of the key. Use one-way screws in the lock so that it cannot be removed. On especially vulnerable windows and patio doors, secure folding metal gates with 5-lever locks or padlocks.

French windows
French and other types of patio doors are just as vulnerable, if not more so, than ordinary doors. To make them more secure fit key-operated bolts, top and bottom, in addition to the supplied lock and, if they open outwards, fit hinge bolts too.

Sash windows
Wooden-framed sash windows should have permanent security bolts fixed to both sides of the upper sash so that the window can only be opened a few inches, and no more.

Casement windows
Unless the catch is broken, hinged casement windows are difficult to open. Make sure all swinging windows fit tightly into their recesses or a wire can be pushed through and the catch can be opened.

Louvered windows
It is easy to remove glass slats from louvered windows. There are special locks, but simply gluing the slats to the frames with strong adhesive will make it more difficult for the burglar.

GOING AWAY

Going out

Even if you are only out for a few hours, the important thing is to make sure your home never looks empty. Do not advertise the fact that you are out by leaving obvious clues such as curtains closed during the day or open at night. An empty garage with an open door is a sure sign of an empty home. Messages on the door and newspapers left outside are other obvious clues. Flowerpots filled with dead flowers left unattended on window-sills reveal you have been away for quite a few weeks already.

Your best ally is a good neighbor who is prepared to go into your home on a frequent basis, and make it look as though it is inhabited. This involves drawing curtains, taking in mail and newspapers, and watering plants.

Going on holiday

When you are on holiday it is ideal if you can find a house-sitter. There are companies that provide this service, but if a friend or relation will do the job, so much the better. If this is impossible, ask a kind neighbor or friend to keep an eye on your home. They should take in deliveries for you, draw the curtains at night and open them again in the morning. It also helps if they can water any plants outside and, if necessary, even mow the lawn.

Before you go
Never leave a message on your answering machine saying you have gone away and try not to tell too many people you are going away. Clear your home of articles of sentimental value. Either deposit them and large amounts of cash in the bank before you go or leave them locked away in a safe. Tell the police the dates you are going to be away and which neighbors have the spare key. Never leave keys in an obvious place, such as under the flowerpot by the door or hanging by the mailbox.

Cancel the newspapers before you go. Make sure a neighbor will take in any large parcels that arrive unexpectedly or ask the post office to hold all your mail until you return. Ask a neighbor to push letters or papers through the mail slot regularly, if it is left sticking out.

Lock all windows and doors securely and padlock ladders together and put them out of sight. Lock up your tool shed for the same reason; your hammer could come in handy for a burglar and

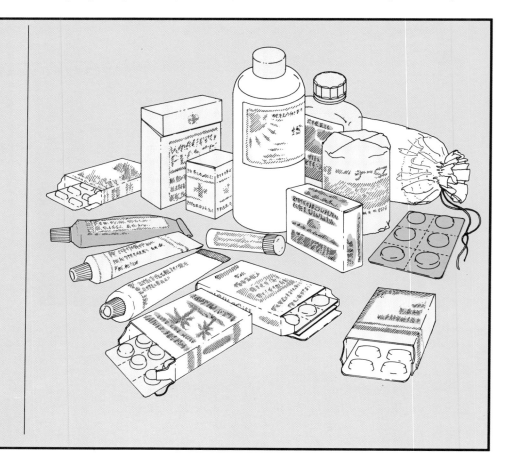

FIRST AID TO TAKE ON HOLIDAY

Travel-sickness pills
Suntan lotion
Antiseptic cream
Crepe bandage
Gauze bandage
Cotton batting
Assorted Band-Aids
Soluble aspirin or Tylenol
Insect repellent
Mild steroid cream (for bites)
Antacid (for stomach aches and heartburn)
Calamine lotion
Mild laxative
Anti-diarrheal tablets
Salt tablets (for very hot countries)
Water-purifying tablets
Any drugs you take regularly

Also take with you a copy of any prescription you are likely to need. Make sure the generic name of the drug is on the prescription as brand names vary.

Make sure you have adequate medical insurance and that you have had all the necessary inoculations in plenty of time.

Pet safety **134**
Burglary **138–9**
Outside **140–1**
Insurance **144–5**
First aid **146–9**

THE SAFE HOME

an old carriage could help wheel the television away.

Invest in several timer switches. The best kinds have several settings so they can come on and turn off a few times during an evening. Set them so you have lights (and a radio) going on and off in different rooms and at different times around the house so it looks as if there is some movement in the house. Install timer switches in the living room, bedroom and kitchen, not in the hall where you would never usually sit.

Helping others

If your neighbors have gone away on holiday, it would be considerate if you could look after their interests without being asked. Keep an eye on their home, garage and garden and, if you see anyone suspicious, call the police.

PETS

If you are out for the evening, lock dogs in and cats out of the home. If you are going away for a longer period of time, ask a neighbor to feed your pet (and exercise it if necessary) and to clean out any cage, tank or litter tray.

Otherwise it may be simpler to book your pets either into a friend's house or into a suitable boarding home. If you are going to have to do this regularly, it is a good idea to get animals used to living away from you at an early age. Make life cosy for them even when away from home: install them in their temporary home with a familiar blanket, some old toys and a bag or two of their favorite food. Let the boarding home know of any idiosyncratic habits they have – for both their sake and that of your pet.

A blanket-lined basket makes a warm and secure bed for a sleepy or penitent dog.

PREPARING TO GO AWAY ON HOLIDAY

Don't forget to:
- Cancel paper deliveries
- Close all windows and doors
- Lock away any ladders
- Lock the toolshed
- Leave on the timer switches for evening lights
- Draw the curtains on the ground floor
- Make sure no taps are dripping
- Shut the garage door
- Water all plants and mow the lawn before you go
- Ask your neighbor to keep an eye open and take in any big parcels
- Book your pets into a kennel
- Put on your answering machine
- Alter the heating-system time clock
- Switch off gas
- Store money and valuables in a safe place

There is nothing more obvious to a burglar than an open garage door – it is an invitation to crime. Similarly, tubs of dried-up flowers are an indication that occupants might not be around. You may be able to make an arrangement with the post office to hold your mail until you return.

INSURANCE

Although you may have to pay high premiums, you can insure against most eventualities, from losing your bicycle to pets getting ill. It is wise to insure your home and its contents and, if you own a car, you are legally bound to take out car insurance. If you are on a limited budget, spend money on basic building and contents insurance together with good security. No matter how much money you are given in compensation for your loss, new items can often not replace those of sentimental value.

Insurance can be useful, however, for replacing, for example, carpets and furniture when your watertank overflows.

Checking your policy

Always read insurance policies carefully and compare policies and quotations from several companies before making up your mind which policy to take. Fill in the application honestly and correctly, otherwise any claims you make may not be paid. Make sure you understand the limits or exclusions that most policies contain. These can sometimes be overcome by paying an additional premium, which may not be very large, but it is essential to do this before a claim arises. Choose reinstatement-as-new coverage, otherwise wear and tear is deducted from payments.

Valuing your possessions

If you want to take out contents insurance, you must work out the value of what you own. Possessions vary enormously from one family to another and the only sure way of arriving at the correct sum for insurance is to go through your own home room by room, writing down what it would cost now to replace each item. Remember to keep all receipts in a safe place: you may need them when you make a claim.

Insure all your records, tapes and discs as well as your furniture and precious objects

BEING WELL COVERED

Engrave bicycles, tennis rackets, televisions, etc with your name and postal code. This will help the police return them to you in case they are ever found once they have been stolen. Special diamond-tipped pens can be bought for engraving glass and metal and pens that use ink that can be read only under ultraviolet light can mark other possessions. Some insurance companies can provide you with these. Do not mark antique items or you will depreciate their value. Do not mark rented pieces of equipment without first checking with the owner.

Jewelry should be valued by an expert or a specialist shop. Usually they will do this for 1 percent of the value of the piece.

Check the details of your contents insurance policy to see whether you can recover the cost of your entire wardrobe and linen cupboard should the need arise, or whether you will be awarded a considerably smaller amount that has taken the amount of wear and tear into consideration.

For future identification, photograph any valuable objects and paintings you have in color against a plain contrasting background. Lay a ruler alongside the article to give an accurate scale.

Photograph silver cutlery or similar objects, clearly showing any distinguishing marks such as crests, initials or hallmarks. Give a copy of the photograph to a friend or relation (or put it in a safety-deposit box in the bank) thus insuring that the burglar will not steal that as well.

When you move be sure to clarify with the moving company whether you or they will be responsible for insuring all your contents. If they are, ask to see the policy and check that your valuables will be well covered. If you are, make sure you take out adequate coverage (although it may be included in your contents insurance).

Even cheap paperback books can be expensive if you need to replace them. If you have several hundred or more, do not bother to count each book but work out an average price per yard (meter) of bookshelf space and multiply that by your length of books.

When calculating the cost of rebuilding your property for a house insurance, seek professional advice. The cost of rebuilding is rarely the same as the market value of your property, especially if you live in a house that is more than one hundred years old.

INSURING YOUR HOME

When you are working out the value of your home contents, use this as a rough guide.

Items	Value for insurance ($)
Carpets, rugs and floor coverings	
Bedroom, bathroom and kitchen furniture	
All tables, chairs, stools, sofas, cabinets, sideboards, books and bookcases, lamps and light fixtures	
Soft furnishings: curtains and their fittings, cushions, blinds	
Televisions, videos, radios, stereos and similar equipment	
Household appliances: stove, refrigerator, freezer, washing machine, vacuum cleaner, heaters, electrical goods, etc	
Cooking utensils, freezer contents, provisions, cutlery, china, glass	
Valuables: gold and silver articles, jewelry, pictures, clocks, watches, cameras, ornaments and collections	
Leisure: sports equipment, bicycles, books, records, tapes, musical instruments	
Children's equipment, clothing and shoes: carriages, strollers, cots, highchairs, toys, books, games	
Garden and garage equipment: furniture, lawnmower, ladders, tools, paints	
Household linen: bedding, towels, table linen	
Clothing and shoes	
Attic: suitcases and their contents	
Total	

When you have worked out the total, add allowance for inflation if necessary and for any items you expect to buy during the year.

SERIAL NUMBERS

Keep these serial numbers: they could be useful to the police if you are robbed.

Front-door key

Car and motorcycle key, chassis, engine and license plate

Bicycle

Washing machine

Dryer

Dishwasher

Stove

Refrigerator and freezer

Food processor

Lawnmower

Vacuum cleaner

Television and video

Radio, tape recorder, stereo system

Binoculars

Typewriter

Computer and word processor

Hair dryer

Camera equipment

Watch

Limited editions

First Aid

BASIC MEDICINE CUPBOARD

The following equipment is suitable for treating most minor illnesses and injuries.

Dressings
- Unbleached triangular bandage (makes a sling to support an elbow injury or strained wrist)
- Sterile white absorbent gauze pads (use dry to dress a minor wound – no cream or ointment necessary)
- Paraffin-coated gauze (for covering cuts)
- Cotton batting (use with soap and water to clean a wound or with baby lotion to clean a baby's bottom. Use also to pad a dressing)
- Crepe or elastic bandages (use to bandage a strained or sprained joint)
- Band-Aids (buy a box of individually wrapped band-aids or a roll. Use on minor wounds or to secure a dressing)
- Open-weave bandages (to protect wounds from dirt and clothing)
- Roll of special adhesive tape (for securing bandages and dressings)

Cleansing materials
- Eyewash and eyecap; ear drops (return to chemist when passed expiry date)
- Liquid and cream antiseptic (for cuts and scrapes. Do not use on burns as these are best left uncovered)

Pain killers
- Soluble aspirin or Tylenol (aspirin is for relieving pain and lowering a temperature. It can irritate the stomach lining, so never take an aspirin for stomach ache. Tylenol is an alternative to aspirin and alleviates the problems without irritating the stomach)
- Cough syrups (a simple linctus to soothe the cough and an expectorant)
- Throat pastilles and antiseptic lozenges
- Mild steroid cream (for bites and stings)
- Oil of cloves (provides temporary relief from toothache)
- Calamine lotion (for soothing bites, stings and painful sunburn. It also helps to relieve itching as in insect bites and stings and nettle rash)
- Arnica cream (for bruises. Do not use if the wound is open)

Stomach disorders
- Mild laxative
- Anti-diarrheal preparation (kaolin and morphine mixture is often used to relieve diarrhea. If it continues visit the doctor in case the diarrhea has been caused by bacterial food poisoning)
- Antacid (taken in tablets, liquid or effervescent powders to relieve stomach aches, heartburn and mild indigestion)
- Travel-sickness pills (take before the journey or as directed by your doctor)

Miscellaneous
- Measuring cup and spoon
- Clinical thermometer (can be used either in the mouth or under the arm)
- Safety pins (for bandages or slings)
- Tweezers (to remove splinters)
- Packet of needles (also for splinters)
- Scissors (a small pair for cutting plasters, cutting away dressings and bandages, cutting nails, etc)
- Insect repellent
- Petroleum jelly (for cracked lips, etc)
- Antifungal powder (for athlete's foot)

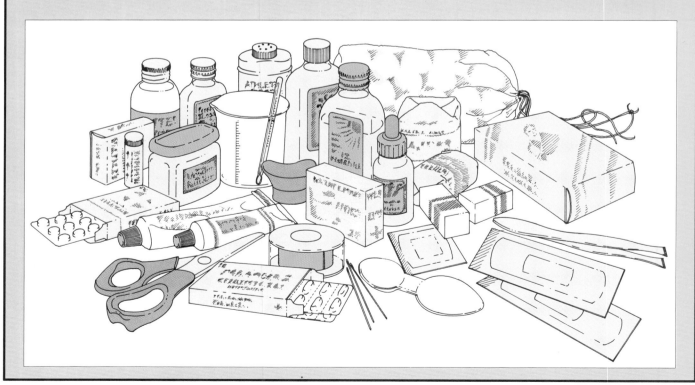

MEDICINES

Always make sure all medicines, pills and cosmetics are out of the reach of children. Lock them up and keep the key in a safe place, preferably away from the cupboard itself. Ideally drugs should be kept cool and dry so it may be better to find a storage space for them outside your bathroom.

Keep your bathroom cabinet tidy and well organized so that everything is easy to find and label bottles carefully. Always follow instructions on medicine bottles and never stop taking prescribed medicines before the doctor tells you it is safe to do so. Take the full course of any antibiotic.

Never save any prescribed medicines you have left over after finishing a treatment and never give prescribed medicines to anyone they were not prescribed for. Keep all dangerous drugs in child-proof containers but make sure elderly people can open them if the drugs are intended for them. Mark each drug you are keeping with the date of purchase, the name of the drug and the reason why it was prescribed.

Better safe than sorry

Regularly check the contents of your cupboard and remove any medicines, pills, cosmetics or perfumes that are old. Ointments and creams should be got rid of if they have separated or hardened, tablets if they have crumbled, capsules if they have broken or melted, tinctures if the alcohol has evaporated and liquids if they have become discolored or have formed a sludge at the bottom of the container.

Get rid of anything that has lost its label – even if you think you remember what it is. All over-the-counter drugs that have passed their expiry date or are over a year old must be removed as well. Do not throw any of these away or put them down the toilet or sink or in the fire but take them to your chemist who will dispose of them.

Pregnancy

Never take any drugs during pregnancy before consulting the doctor. If you are in the middle of a prescribed drug and find yourself pregnant, ask the doctor whether or not you should continue with the treatment.

USEFUL EXTRAS

A bag of frozen peas (excellent as a cold compress because it molds easily to your body. It numbs pain, especially after stitches, if placed gently on the afflicted area. It is also useful when a child has fallen over, to prevent undue swelling. You can use an icepack instead)

Plastic bag (if you are suffering from a sore throat, wet a cloth with very hot water, wring it out, fold it twice and place it across your throat over the sore patch. Tightly wrap a plastic bag around your neck, covering the cloth so that it does not leak, and wrap a warm scarf on top of that)

Salt (a handful or more of pouring, rather than sea, salt added to your bath for several days will help clean and heal a wound)

ALTERNATIVE MEDICINE

If you wish to try alternative medicine, let both your orthodox doctor and the alternative practitioner know about each other. Tell each of them what the other has prescribed and about any medicines you are taking or treatments you are already having.

Make sure that you go to a fully qualified practitioner: not all those who practice are. There is no national umbrella organization, but regional associations may be able to advise you. The main branches of alternative medicine are those listed below:

Acupuncture
An ancient Chinese treatment, acupuncture consists of inserting fine needles into living tissues of the human body. The idea behind this is to restore the balance of the body's "vital energy," which acupuncturists believe is upset when you are ill or in pain. Acupuncture is known to relieve pain and to act as a local anesthetic. It is used to treat a whole range of conditions, from headaches to sprains, pulled ligaments, and even strokes. Some general practitioners now offer acupuncture as an optional treatment, and it is proving to be most successful.

Homeopathy
Homeopathy works on the principle of treating like with like. Diagnosis and treatment take into account the person as a whole as well as his individual physical symptoms. Homeopathic remedies are based on natural substances, diluted many times over, whose characteristics correspond to the patient's own mental and physical state. Given in minute doses, they are designed to stimulate the body's own healing powers without the use of drugs.

Homeopathic remedies are now available over the counter at many drugstores and health-food shops. you may feel it is worth trying these sometimes, to cure a particular ailment, before resorting to prescribed drugs. But for a full diagnosis you would need to see a qualified homeopathic doctor, who will assess your problem in a holistic context and prescribe treatment accordingly.

Osteopathy and chiropractic
Both treatments involve the manipulation of bones and joints in order to resolve their proper alignment in the body. Whereas chiropractors concentrate on disorders arising from the spine and nervous system, osteopaths believe that manipulation can also help other conditions by generally improving the patient's blood circulation.

MINOR COMPLAINTS

If any of the problems mentioned below are persistent, recurrent or worsening, do not hesitate to consult your doctor.

Athlete's foot

Athlete's foot is a fungal infection that is usually picked up in showers, swimming pools or other warm, wet places. The patient will notice cracks in the skin, which may sting, and blisters and scaling between the toes. Rub away the damp patches and scales with cotton batten and always dry the foot thoroughly. Use a fungicidal cream twice a day. Seek medical advice if the blisters are oozing or the problem does not go away in a reasonable amount of time.

Black eye

A black eye is just a bruise, caused by bleeding beneath the skin. To lessen pain and reduce swelling, apply a cold compress, such as a bag of frozen peas or ice cubes, or a cold cloth, to the area.

Bleeding

A small wound should stop bleeding on its own. Always clean the wound well with cold running water and dry it off carefully.

Blisters

Blisters are formed as a natural protection to the body where it has been bitten, burned, rubbed or chafed. If the cause can be treated, do so. Do not prick the blister as the wound may become infected. Instead, cover it with a well-padded band-aid. The blister will soon subside; the skin will harden and eventually fall off. Do not disturb the natural healing process.

Boil

Unless they are recurrent, boils rarely need any special treatment. Never squeeze a boil as you will spread the infection to other parts of the skin.

Bruises

Once a bruise has formed there is little that can be done to remove it. Rubbing arnica cream into the area or covering it with a cold compress the moment it has been injured may stop the bruise forming, or at least prevent it from becoming too big and unsightly.

Burns, minor

Hold the burn under cold running water or place it in cold water (or any other cold liquid available) for ten minutes or until the burned area has cooled down and the pain has lessened. Then apply a dressing, such as a piece of clean gauze or a freshly laundered cotton handkerchief, to protect the burn from dirt and damage. Never put fats or ointments onto a burn and do not break blisters or remove any loose skin or anything else that is sticking to the area. For major burns, it is essential to seek medical advice at once.

Choking

Choking is caused by the windpipe being blocked. Tell the patient to put his arms straight up in the air and thump him firmly several times between his shoulder blades. A small child should be held upside down by his feet and then thumped; a larger child should be placed face down over your knee and thumped between the shoulder blades. If the choking continues and the patient turns blue, give him or her mouth-to-mouth resuscitation and get the patient to hospital.

Colds

The common cold is infectious, highly contagious and cannot be cured by an antibiotic. This means it has to run its own natural course. Symptoms are a running or stuffy nose, a headache, sore throat and cough, although the patient can also develop a temperature. A cold can last from a few days up to a few weeks. The patient should keep warm, drink plenty of fluids, take vitamin C and eat well, if he feels like it. He can go to bed but this may not be necessary. If necessary or if the cold is accompanied by a headache or sore throat, take aspirins or paracetamol regularly to relieve the pain and reduce the fever.

If the cold is accompanied by an infection of the middle ear, the lungs or the sinuses then medical advice should be sought. If the patient is a young baby and the cold is preventing him breathing when feeding, it is wise to seek medical advice.

Cold sores

Cold sores last about ten days to two weeks and are slightly swollen, red patches usually around the lips or nostrils. Small blisters appear, turn yellow, crust and then flake off. Cold sores are not infectious but can be passed on by direct contact, such as kissing. They can also be passed on from one part of a patient's face to another if he repeatedly touches the cold sore and then touches another part of his face. Use calamine lotion to soothe and dry the blisters, or seek medical advice.

Conjunctivitis ("pink eye")

Conjunctivitis is an inflammation of the outer covering of the eye that makes the eye look red and may produce a sticky discharge inside the lids. It can feel itchy and sore. It is caused by bacteria, a virus or an allergy and is highly contagious. Do not share a towel with anyone with conjunctivitis. When the patient first develops "pink eye," check to make sure there is nothing trapped underneath his eyelid. Remove it if there is. Bathe the patient's eyes in warm boiled water several times a day by dipping cotton batting in the water and then holding the cotton batting against the eye. If the eye feels sore, then keep it closed by taping a small pad of cotton batting over it. If the eye feels very sore or has not healed after a few days, seek medical advice.

Constipation

The patient should not take laxatives until he has tried eating properly for a few weeks. He should change his diet to include plenty of raw fruit and vegetables, wholewheat bread and bran and he should drink lots of water.

Coughs

The purpose of a cough is to remove excess mucus by bringing it up into the mouth where it is swallowed and any germs in it are killed by the acid in the stomach. A productive cough is one that brings up mucus and is serving a useful purpose. An unproductive cough serves no purpose and is a response to irritation. No matter which the patient has, he should stop smoking immediately and start drinking lemon juice mixed with hot water and honey to taste. Unproductive coughs should then be treated with cough-suppressant medicines or cough drops. Productive coughs should not be suppressed, but you should give the patient an expectorant medicine to help get rid of the phlegm. If the patient begins coughing up discolored or sticky sputum then medical advice should be sought as bronchitis may have developed.

Cramp

Cramp is a sudden and painful tightening of a muscle or group of muscles that makes movement difficult. It can

be caused by cold, overworking of the muscle or sweating, and it can also occur in bed at night. Try massaging the affected muscle firmly for a while, or stretching the muscle and then quickly bending it. If it occurs repeatedly in bed, raise the foot of your bed by about 6 in (15 cm) and make sure your bedding is loose.

Cuts, grazes and scratches

Clean the wound by washing in cold or warm water and wiping any dirt away. Use mild antiseptic either in the water or as a cream. If the cut is filled with dirt, seek medical advice in case an antibiotic or anti-tetanus injection is needed. Otherwise leave blood to clot, and cover the wound with an adhesive or nonadhesive dressing and bandage.

Diarrhea

If the patient knows what has caused the diarrhea he will probably be better soon. Until then, he should drink lots of fluids and should not eat unless he feels like it. If he has to go out and will not be near a toilet he should take some kaolin. Follow the instructions on the bottle. (For acute diarrhea, see Vomiting below.)

Dog bite

If the skin has been pierced, seek immediate medical help. There may be a risk of rabies.

Fever

A fever is a high temperature and is almost always a sign of infection. The average normal body temperature is 98.6°F (37°C), although young children and many adults have a temperature either a little higher or lower than this figure. A fever is said to start at 100°F (37.8°C) and you should seek medical advice if the patient's fever reaches 101°F (38.3°C).

Hay fever

Hay fever is an allergy usually caused by pollen, animal hairs or household dust. The patient will suffer from sneezing, a watering nose and often a burning or itching sensation. Seek medical advice in the winter or early spring as the doctor may be able to make the patient immune with a series of injections.

Headache

If the patient can work out why he has the headache he will be closer to getting rid of it. If he is hungry he should eat a light meal. If he is tense he should try taking deep breaths of fresh air or massaging his neck or temples. Otherwise he should lie down in peace and quiet and take a pain-relieving drug, such as Tylenol. If the patient has recurrent headaches he should seek medical advice (see also Migraine).

Hiccoughs

Most hiccough attacks go away within an hour. If the patient's attack has gone on for longer or is particularly severe, seek medical advice. Try drinking a glass of water from the wrong side of the glass (the side farthest from you), gargling with plain water for a minute or two, eating a large spoonful of granulated sugar or holding your breath and swallowing quickly as often as possible.

Indigestion

Many people find one or two special foods give them indigestion so they avoid it by not eating those foods. Otherwise a glass of milk or an antacid will help relieve indigestion. Or lay the patient down with a hot-water bottle placed on his stomach. Recurrent indigestion could be due to a stomach ulcer, so the patient would be well advised to seek medical advice.

Influenza

Influenza is an infectious disease caused by a virus. Its symptoms are pains in the joints, fever, headache and occasionally a cough and pains in the throat. These are sometimes over in a few days, but the patient may feel weak for a week or more. A patient should be told to go to bed and keep warm. Staying at home reduces the likelihood of passing the influenza on to other people. Patients should drink plenty of fluids and take two aspirin or Tylenol every four hours to relieve the pain and reduce the fever. If the patient is otherwise healthy, there is no need to seek medical advice, but an elderly person or anyone with chronic bronchitis should tell the doctor soon to avoid further illness.

Ingrowing toenails

Ingrowing toenails are generally caused by ill-fitting shoes and are less likely to occur if the shoes fit better and if toenails are kept short and cut square, rather than rounded. If the edge of the patient's toenail has grown into the side of his toe and the swollen area has become painful and infected, seek medical advice.

Insect bites and stings

Treat them at once with calamine lotion or with a solution of bicarbonate-of-soda (hold a piece of cotton batting, soaked in the solution, over the sting) or with an antihistamine cream. All of these will help to ease the itching. Then cover the bite with a Band-Aid to keep dirt out. Remove bee stings with tweezers, trying not to squeeze the sting as you will push more venom into the wound.

A few people are allergic to insect bites and will suddenly find breathing difficult. Seek medical attention at once. When bites cause skin irritation, apply calamine lotion frequently to soothe the itching. Do not scratch or the skin will be damaged further, and this could very easily lead to infection.

Migraine

In migraine the patient has a severe headache accompanied by a feeling of patterns or lights in front of the eyes and possible nausea or vomiting. The patient should seek medical advice as migraine is a distinct illness.

Mouth ulcers

Single mouth ulcers are due to a virus infection or broken teeth or ill-fitting dentures. If mouth ulcers are recurrent the patient should visit the dentist. Otherwise pain can be relieved by a mouthwash, mouth cream or pastilles.

Nettle stings

Cover with calamine lotion or antihistamine cream.

Nose bleeds

Tell the patient to lean forward, breathe through his mouth and pinch the soft part of his nose for about ten minutes or until the blood has clotted. He should also spit out any blood that gets in his mouth as swallowing it may make him sick. If the bleeding has not stopped after twenty minutes, seek medical advice at once. Once the bleeding has ceased, clean the patient's nose and mouth with warm water; do not use hot water as it may disturb the clot. The patient should not blow his nose, sniff or drink any hot drinks for a few hours after the bleeding has stopped.

Rashes

Rashes may be due to heat or to an allergy. Has the patient recently changed his soap, cosmetics or washing detergent? If so, he should change back. Rashes on children often have an internal cause and may mean the child has one of the more common infectious fevers, such as German measles or roseola. Relieve the symptoms with calamine lotion and seek medical advice, especially if there are tiny blisters in the rash.

Sore throat

A sore throat is an inflammation of the throat tissues which can be due to infection or to inhaling dust or smoke. The patient should stop smoking and drink a lot of hot drinks, especially lemon juice mixed with hot water and honey. He should gargle with soluble aspirin (and then swallow the aspirin) or a suitable antiseptic liquid and suck antiseptic throat lozenges as necessary.

Splinters

Soak the splinter and surrounding area in warm soapy water for a few minutes and then remove the splinter with a pair of tweezers or a sewing needle that has been sterilized (hold it in a flame for a second). Then rub a little antiseptic cream on the area and leave it free to the air. Never try to remove the splinter by squeezing the surrounding skin. Many small splinters are eventually expelled by the skin growing and just get rubbed off. If a splinter becomes infected, break the skin over the pus with a sterile needle. The pus will drain away and the splinter should become free.

Sprains and strains

A joint can be strained if it is bent farther than normal. A sprain is often indicative of the ligament around the joint getting torn. There is then bleeding under the skin which causes swelling and bruising. Remove anything that is restricting the swelling and apply a cold compress, such as a bag of frozen peas or a cold wet cloth, to the swelling. Often the best treatment for a sprain is rest, so do not walk on a damaged joint. Do not hesitate to seek medical advice if the swollen joint is painful.

Stomach pains (see Indigestion)

Sty

A sty is a painful, red swelling at the base of an eyelash and often the patient will have several, one after the other. They usually last for several days each and then just disappear, but you can speed the recovery by applying hot compresses of cotton batting soaked in hot water to the sty. If you are at all worried, seek medical advice.

Sunburn

Move into the shade and soothe the skin with a cold cream or calamine lotion. Give the patient plenty of fluids to drink and a couple of aspirin or Tylenol. If the skin is blistered, do not break the blisters but seek medical advice. If the sunburned person is shivering or vomiting, seek medical advice as they may have sunstroke. If possible, prevent sunburn by avoiding intense sunlight if you are not used to it.

Toothache

Seek dental advice as soon as possible. For temporary relief, give the patient aspirin or Tylenol or lay a warm, light hot-water bottle on their cheek. Try painting the tooth with oil of cloves.

Vomiting

If possible, remove the patient from the cause of his nausea, lay him down flat and keep him warm. After a few hours give him a little water to drink. For the following forty-eight hours make sure he eats carefully – rusks, boiled rice, plain potato, etc. If the patient has acute vomiting or diarrhea, mix $\frac{1}{2}$ pint (250 ml) water with a tablespoon of sugar and a teaspoon of salt, which he should slowly sip. He should not eat for twenty-four hours afterward.

CALLING THE DOCTOR: ADULTS

Even seemingly unimportant things like voice-loss, coughing, dizziness, indigestion, loss of appetite and sleeplessness can all be symptoms of a more serious illness if they are persistent or recurrent.

Call the doctor if...
- you are feeling really ill or have been feeling mildly ill for some time and do not seem to be improving, or if you think you may be suffering from an infectious illness
- you are continually gaining or losing weight; if you never seem to be hungry; if you have any difficulty in swallowing or if you have an abdominal pain which lasts for longer than six hours, especially if it is accompanied by vomiting and loss of appetite
- you feel tired all the time, even though you are sleeping a lot; if you have a persistent headache; if you are feeling severely anxious or depressed or if you are having sleepless nights
- it hurts when you pass water and you find you want to do so frequently; if you have an unusual vaginal or penile discharge or any blood in your urine; if you have a change of bowel habit or if you have an excessive thirst
- you have an unusual and persistent cough without having a cold, or a cough producing green sputum or hoarseness or a loss of voice that lasts for longer than a week
- you have an unexplained rash that has lasted for longer than a week; a change in the color of your skin or complexion; sores that do not heal; boils around your nose or upper lip; a change in your moles or birthmarks or swellings or lumps anywhere on your body, even if they are painless
- you have continued or recurrent pain anywhere in your body; if you have acute joint pain or stiffness or swelling or if you have painful feet which are affecting your mobility (especially if you are over sixty)
- you are having serious difficulty in breathing, continuous backache or if you have a gripping central chest pain, especially if you are over thirty-five
- you have unexplained or severe bleeding from the skin or any body opening (such as your rectum)
- you are giddy or weak and falling over a lot; if your hearing is getting worse; if you have visual problems such as double or blurred vision or if you are unconscious for any reason, but especially after injury
- you are pregnant

CHILDREN

Never worry about troubling the doctor if you know your child is ill, even if he has no obvious symptoms.

Always call the doctor for a child if...
- he has a fit or convulsion, or if he turns blue or very pale, especially if accompanied by a high temperature
- he has quick, difficult or grunting breathing
- he has had a high temperature (that other obvious sign of illness) that has lasted for three days
- he has had a high temperature that drops, then suddenly rises again
- he has a low temperature accompanied by cold skin, drowsiness, quietness and limpness
- he appears listless for no apparent reason and does not seem to know you
- he has been vomiting or suffering from diarrhea for over six hours
- he goes off his food suddenly for no obvious reason, especially if he is under six months old
- he is dizzy, especially if he has bumped his head
- he has a bad pain on the right side of his stomach and feels sick
- he has a headache together with dizziness or blurred vision

Even if you have visited your doctor within twenty-four hours, if your child is not improving or is getting worse, call him again.

THE BEAUTIFUL HOME

Making Improvements

Few people are ever totally content with their homes. It could just be that the living room never has enough comfortable chairs, that there is not enough storage space in the kitchen or that the yellow gloss paint you used in the bathroom is beginning to chip. Maybe you are not even sure what is wrong, but something always bothers you when you enter a certain room.

To help you work out how you intend to improve your home, study photographs of rooms. Think what it is that appeals to you. Is it the fabrics used, the style of the furniture, the mixture of patterns, the simplicity of color or the softness of the lighting? On the other hand, if it is the size of the room or the view from the window that appeals to you, you may have problems re-creating something similar in your own home.

Think about the photographs and the suggestions below and on the following pages and you may begin to get an idea of how to achieve the changes you are really aiming for in the easiest and cheapest way.

It is always easier to plan a room from scratch around a painting, a rug, curtains or a collection. But where this is not possible, you can still make changes that will improve your home. The first step is to take a critical look around you. Be courageous. It may mean getting rid of things you have had for some time. This is difficult decorating, but with a little thought your home can be beautiful too, and can work in the way you want it to.

Could you change it?

It is essential never to keep anything just because you do not want to hurt the feelings of the person who gave it to you. If you do not like it – or if it does not work in your home – store it, sell it or give it away. Compromises may be what make life go smoothly, but not in decorating. A home will never be beautiful if it is filled with mismatched objects that you do not like. It is your taste that will make your home look right to your eyes, not your taste plus Aunt Joan's and her Christmas gifts.

Does it work?

By now you have probably developed a pattern for living in your home. You instinctively go to one room for cooking, another for sleeping and another for washing, but what about less obvious activities? Where do you go for sewing, for practicing the cello, for watching television, answering letters, paying bills or when guests come to dinner? Often rooms, usually living rooms and dining rooms, do not work well because their functions are unclear.

Think of the way you live in your home and make a list of all the things you do and where you like doing them. Then see if the rooms really work the way they are. Do not worry if the layout of your rooms is constantly changing. It is only in magazines that rooms look immaculate. Most people alter their homes constantly and are forever pushing a chair from one room to another or shifting the sofa around – so start pushing and stop worrying.

Does it suit you?

How do you feel when you are in each of your rooms and, more importantly, how do you look? It is essential that you both look and feel attractive in your home. If your wardrobe is filled with blues, yellows and greens then your home should be too. There is no point having a pink and brown home when you feel dowdy and depressed wearing those colors. Always hold carpets, fabrics, wallpapers to your face when buying; look in the mirror to see if they suit you.

A stylish solution

If you always dress very simply with straight, sharp lines and few frills it makes little sense to have a home cluttered with lavish curtains, endless knick-knacks and floral patterns. Your home should mirror your style as well as your complexion.

Look around you and decide whether you have been collecting things because you like them, because you need them

ADDING TO AN EXISTING SCHEME

Use a separate sheet of paper for each room and stick all the new wallpaper and paint swatches and fabric samples for each room together on the appropriate sheet. It will let you see how patterns and colors blend.

Keep the sheet of paper in the room for several days, sticking it on one wall after another and looking at the colors carefully in both daylight and artificial light to see if they still work.

If you have to match existing carpets, curtains or wallpaper, take samples with you so that you can match them carefully, checking them at different times of day.

or because you thought they would make your home look more fashionable. Never do anything to your home that does not feel right. You can never emulate someone else's style, so why try? Your home should reflect you and your style. If you do not like something that is in vogue this year then do not be influenced by it. This year's fashions become last year's quickly enough and then you are stuck with them.

Does it suit your lifestyle?

Have you got boisterous children and pets? If so, is an all-white room really ideal? Pale colors are soft, pretty and easy to live with – visually. They are not appropriate to a lively family home to which patterns or bright washable fabrics, such as corduroy, denims and linens, are far better suited. Your home should be designed to fit your life: it is no good pretending you are something that you are not. Delicate china or glass objects, for example, are incompatible with toddlers – unless you lock off a room and keep the children out.

Are you using the right materials and colors in the right rooms? An expensive carpet in the nursery is a waste of money and a constant headache. Dark, sophisticated curtains in the laundry room are another unnecessary expense. Keep your head and spend money in rooms where you are going to appreciate rather than regret it.

Does it suit the building?

Try and complement the style of your home rather than ignore it. Do not take out period features, such as Victorian sash windows, tiny Tudor-style panes or beautiful fireplaces. Similarly, do not straighten floors, walls and doors that are crooked and uneven. All these things are part of the charm and character of your building and you should enjoy living with them.

On the other hand, do not be tempted to add inappropriate features to your home. Putting a pine nineteenth-century fireplace (even if you have wanted one for years) in an Edwardian room does not work. The intricacy and frivolity of the Edwardian style of architecture will be underplayed by the plain, simple wooden mantel – which in turn would look warm and inviting in an early nineteenth-century home.

In need of a focal point?

Could it be that what is wrong with your living room is that the main focus is the television rather than the fireplace? Does the seating area seem to have no coffee table or central rug holding it together? Or does the room lack a single beautiful item, such as a painting, a grand piano or a stunning palm tree that everyone can admire?

Features come in all shapes and sizes – and all price ranges. A wall covered with gilt-framed pictures painted by your child is as eye-catching a feature (although it may be not as good an investment) as the work of an old master. You may even feel that covering one wall with a stunning wallpaper is preferable to having it blank.

Why not make a low-level, built-in storage area stretching across the entire room, and cover it with cushions? It would be a wonderful seat or lounging area, a useful storage space as well as a

spectacular feature. Or you could consider laying a secondhand parquet floor in your living room and covering it with rugs instead of a fitted carpet? Not only would it look unusual and be easy to clean but it would also be ideal for parties, when rugs could be removed.

Any money to spend?

If you have any money to spare, spend it on essentials, not frills. It is easy to get carried away and spend too much on the first thing that catches your eye. But it is more important to think carefully about your priorities. A chest of drawers may cost more than a pretty lamp and shade, but it may be more essential to improving your room. The basics in a room must be right, so do not rush any decisions and always buy the essentials first. Once you have got these right, take your time to consider all your other purchases.

Above An expanse of mirror is one of the best ways of ''enlarging'' a room.

''ADDING'' SPACE

Mirrors will give you light, and the illusion of mystery and space. Place a mirror on the window wall to look as if there was an extra window, or put one opposite the window for more light and a further view. Add a mirror over the mantelpiece for dignity, scatter several mirrors with gilt frames around a room for opulence or place a mirror along the edge of your bath for fun bathing.

Covering an entire wall with a mirror will make the wall disappear and the edges of the room dissolve. Although this can be effective in a room, it may also make you feel a little uneasy. In a hall a mirror near the front door is essential to check your appearance when coming in or going out.

Storage 10–17
General cleaning 18–25
Around the home 36–43

Your home workshop 58–61
Energy saving 62–69
Electrical maintenance 76–7
Decorating 78–85
Flooring 86–91
Furniture & furnishings 92–3

Room by Room
LIVING ROOMS

As its name suggests, a living room is different from a sitting room, a drawing room, a study, a parlor or a den. It is a family room where you should be able to live and relax in comfort, with friends and family, reading or listening to music. It should feel cosy in winter and bright and cheerful in summer, and it should not be so precious that you dare not take your children in there for fear they will cause chaos.

Two atmospheres in one

Your living room should also reflect the different seasons. In winter you will want a warm and intimate room, filled with soft, welcoming objects and lined with thick, heavy curtains. A lit fire surrounded by comfortable chairs and a

furry carpet to lay your feet on will complete the picture. In summer you need a room that works as an extension of outdoors. It should be cool yet sunny, plant-filled, light and airy.

The simple answer
In winter, seating can be focused around the fire and, in summer, around the windows. In winter, chairs and sofas can be covered with rich velvets, corduroys and brocades and, in summer, a loose plain or floral chintz cover can be thrown over them. In winter, windows can be covered with thick curtains, which are taken down in summer to reveal cream-colored roller blinds. Floors can be strewn with beautiful warm rugs, which can be taken up and stored in summer, and flowers can be dried in winter and fresh in summer.

Above A comfortable, cosy living room is the heart of a home. Despite the geometry of this room, its layout and warm furnishings give it a cosy feel and encourage relaxation.

FIREPLACE

As the fireplace is so often the focal point of a room, it should be pleasing to look at and should suit the character and period of your home. If it does not, consider replacing it with one that will.

Fill it with a real fire or flame-effect gas fire in winter and pots of fresh flowers in summer. Alternatively, choose an impressive dried-flower arrangement for the whole year round.

Creating a relaxing room

As you are mainly seated, rather than standing, in the living room, make everything low level. Hang pictures low: if you own a few small pictures rather than one large one, place them to the side of the mantelpiece rather than directly above it. Keep arrangements intimate, rather than grandiose.

Chairs should be a pleasure to sit on, and each piece of furniture should have a function, even if it is just to delight the eye. There should be enough tables so that everyone can have somewhere to place his drink without having to put it on the floor where it can easily be spilled. Tables are also essential for siting lamps, as well as ashtrays and other bric-a-brac.

A change of plan

The layout of your living room will be determined by the floorplan and the position of doors, windows and fireplace. It will also depend on the use the room has. Plan the room so that as many different activities as are necessary can take place at the same time. One person should be able to read, while another watches television, or your entire family plus a few guests should be able to sit down together and talk or play a board game. Access to the television, stereo, doors, light switches and windows should not be impeded.

Creating more space

You may want room for a piano, a stereo, a liquor cabinet, bookshelves, or even a desk, so keep areas clear or make it easy to push a sofa out of the way when friends come around. Put furniture on castors so it can easily be moved. Do the same with the television – keep it out of sight in a cupboard, so you do not automatically turn it on when you go into the living room. You can roll the television and video out into view when there is something on that you particularly want to watch or record, or if repairs need to be made.

FLEXIBLE SEATING

A living room should be a flexible area with furniture and lights that can be moved around easily. A useful arrangement is to have seating placed around the fire with a separate area for study. Seating around the walls is better suited to a waiting room than a living room. People must be able to stretch their legs when seated and if possible conduct conversations with others at right angles or in front of them, rather than to their side.

A symmetrical arrangement of sofas and chairs makes a room more formal; lots of different shapes and sizes make a room cosier. A three-piece suite is not very flexible and a three-seater sofa is usually only sat on by two, so is a waste of space. Two two-seater sofas and two easy chairs or one two-seater and two easy chairs are preferable combinations.

Below Two rooms of the same shape and size can be given a completely different feel by arranging their furniture in various ways.

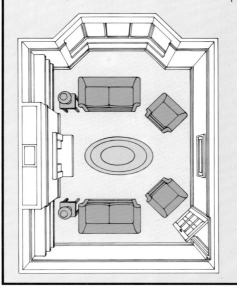
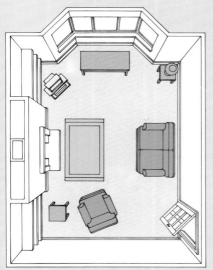

LIGHTING – THE INSTANT TRANSFORMER

As with everything else in the living room, the lighting should be flexible. Make sure you have enough lights, plenty of power points – so that lights can be moved – and dimmer switches, so that the intensity of the lighting can be altered according to the mood you wish to create.

Ceiling lights are inflexible and, although they cast a useful, general light, can be harsh and monotonous. Fit recessed directional downlights or, where possible, replace them with table and standard lamps. If you have a hanging light, position it off-center and bring it down low over a coffee table.

Living-room lighting should be restful and yet you need sufficient light at strategic points – for reading, sewing, deflecting the light of the television, accenting pictures or ornaments, playing board games, etc. For this, low-level lamps carefully situated around the room are ideal. Use more lamps, rather than fewer, and fit them with low-wattage bulbs for a softer light.

Any arches or alcoves with shelves or bookshelves can also be illuminated. This will look especially effective if the shelves are glass.

KITCHENS

Few things are more infuriating than a kitchen that is not working properly. There may be too few work surfaces, too little light where it is needed, nooks and crannies that are constant dirt-traps, or not enough storage space. Or you could be having to walk too far from the stove to the sink with heavy pots and pans of boiling water.

The kitchen is an expensive and complex room to redesign, so you must take time to make decisions. Each kitchen has its own problems, and what will suit one family may not necessarily suit another – or fit in the room available.

You should first decide what is wrong with your present arrangement and what you want from a new kitchen. Is it simply a room to cook in or will you also be eating and entertaining in it? Will it have to double as laundry room, larder, nursery and study as well? Have you got all the appliances you need or will you be buying more in the future? If so, they all need to be stored somewhere. Ask yourself as many questions as you need to determine exactly what kind of kitchen you would like, how it will work and what you will want to put in it.

Choosing your atmosphere

Do you want an old-fashioned, countrified kitchen with a cosy atmosphere reminiscent of pickling vegetables and making jam? Or do you want a rather more stark, clinical, high-tech kitchen that will be easier to look after, and possibly even to cook in, but may be less conducive to relaxed eating? There are any number of styles to choose from, ranging from fitted wooden country-style units to free-standing space-age formica cupboards.

Whatever solution you opt for, your kitchen should be a light and cheerful place to be – after all you will be spending quite a bit of time in it. But remember that, irrespective of your environment, your kitchen layout is of vital importance in saving you much time and energy.

KITCHEN LAYOUT

An ideal kitchen layout is based on a triangle, not necessarily with equal sides. One point is the oven and/or stove, another the sink (preferably situated under the window for both light and a view) and another the fridge. These three points are your main work areas and in between them should be work surfaces and storage space. If the triangle is located at one end of the room it means that the other end of the room can be used for different activities.

Smaller kitchens

If your kitchen is too small, you may have to compromise by placing all the fittings along one wall in a "work surface, stove, work surface, sink, work surface" arrangement – with the fridge under one of the work surfaces. This is the very simplest plan, but provides probably the most difficult kitchen to work in.

One step up is the galley kitchen, when the units are situated on two facing walls. You will need to allow at least 2½ ft (75 cm) between the units and will have to stop your family using the kitchen as a corridor as it will be too dangerous. This arrangement is ideal for a small room, but it requires a certain amount of tidiness from the chef. The best way to arrange a galley kitchen is to have the sink and stove elements on one wall and the fridge and oven on another. If a little bit more space is available it will allow you to place an island, or simply a table, in the middle, which can be used as a seating area or to accommodate chopping boards.

Larger kitchens

A larger kitchen is easier to design and more satisfactory to work in. Both an "L"- and a "U"-shaped kitchen are easy to cook and live in, with the "U" shape being slightly preferable as it allows for the most surface space and the minimum amount of walking around from one area to another. Place the sink in the center of the work triangle (and the "U" shape), with the fridge to one side and the stove and oven to the other side.

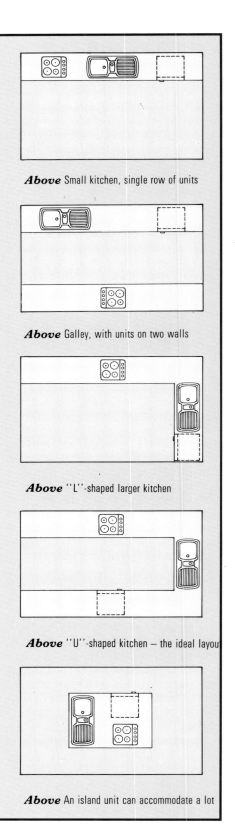

Above Small kitchen, single row of units

Above Galley, with units on two walls

Above "L"-shaped larger kitchen

Above "U"-shaped kitchen – the ideal layout

Above An island unit can accommodate a lot

General principles 106–7
Kitchens 108–15
Special considerations 130–4
Household emergencies 135–7
First aid 146–9

Making improvements 154–5
Dining rooms 160–1
Style & color 166–75
Furnishings 176–83
Furniture 184–7
Entertaining 196–9

THE BEAUTIFUL HOME

STORAGE SOLUTIONS

A kitchen always looks most manageable if work surfaces are clear when you want to start cooking. This means you may want to add to your storage space: for food (fresh, frozen and groceries), wine, cutlery, china, pots, pans, utensils, cleaning products and equipment, recipe books and large, decorative serving dishes and platters.

Shallow, open shelves are easy to use but equipment kept on them will quickly get greasy and dusty. A pegboard to hang cooking utensils on is very useful, as is a knife rack. Keep sharp implements well away from children.

Sliding doors on units often leave a dead space in the middle, too many deep drawers cause chaos and confusion, and items stored too high up mean perching on a chair or ladder whenever you want to get something out.

Everyday items are best stored at eye or hip level, and pots and pans should not be stacked but kept easy to get at.

REVAMPING YOUR FITTED CUPBOARDS

Most fitted cupboards are designed so the doors can be removed and replaced, but if you want a cheaper – and quicker – solution, it may be easiest to paint them a flat color or with a paint finish. You could even paint them *trompe l'oeil*, possibly suggesting the beautiful old copper pots and pans or food boxes you would like there to be behind the doors.

Otherwise you could add dimension to the doors by sticking thin wooden panels along their edges and painting them a subtly different color. Even simply changing the knobs may make such a difference that nothing else will be necessary to do.

A fresh paint color and a change of knobs or handles can inexpensively transform the look of your kitchen.

Ideal work surfaces

A single-level work surface is easier to install and keep clean, but ideally each task should have a different height of surface to avoid backache and to make tasks easier to perform. Chopping food, for example, should be done at a lower level than rolling pastry.

The easiest height to determine is that of the sink. Simply stand up and stretch out your forearms in a straight line. The bottom of the sink should be the height the tips of your fingers reach, otherwise you could put an unnecessary strain on your back. Work out the rest of the worktops from this height. Always leave a recessed space under your units for your toes.

LIGHTING WORK SURFACES

It is important that you do not cast a shadow over what you are doing. One solution is to place tungsten or fluorescent tubes under wall-hung cupboards to shine light down onto the work surfaces (do not store food above these lights as the heat rises).

Make sure the sink and the top of the stove are well lit at night – strategically placed spotlights could be the answer. All the lights in your kitchen should be individually controlled so that you do not necessarily need to have them all on at the same time.

DINING ROOMS

Unless you have a large home with a few rooms to spare or enjoy formal entertaining, there is no need to have a separate dining room. Often a more relaxed atmosphere is achieved by eating with friends in the kitchen, and the chef will not be excluded from half the conversation as he or she rushes to get the next course.

The dining room tends to double as a study or playroom or be a part of the kitchen or living room. But if you want a separate dining room you should designate a room that is near, and preferably next to, the kitchen so that you do not have too far to walk back and forth with plates and dishes.

A separate dining room is an enjoyable luxury.

Creating the right atmosphere

Your dining room should be a warm, relaxed room with a stimulating atmosphere. The chairs should be comfortable, the table should preferably be circular to encourage group conversation and there should be enough room round it for guests not to feel cramped. To seat six people a round table should ideally be about 4½ ft (1.35 m) in diameter for comfort and convenience.

The lighting should be soft, with the table as the focal point, and cutlery, dishes, linen and glassware should be simple, clean and beautifully presented. Candles are good for creating a cosy atmosphere for evening meals.

Suiting your lifestyle

Once you have chosen the room you wish to eat in and are about to redesign, think about your lifestyle. When will you be using the room and with whom? Will you be eating in the dining room for breakfast, lunch, and dinner with your family – including small children? Or will it be used mainly for entertaining: formal parties at night or casual Sunday lunches? How many people do you enjoy cooking for? What else do you plan the room to be used for?

Sunday lunches

A dining room used mainly for breakfasts, lunches and summer tea parties would ideally be almost an extension of the garden. It might double as a conservatory, where your green fingers could be displayed, or it might be painted white and green and have vases of flowers scattered liberally around. However you plan it, the atmosphere should be casual, sunny and open.

Dinner parties

A room used mainly in the evening should act as a womb-like space, enveloping guests in a cosy cocoon that stops them worrying about the world outside. A view is not important; what is important is the table in front of them and the atmosphere in the room.

Dining room and...

If the dining room is sharing a function, for example becoming a playroom or study area by day, it must have enough storage space for traces of its other life to be quickly removed. Toys could be swept behind a curtain across a partition. Typewriters and telephones should be able to be lifted up and shut away in a cupboard where they will not get dusty. Books and pictures or prints,

LIGHTING

By far the most flattering and effective lighting for a dinner party is candlelight – but make sure you have enough candles so guests can see what they are eating. Otherwise a light hung low over the center of the table is a simple and less formal solution. Install one that can rise and fall, hang it high enough so that guests can look at each other across the table and fit it with a dimmer switch so the light can be soft and intimate. Add supplementary lighting around the rest of the room.

whether children's or grown-ups', never go amiss in a dining room and may make an interesting feature.

Conversely, you may wish to make the dining room disappear during the day. Think about buying a table that can be folded up or an expanding table, with wings or leaves. Chairs could either be folded and hung on the wall or used around the house, some in the bedroom, some in the corridor and some in the hall.

Informal dining rooms

The informal dining room is light and cheery. The atmosphere is casual and friendly; food is rough and ready, but tasty. Cheerful plastic tablecloths and paper napkins protect the table and the guests, the china is harmonious without necessarily matching, the water comes in a pitcher and not in a bottle. Colors are bright, sunny, spacious; patterns loud and bold – guests relaxed.

Formal dining rooms

In a formal dining room there should be a feeling of opulence – possibly even decadence. The wooden French polished table should shine, the crystal should sparkle, the candles should glow, the mirrors should reflect, the silver should glisten and the linen should be starched. Everything should be perfect and there should even be an element of excess: too many courses, too many decanters, too many cigars, too much conversation, too many guests and too much washing-up afterwards!

UNIFYING AN EXISTING SCHEME

A simple and effective way of unifying a set of different dining room or kitchen chairs is to give them all the same cushion cover. If you paint the chairs all the same color their different shapes will contrast with each other in a most original way. Or you can leave all the chairs in natural wood but make the same style of tied cushion for each chair, using a different color (or pattern) for each one – of four different colors for eight chairs.

To do this, buy as many thin feather cushions (or use thin foam cut to size) as you need. Then cover the cushions with the fabric and add two ties to each of the back corners of the cushions, which you can then tie in a bow round your chairs. You can play with the theme by piping the cushions with a contrasting color, or adding a frill to the edge of each cushion. You can even cover the back of each chair as well with another matching cover.

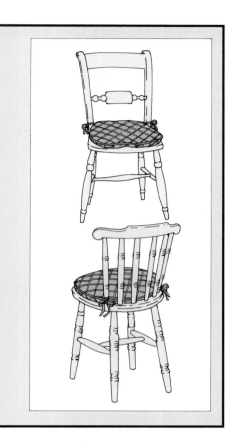

ADDING A ROOM DIVIDER

If a room is sharing activities you may feel you want to split it in two, and possibly with something less permanent than a new wall. Much mystery is lost when one arrives at a friend's home for dinner, sits in the living room and sees the dining room table already laid waiting at the other end of the room. It is much better if the table is screened off by a curtain, a roller or Venetian blind hung from the ceiling, a folding screen or a purpose-built unit.

Dining tables in kitchens need not necessarily be screened off. However, a low-level kitchen unit will provide not only more storage, but also more chopping space and will make the dining area feel more private.

A dining area within a kitchen can be partially screened by a low-level unit.

BEDROOMS

Your bedroom should act as a refuge to which you can retire from the world and its problems. Ideally it should be next to a bathroom and should have enough space for you to store all your clothes, shoes and surplus bedding. Moreover, it should feel like you – after all, it is the one room in the house that is yours alone. So ask yourself whether it has the right atmosphere for you.

Are you an early riser?

Before electricity was invented, houses were designed with east-facing bedrooms to catch the sunrise. If you have a choice of rooms, decide whether you like being woken by the sun in the morning or would rather watch it set in the evening. Whatever your preference, make sure the curtains are heavy enough to block any bright lights or noise from the outside world.

Bed coverings

If your bed cover looks boring, try throwing something different over the bed. The traditional patchwork quilt will tie in with many colors already in the room. A large piece of lace placed over a paisley eiderdown or even over a brightly colored duvet would look romantic and feminine, a fake fur would look sexy, as would a highly impractical velvet cover, and an old, worn rug would create an Oriental atmosphere.

Floor coverings

The point about floor coverings in your bedroom is that they should feel cosy underfoot when you have to get out of bed. If you do not have a wall-to-wall carpet, scatter rugs about liberally to stop your feet from getting cold. The bedroom is the one room in the house where you can afford to be impractical – so indulge yourself. If you want fragile Persian rugs you can use them here.

Cushions on the bed make your bedroom look attractive by day; bedside lamps give gentle light and facilitate night-time reading.

CHANGING THE COLOR IN YOUR BEDROOM

Whereas warm pinks and yellows in a bedroom will capture and enhance even the subtlest rays of the winter sun, cool greens and blues will give a warm, sunny room a cooler, fresher feel. A white bedroom will reflect whatever light is outside the room and act as a good backdrop for bold pictures and patterns.

Soft colors, such as gentle pinks, warm tobacco and earthy terracotta, will make a bedroom seem comforting, but could be overpowering in a hot south-facing room. A vivid color may be romantic and welcoming when you are feeling strong but prove too stimulating if you are convalescing.

A CHANGE OF LIGHT

Bedrooms need a soft, romantic light, but on occasion also lights for reading, and brighter lights for finding clothes, dressing and applying makeup. Lights on dimmer switches may be best.

If you have to get out of bed to turn out the light, now is the time to make the change. Install bedside lights on both sides of the double bed so you can read independently. Your clothes cupboard could have a concealed light and make sure the light on your dressing table shines on your face, not on the mirror.

CHANGING CHILDREN'S BEDROOMS

When thinking about changes to your child's bedroom or playroom, bear in mind that she may be using it for a number of years to come. Although clowns and trains on the walls may be suitable now, posters of rock stars may be covering the walls in a few years' time. Keep fixtures and fittings simple and ageless: your child's possessions will always express her perfectly.

It is simplest to redecorate your child's bedroom in straightforward neutral colors. They are easy to keep clean and are soothing for your child to sleep in after the excitement of the day is over. Remember it is easier to repaint rather than repaper a room.

If you have a room available, the child's bedroom should be near yours so you do not have to worry about him at night. For a toddler, check that lights are firmly fixed to the walls so they cannot be pulled over and fix window bars.

Extra shelves are useful as the number of books, toys and other possessions increases. A chest of drawers is easier to store children's clothes in than a wardrobe. A spare bed for you to sleep in when your child is ill and a comfy nursing chair will also make a difference to your life. Some pieces of furniture can grow with your child: for example, you can buy a changing unit that turns into a desk and a cot that becomes a bed for a young child.

CHANGING THEMES IN CHILDREN'S ROOMS

The nursery should be a bright, stimulating room where young children can enjoy living, playing and learning. You can change its theme every now and again by sticking cheerful sheets of wrapping-paper or pictures painted by your child himself onto the walls – they can be removed and replaced by new papers or pictures with little trouble and expense, especially if the wall behind is cork or painted with an oil-based paint.

Where you have your nursery depends on whether or not you are with your child during the day or if you have help. If you are alone with your toddler, it is easiest to have the nursery next to, or even include it as part of, the kitchen, provided it is safe. As children grow up, the nursery will have to become the playroom or study and older children will prefer a room of their own as far away from you as possible.

Once your child is beginning to assert himself, help him on his way. A teenager will not want a child's room any more, but will appreciate a place where he can play loud music, read his magazines and keep his extensive wardrobe. Remember that the room belongs to him and, unless a decision he makes upsets you greatly, let him have his way.

A child's room can be tasteful as well as bright and cheerful; make bold use of color against a neutral background to achieve the right balance.

BATHROOMS

The bathroom is such an intimate room that it is important that your taste is reflected in it – even if it conflicts with the other members of your family.

There are many cheap ways of adding personal touches to the bathroom. You could buy sets of luxurious towels, which you can monogram for fun. You could cover any available surface with pots of humidity-loving plants or fill shelves with collections of knick-knacks or china or glass – either appropriate to the bathroom or otherwise. More expensively, you could redo all the fixtures and fittings. There are so many styles of tiles, taps and toilets that you can make your bathroom as unique as your imagination allows.

Creating a new atmosphere

Anything unexpected makes a bathroom more welcoming and less a purely functional area. For example, a collection of nine Redouté rose prints beautifully framed and hung in three rows of three over the bath would add an elegant and striking note. A richly covered armchair could introduce an unexpected dimension to family bathing and a large collection of hardback books would lend an air of sophistication.

On the other hand, if you want your bathroom to be streamlined and feel like a 1930s hotel bathroom or even like the capsule toilets in an airplane, you could add tiles, marble, chrome and thick white towels to enhance this effect. No softening touches are necessary.

Is the layout right?

The layout of your bathroom is important. Is there enough space for your knees when sitting on the toilet? Do you have room to get in and out of the bath while someone is standing at the basin? Can you get to the washing machine without having to sit on the toilet? Make sure the towel rail is where you want it, next to the bath, and not on the other side of the room, and that you have plenty of shelf space next to the washbasin for everything that you need – and more besides.

Now is the time also to consider whether you would like two basins for shared morning ablutions if you have the same timetable.

Have you enough space?

If your bathroom has not got a toilet, remember that toilets can be fitted into minute spaces. Equally, if you are considering fitting an extra bathroom into a small space, it is useful to know that basins come in all shapes and sizes, including shapes for corners, and that baths need not be long and spacious but can fit into a corner or simply be big enough to sit down in. Showers take up even less room of course.

Use the back of the bathroom door for hanging things on and box in basins, toilet tanks and baths so you can store cleaning materials and other equipment under them. Make use of hanging shelves and corner cupboards or shelf units for storing cotton batting, toiletries, makeup and shaving materials. An extending shaving mirror, with a concertina arm, can be fixed to the wall and pulled out when needed.

COLOR IN THE BATHROOM

Bathrooms tend to be predominantly white, blue or green – perhaps to recreate a natural, water atmosphere or to suggest hygiene.

If you are thinking of repainting the bathroom, remember it must be clean and hygienic to relax in, but does not have to be white. Pale yellow is cheerful and sunny – ideal for an early morning shower – and pink is a soft, gentle, welcoming color for a bathroom at any time of the day or night. Wallpapers can also look very effective, especially if they tie in with the color scheme of a neighboring bedroom.

CHANGING THE LOOK OF YOUR TILING

One cheap way of altering the look of your bathroom is to change your tiles. You can either paint them another color, or several different colors to achieve a patchwork-quilt effect, or you could apply old-fashioned transfers to them.

Alternatively, you could simply change the color of the grouting. By making the grouting a complementary color to your tiles you will achieve a strong, graphic grid pattern on your wall. You can do this either by simply painting over the

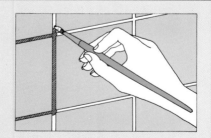

existing grouting using an oil-based paint, a small brush and a firm hand or, if the original grouting is old and worn, you can remove it first and re-grout with a different colored grout.

NEW LIGHTING IN THE BATHROOM

Always make sure that you follow safety regulations when putting in additional lighting in the bathroom.

A dimmer switch attached to your central light will help you relax in a late night bath. To bring extra light into the bathroom fix wall lights on either side of mirrors or above mirrors for applying makeup or shaving.

Imaginative use has been made of the wall space in this high-ceilinged bathroom.

Style & Color
PERIOD MOLDINGS

WHAT TO DO WITH CLASSICAL MOLDINGS

If you live in a grand house with classical moldings, it may be correct and attractive to pick out parts of the detail in gold leaf. Otherwise a standard nineteenth-century ceiling is simply best left alone.

Palladian ceiling moldings were frequently treated with subtle tinted color washes, but unless you have superb color sense and the kind of ceiling moldings which would have been treated this way, it is probably safer to paint all decorative plaster details in white or broken white and leave the color to the background.

If your home has any original features you should try and restore them as they will give more character to your home than almost anything you can add yourself. If all the features have been removed, look at those in your neighbor's homes (if they are identical to yours) or consult specialist books on the architectural detailing of the era in which your house was built and try and put some of them back.

Hidden or removed features

In the 1960s staircases, doors and fireplaces were often covered over with sheets of plywood to make cleaning easier and to give a futuristic, linear feel. If all you need do is remove the plywood to find an original treasure underneath, then do it. Otherwise there are shops specializing in selling doors and

fireplaces which have been ripped out of old homes. Make sure the mantelpiece and grate are both the correct period for your home and the correct proportions for your room and check that any replaced door fits.

Old baseboards, architraves and shutters were often removed and replaced with something simpler or nothing at all. It is worthwhile, though expensive, to ask a carpenter to copy any original features you still have as they will suit the room far better than any cheap, modern copy could do.

Above Deep cornices in a classical style are often found in the high-ceilinged rooms typical of eighteenth-century houses.

Top right A decorative molded cornice can be restored to its former glory once the layers of old paint or distemper are painstakingly removed.

RESTORING A CORNICE

Often modern partitions have been put up in houses ignoring cornices that follow the original borders of the room. You probably will not want to take the partitions down and turn three small rooms into one large one, but you may want to restore any cornice in which the pattern has been clogged up by paint. It is a messy job, so do it before you decorate. Then consider how to paint it – a white cornice on a colored ceiling looks most striking.

Use a damp sponge to see if the old paint can be removed with water. If it can, empty the room and cover the floor with dustcloths.

Fill a plant spray bottle with water and spray a 12 in (30 cm) length of the cornice

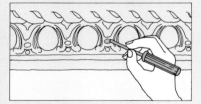

Leave it for half an hour and then carefully scrape out the paint with a screwdriver or other pointed object.

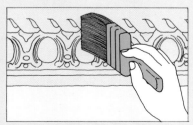

Finally brush out any loose or flaking material until only the plaster is left.

RESTORING ORIGINAL FEATURES

Ceiling roses
Like cornices, ceiling roses can be cleaned and restored. They can also be added if yours have been removed. You could ask a specialist to copy an existing one elsewhere in your home, or you can buy quite effective copies made of fibrous plaster or Anaglypta (relief wallpaper) which can simply be stuck on. Again, be sure you get the pattern and proportions correct for your home. Just because a rose is sold as "nineteenth century," it does not mean it will be appropriate for all houses of this period.

Picture rails
The Victorians and Edwardians used picture rails; if your home is of this period it would be appropriate to reinstate them if you wished to. Picture rails are not only useful for hanging pictures, but also have the effect of making a tall room look lower and a large room smaller, which can be desirable. The area above the picture rail can either be painted the same color as the rest of the wall or be given a different treatment.

Dados
The dado is the lower part of a wall and differs from the upper part in color or material – in the case of wainscotting, for example, the dado is wooden paneling. In halls, you may want to bring back the dado and chair rail (the horizontal rail dividing the two sections of the wall); you could paint the dado with a washable oil-based paint and treat the wall above the dado along with the rest of your decoration.

In nurseries why not cover the dado with blackboard paint and give children a box of chalks?

Walls & ceilings 36–7
Floors 38–9
Furniture & soft furnishings 42–3

Decorating 78–85
Flooring 86–91
Furniture & furnishings 92–3

COLOR

Changing the color of a room can alter both the size and feel of the room completely. When choosing a new color, the decision should never be completely arbitrary. Imagine your home as a whole: try to let color link the rooms and unify the house. By using the same carpet throughout or the same wall color, you can make your home look larger.

Color and light

In a subdued northern light, soft colors are often the most successful. In contrast, vivid colors work wonderfully in the brilliant southern sun.

When choosing new colors, study each room carefully. Never rush into painting a dark room a light color in an attempt to cheer it up: dark rooms can be most effective and very cosy.

Color and light are closely related. A room that faces north should have a warm color scheme: you can afford to use rich deep yellows, pinks and browns. A sunny room can take pale, cool shades or harder colors, such as grays, lilacs and blues. It does not mean that you have to have different colored carpets throughout your home: a neutral color suits both warm and cool colors, with rugs added for extra color and interest.

Color and size

Color can be used to change the shape and proportions of a room. Light colors will give you a feeling of spaciousness; dark, rich colors a feeling of warmth and cosiness – especially useful in a large and cold room.

Low ceilings can be made to appear higher if the ceiling is painted a lighter color than the walls. If you want to bring a ceiling height down, add a picture rail and paint the ceiling down to the picture rail a darker color than the rest of the walls. By painting alcove recesses a dark color, they can be made

to disappear, which will highlight any fireplace or wall between them. By making carpet, walls and curtains the same pale color and by keeping strong colors in the center of the room, a small room can appear more spacious. Otherwise it is almost always better to have the floor darker than the walls and ceilings as it will give solidity to a room – an effect which can easily be achieved by throwing a large rug over a pale carpet.

Various color schemes

Monochromatic schemes use shades of one color only. Monotony is avoided by varying the values and intensities of the color. Further interest is added by contrasting texture, patterns and materials (china, glass, wood, etc) within the one-color plan. The addition of black or white to monochromatic scheme is sophisticated and subtle.

Related or harmonious decorating schemes use three colors adjacent to each other on the color wheel, all of which share a common base color. One such scheme might use yellow with yellow/orange and orange; another yellow/green, yellow and yellow/orange; another blue/green, blue and blue/violet. To avoid dullness in your decorating scheme, use colors of different values and intensities.

Contrasting or complementary schemes use opposite colors such as orange and blue, yellow and violet, red and green. Each scheme therefore uses a cool and a warm color which are intensified by being used together. The colors used are rarely as bright as those shown on the color wheel, but tints and shades of these colors.

Primary schemes use several, or just one, primary color with white. The primary colors used need not be pure Black and white used with yellow/green with highlights of blue/violet can look striking. A primarily white room used with red/violet, blue/green and yellow/orange will look larger, the primary colors forcing the room apart.

PERIOD WALL COLORS

It is difficult to know what colors originally looked like when they were newly applied. Even if we did know, we may well find we do not like them.

Eighteenth century

In the mid-eighteenth century the two main wall colors were pea green and stone. Other colors used were olive, sky blue, orange, lemon, straw, pink, blossom and "fine deep green." The oil-based finish used on walls and woodwork would have resembled today's eggshell rather than gloss. Doors were painted black or dark brown and window frames were white. By the end of the century, when the Adam brothers were influential, colors were based on classical sources and nature, with deep reds contrasted with white and pale greens and blues.

Victorian and Edwardian

Colors in the Victorian era tended to be rich, heavy and gloomy. Maroon, deep blues and dark brown were popular for woodwork and went with yellow, purple and green fabrics and wall-coverings.

The Edwardian home used pastel shades for large areas, picking out ornaments and details in brighter colors. In the 1920s style-leaders used pillar-box red, black, royal blue, deep green and gold, whereas popular taste chose creams, buffs, whites and yellows.

Modern colors

By the 1930s pastel colors were everywhere – the more unusual the better. Gray, lemon yellow, mauve, beige, silver, coral and white were the favorites, used against wood surfaces.

In the 1950s Le Corbusier's primary colors began to be used along with black, pale pink, turquoise and cream. Ten years later vibrant pinks, oranges, purples and violets took their place and the 1980s saw them softening into rusts, beiges, corals and browns.

Opposite Original, even daring use of color can be extremely successful if it is well planned.

COLOR WHEEL

The color wheel illustrated here is the basis of color theory and of all considered color schemes in decorating.

In its most basic form the color wheel is made up of twelve colors. The primary colors (yellow, red and blue) are so called because they cannot be made from mixtures of other colors.

In between them are the secondary colors (orange, violet and green). Each of these is made from mixing equal amounts of the primary colors. Orange is made from equal amounts of yellow and red, violet from equal amounts of red and blue and green from equal amounts of blue and yellow.

In between the secondary colors come the intermediate colors, of which there are hundreds – though only six are shown here. These colors are mixed from equal parts of their neighboring colors, for example yellow/orange is mixed with equal parts of yellow and orange, and so on.

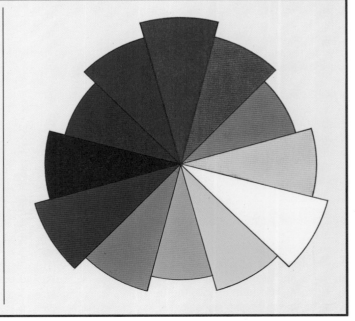

PAINT FINISHES

Paint finishes are not only fun to do but also can be used to change any surface in your home, whether woodwork or wall, into something unique. For, no matter how expert, no one else will ever be able to copy exactly what you have done. Paint finishes can help disguise uneven wall surfaces and poor plasterwork, and they can also add depth to flat walls.

The essential thing is to prepare the surface to be worked on very carefully, and not to get carried away – paint finishes look best as detailing.

Techniques of paint finishes

Several techniques are described below, and they can be effectively combined. Try out each finish before you begin and, if you can, work with someone else (one of you applying the glaze or wash and the other removing it) as the most difficult part is often achieving a consistent result over a large area. When working on your own, it is usually best to work in 2 ft (60 cm) vertical strips, making sure you do not overlap them as you go.

The paint finishes described below are known as "distressed" finishes, because they are all to do with broken color. In each case you start by painting an opaque background of either oil- or water-based paint, on top of which you use a glaze or wash – but only once the background color is completely dry. The various finishes are produced by the tools used (combs, sponges, rags etc) and the colors chosen.

Choose your colors carefully. If you mix too many strong colors they cancel each other out. Start by slowly adding colors and experiment.

Special effects in context

At the end of the seventeenth century, rich and special effects, like elaborate marbling and graining, were carried out by professional painter–decorators on doors, pillars, banisters, alcoves and occasionally walls. These decorators also specialized in painting walls with glazed effects. These were achieved by applying thin washes of transparent color over paler, often white, grounds so the paler background seemed to glow through. When it became possible to buy ready-mixed paints, the days of the subtle paint finishes were numbered: the house servants painted the walls.

Graining and marbling returned to favor at the end of the eighteenth century and remained popular until the twentieth century.

GLAZES AND WASHES

All paint finishes use glazes or washes. A glaze is a thinned oil-based paint and a wash is a thinned water-based paint. Glazes come in three finishes: matt, mid-sheen or gloss and are richer and have a more sumptuous finish than washes. Washes are softer and fresher looking and can either be matt or mid-sheen.

Glaze has either a transparent or a semi-transparent finish and can be bought ready-tinted or you can color it yourself. The correct ratio of paint to solvent, both with glazes and washes, is generally 1 to 3, but you should experiment. The weaker the color, the more transparency it will have and the quicker it will dry.

Recipes and equipment

If you want to make your own glaze, here are three recipes, each of which can be tinted using artist's oil colors.

- Boiled linseed oil and turpentine (1 to 3)
- Transparent oil glaze and mineral spirits or turpentine (1 to 1)
- White undercoat, flat oil or eggshell and mineral spirits or turpentine (1 to 3)

If you want to make your own wash, thin vinyl matt paint with water (1 to 3) and then, if necessary, alter the color using artist's gouache.

When carrying out any paint finishes, it is important to keep a rag soaked in turpentine (if using a glaze) or water (if using a wash) by your side so you can control the amount of paint in the brush, roller, sponge, comb or rag. As with all new skills, this will seem easier and you will become more and more accomplished the longer you practice.

Left Marbling is a technique that imitates the appearance of real marble, but looks more effective done in an impressionistic way rather than as a slavish copy. Start with a base of pale-colored eggshell or semi-gloss oil-based paint, and cover this with a lightly tinted oil-based glaze. Finally add the veining to the wet surface freehand, using a sable brush and ''feathering'' the paint out.

COLOR WASHING

Color washing is a traditional technique used in oil painting. It involves using thin top coats of color over paler backgrounds so the pale colors glow through and enliven the finished color.

You can color wash using either oil- or water-based paints. You begin with a dry surface that has already been painted with a pale color or white. Using a large brush and exuberant, sweeping criss-cross strokes — some of which should show — you paint over the background with a thin film of tinted wash made by thinning down water-based paint or diluting glaze (1 to 9 paint to solvent) so it is almost transparent. Textures can vary from translucent to almost opaque and the finished effect is warm and lively.

Distressed paint finishes

Dragging

The dragging effect, resembling a fine, striped texture similar to natural fiber, works by removing the color using a fairly firm brush. First you paint the wall with a thin glaze or wash and then you drag the brush over it to remove the paint. This is best carried out by two people, one painting on the glaze, another dragging it off.

Rag-rolling

Rag-rolling is a technique done with a rag. The rag itself can be of any fabric and used in any shape, although the standard shape is to bunch the rag into a loose sausage.

One way of using the rag to give the impression of crushed velvet is to roll it down the wet glaze or wash and let it remove some of the color. Another way is to press it on the wall over the wet color in different directions, giving a softer, more mottled look. Both of these techniques are again best done with the help of another person. A third technique is to dip the rag itself into the glaze and then rub the surface with a polishing motion until a soft textured, cloudy finish is produced.

Above Color washing adds interest to an otherwise plain wall.

Spattering

Spattering can be messy. It involves flicking specks of paint onto a surface using either a coarse-bristled brush, or a spray which will give a fine misted effect. Varnish the surface once you have finished to protect the end result.

Sponging

Sponging can be done in two ways. One way is to dab one or more glaze or wash colors over the base with a natural sponge. The other way is to paint the glaze or wash straight onto the base, and then dab the sponge over the top, removing some of the wet glaze. The first effect has a soft, cloudy look, the second more of a mottled effect.

Stippling

A stippled finish is produced in the same way as a dragged one, only using either a small, hard-bristled stippling brush, a dry rag or a paint roller (as long as the roller does not slide over the wet glaze). You simply press the brush, rag or paint roller into the wet glaze or wash and when you remove it some of the wet color will have lifted off as well. The finished effect is of tiny specks of color over an even base.

171

Walls & ceilings 36–7
Floors 38–9
Stain removal 50–3

Preparation 78–9
Painting 80–1

ILLUSIONS WITH PAINT

Illusionist paint finishes which imitate real materials can be very effective, but may be more difficult than you think. Take time to study the material you wish to imitate very carefully before trying your luck.

The techniques

Faux marble
Marbling is done quickly with a layer of glaze being introduced and worked on and then another layer added before the first has had a chance to dry – with the result that the colors bleed into each other. Veins are drawn as thin lines in a darker color, using a fine brush, and then smudged with a rag, feather or twigs while still wet. Unless the surface you are marbling is black, it is best to work from light to dark, using several coats of dirty-white glaze with a little black or raw umber added. Varnish the painted surface to protect it.

Faux tortoiseshell
Tortoiseshelling is probably the most difficult illusion to do well. First you paint a base coat of yellow oil-based paint thinned 3 to 1 with mineral spirits. You leave this to dry before painting on top a coat of varnish,

Above Faux marble panels bring a touch of grandeur to a room.

FAKE PANELING

Fake panels can be painted around a tall room to bring your eye level down or simply on a flat door to give a feeling of depth. The panels themselves can be painted a few tones darker or lighter than the surrounds and the shading should be appropriate to the location of your window and the angle of light. Stipple a little extra white on two sides and a little extra gray on the other two.

First position the panels using masking tape, strips of paper, a plumb bob and a spirit level. Try a few arrangements. Then pencil lightly round the panels and begin painting.

thinned 2 to 1 with white spirit or turpentine, and tinted brown. When still wet this is manipulated with a brush into broken diagonal bands. Then dots of varnish are added between the marks, and lines of darker colors (black and burnt umber oil paint) are painted on top and softened with a large, soft, dry brush. Varnish when finished.

JUST AN ILLUSION

Both *trompe l'oeil* and murals can be used seriously or for fun. A staircase glimpsed through a hallway can grandiosely enlarge the size of your home and a fake, but perfectly painted, tiger-skin rug lying on your wooden floorboards can bring a smile to whoever has carefully avoided walking on it. A mantelpiece filled with glamorous invitations and priceless Staffordshire china dogs or a bookcase of rare leather-bound books can make friends envious – until they realize they are not really there at all.

Simple *trompe l'oeils* that are easy to do are black and white checked tile floors – cheaper than vinyl. Or for fun you could paint on your floor the shadow the sun might cast if it were at this moment shining through your window. You can also stick prints on your walls and then paint a simple frame around them. On your kitchen table you can paint place settings using china and cutlery you would love to have or a cheerful tablecloth, which will look better and better as it ages.

If you do not have a lot of furniture, paint a mural. On lining paper or a white vinyl matt wall, use a thin gray wash to paint a particular furnishing scene, like a stage set. It could be a Louis XV bureau surrounded by two matching chairs and an ornate gilt mirror, or a simple column with a Grecian urn on top or even Michelangelo's *David*.

Faux wood
The basis of wood-graining is dragging, using a glaze slightly darker than the ground coat. Wood grains are faked by drawing a comb or dry brush through wet glaze. Knots are faked by using the edge of a cork and heart wood lines are faked by pressing pieces of string into the wet glaze. Look at samples of wood to see what sort of effect you want. Bamboo can be copied as well, either realistically or so that it looks obviously fake. The most helpful tip is only to try to copy bamboo on already rounded woodwork or plaster.

A cloud-filled sky is an amusing and fitting *trompe l'oeil* effect for a ceiling,
reminiscent of an Italian *palazzo*.

STENCILS & BORDERS

The earliest stenciled patterns to be found in homes imitated the sumptuous fabrics their inhabitants had seen in great houses. The pineapple was a favorite pattern as it was easy to copy.

Stencils are a quick and accurate means of reproducing a pattern by hand. You probably did your first stenciling as a child and, without thinking of it as stenciling, you may well have used a doily to decorate the top of a cake by sprinkling icing sugar through it.

Stencils can transform a boring wall or piece of furniture and can make floors and fabrics more unusual. You can use them as borders, for all-over patterns or for central decoration, depending on the look you want to achieve. Either buy stencils or make them, but remember that each pattern needs "bridges" to hold it onto the edge of the card.

Why not make the pattern on your china into a stencil and use it as a border on kitchen curtains or as a central feature on kitchen tiles? Or make a stencil of your child's favorite toy and stencil it on his pillowcase and duvet cover?

Stenciling can be used to decorate plain tiles, provided an oil-based paint is used, and will enhance a simple, modern hearth.

Replacing features

Often features (chair rails, cornices, picture rails) in old houses have been removed, leaving a room that somehow feels wrong – too tall, too large, just out of proportion. Replacing the feature with an accurate copy of the one that has been removed can be expensive. You can play the same visual trick using paint, wallpaper or wallpaper borders.

Borders can highlight architectural features or replace missing ones. If you use them instead of picture rails or cornices they will lower a high ceiling. Fake a chair rail or architrave with a stenciled border or a simple painted stripe to add interest to a boring wall.

If you are using paint to solve a problem in your room, take care that you get the proportion exactly right or the dimensions of the room may look worse, rather than better. If any of your neighbors still have original features, measure them in distance (from the floor or ceiling) and in width so you can copy the feel, if not the materials.

TECHNIQUES OF STENCILING

Either draw your design freehand or use carbon paper to copy a pattern you like onto a piece of traditional oiled stencil board or any other waterproofed paper or card. Then cut out the pattern, using a scalpel or small craft knife, keeping the blade sharp. Place cardboard, a cutting board or a sheet of plate glass under the knife or you may ruin a surface underneath. Trim off any rough edges.

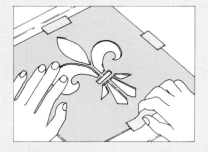

Using masking tape, stick the stencil in place on the surface you wish to paint. It will help if you have covered the surface with registration marks so that the pattern can be accurately moved each time. You should make a separate stencil for each color you plan to use and you must make sure all the registration marks match up.

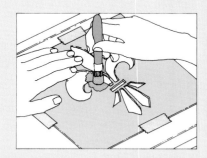

Using a coarse stencil brush, lightly stipple on the color, working in circular movements. Keep the brush and stencil as dry as possible – dab off excess paint before starting – and use quick-drying paint: diluted acrylic paint is ideal, as is oil-based Japan paint. Wait for the first color to dry before applying the second.

TURNING CORNERS WITH STENCILS

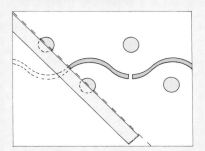

If you want to stencil a border, corners may prove complicated. If possible, adapt the pattern so the corner appears natural. Otherwise miter the corner. Draw a diagonal into the corner and mask off one side of the diagonal. Continue the wall you are stenciling into the corner, not going over the diagonal.

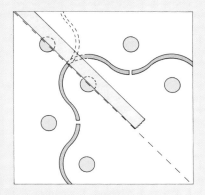

When the paint is dry, mask off the bit you have just painted and stencil down the other side. Alternatively, try turning the stencil over so you are painting through the back of it. Stencil two walls through the top of the stencil and two walls through the back of the stencil.

Decorating . . .

. . . *with ready-made borders*

There are now plenty of designs available in ready-made friezes and borders. You can buy them to match existing wallpaper or curtains or use them on a plain, painted wall.

. . . *with cutouts*

It is not difficult to cut out magazine pictures or find some old transfers and use them on the wall or floor as a border. Simply glue them down and cover them with several coats of varnish. Pale blue walls bordered with animals could look charming in a nursery.

. . . *with stripes*

The simplest border is a painted stripe, or several, which can be easily achieved by sticking two straight parallel lines of masking tape on your wall and painting between them. Be careful when you remove the tape. Painted plaster walls are best for this treatment because they provide a smooth, hard surface.

A variation on the simple stripe makes an effective feature in a modern, uncluttered bedroom. It adds interest to a plain wall and pulls the room together by picking up colors used elsewhere.

Cleaning materials 20–1
Furniture & soft furnishings 42–3
Stain removal 50–3

Furniture & furnishings 92–3
Upholstery 96–7

Furnishings

CURTAINS

Up to now you may have made do with the curtains left by the previous occupier of your home, or just hung up your old curtains which have never quite fitted properly. Since curtains set the style and mood of the whole room, it is important to get the window covering right. So start by taking a critical look at how your windows are dressed.

If your existing curtains are definitely a mistake can you move them anywhere else in your home (or remake them as blinds)? Or can they be reused on the same windows as the lining and interlining? In this case all you need to do is add a new fabric on top – which will certainly save you some money.

If you are quite happy with your existing curtains but just feel they could do with being spruced up, you could add frills, piping, braid, tiebacks and even a valance in a contrasting fabric.

If you want to start from scratch again, the simplest, and one of the cheapest, window treatments is casually to drape a sheer fabric over your window, using a brass or wooden pole. This softens the stark outline of the windowframe, filters the sunlight and covers the blackness of the glass reflection at night. Use lace, muslin, voile or lawn rather than resorting to the predictable net curtain – and remember to keep the curtains clean. If you would rather use an opaque fabric why not buy a long strip of a fabric you could not afford to cover an entire window in and drape it over a pole with exotic finials?

Ornamental poles

It could be that simply changing your curtain heading, for example, from a plastic track to a decorative pole, might be enough to make all the difference to your window. Poles are available in a range of both metal and wood, with elegant finials in acorn and globe shapes – even as hands holding up the rod. Wooden poles can always be painted to match the color of your walls or you could cover them with the same fabric as the curtains – this only works for poles supporting curtains that remain

Above Adding fringing and matching tiebacks provides the perfect finishing touch to a pair of unlined curtains made of a plain, inexpensive fabric.

open or poles with hidden tracks, otherwise the fabric will get scratched.

Are your curtains the right length?

It is, of course, easier to shorten existing curtains than to lengthen them. You could even use the leftover fabric to make a valance, tiebacks or some cushion covers. There are three standard lengths of curtain: floor length $\frac{1}{2}$ in (1 cm) above the floor – or trailing on the floor a little, which is romantic but impractical; sill length $\frac{1}{4}$ in (5 mm) above the sill, ideal for kitchens, bathrooms and nurseries where a less formal look is required; or apron length $\frac{1}{2}$ in (1 cm) above the radiator, for a more formal look, but so the curtains will not block out any heat or get singed.

Are they too short?

If you have several old, identical curtains you wish to reuse but they are too short you can join them together to make one full-length pair of curtains.

The join should be at sill height or approximately one-third of the way from the top or from the bottom of the curtain. If you sew the two curtains together so that there is a flap where they meet (i.e., by sewing the lower curtain about 3 in [7 cm] above the hem of the top curtain, but behind it), the join will then become a feature.

Are they full enough?

On the whole, the thinner the fabric, the more you need for the curtain to look full and not skimped. If your curtains have been moved from another, smaller window they may well now look skimpy. You could cut your existing curtain into strips and sew smaller strips of a contrasting fabric in between them to widen the curtain – or you could use the contrasting fabric to make a border on three sides (left, right and bottom) of the existing curtains.

If your curtains just look too flimsy, it is easy to line and interline them. Curtains hang better if they are lined, and are still warmer and more substantial if they are interlined. You can either sew a lining to the back of the curtain or simply attach it to the heading tape with curtain hooks.

Do you like the pattern?

If you are stuck with curtains with too dominant a pattern, you could always dye them a darker color, although you take the risk that they may shrink. For a more subtle, faded look, a useful tip is to dip your curtains in a bathful of cold tea for one or two minutes, depending on the depth of color you want. Otherwise add a plain colored border (about $2\frac{1}{2}$ in (6 cm) wide) to the outside and bottom edges of the curtains about 4 in (10 cm) in from the edge and make tiebacks and even a valance out of the same fabric to soften the effect.

Are they too plain?

If your curtains seem generally colorless and dull, you can always add a border of a contrasting plain or patterned fabric or add a cheerful tieback and valance. To give an extra dimension you can always quilt the fabric or add an applique pattern of your choice.

PAINTING CURTAINS

Using fabric paints, you can stencil a pattern onto old curtains or blinds in the same way as you would stencil a wall. Or you can paint freehand – a mural is one possibility or simply turn plain curtains into striped or gingham ones – even the odd irregularity will add interest. Although this may seem like a lot of work, it can be well worth it. First of all, you will be creating a pattern that is totally original, and second, you can achieve a very luxurious-looking pattern at a fraction of the price the real thing would cost to buy.

1 Having marked out the depth of the border in pencil on the curtain, mask the edges of the border to prevent the paint from bleeding. Then paint in the base color and border.

2 Tape down the stencil, making sure it is evenly placed on the border. Paint in the colors of your choice.

3 When the paint is dry, carefully remove stencil and tape to reveal the pattern beneath.

4 Paint additional details by hand to give a looser effect to the final border.

CURTAIN HEADINGS

If you want to give your curtains a new curtain rod remember that it can alter not only the shape of your window but also the character of the whole room.

Box valance
A valance is a stiff three-sided shelf, fitted to the wall above the window recess that hides the top of the curtain and the track. It also provides impact, softens incoming light and finishes off the curtains. Box valances are made of plywood covered with fabric and the lower edge can be cut to any shape.

Draped valance
Draped valances are soft and simple, but with the voluptuousness of festoon blinds.

They are made with a strip of fabric, twice the depth needed. You simply sew curtain tape on the wrong side at 9 in (23 cm) intervals – or whatever width is appropriate – and draw the cords up.

Valance frill
A valance frill is softer than a valance, consisting of a straight line or a curved shape of frills or gathers. A straight-line valance frill is usually 6–8 in (15–20 cm) deep and looks particularly effective with a $1\frac{1}{2}$ in (4 cm) border at the bottom.

Swag valance
A swag valance is a formal window treatment that is equally effective without curtains. The swag is the draped fabric in the middle, and at either end are pleated cascades that act as a frame for the window.

Swag valances can be highly ornate: they may be fringed, lined with a contrasting color fabric, decorated with braid or tassels and bows, or rosettes can be added where the swag and cascades meet. A similar, less formal effect can be achieved by artfully draping a long length of fabric around an ornate curtain pole.

OTHER WINDOW TREATMENTS

If you are bored with your curtains, why not remove them and replace them with a different window treatment? There are many others that will work just as well – or better.

Obscuring a view

If you do not need curtains for warmth, but want to block out an ugly view and still let the sun in, you will probably not want to shut off the window completely. One solution is to hang glass or wooden shelves across the window and fill them with interesting glass jars. Other solutions are to grow large plants on the windowsill, to cover the bottom half of the window with a mirror or to use a roller blind the wrong way round so that it pulls up from the bottom.

Shutters

Another alternative is shutters, which offer security and privacy. Since they vanish completely when folded back, they are ideal for a room that does not receive much light. They can always be stenciled or covered with fabric to make them appear cosier at night. And they can be cut in half, like barn doors, so the bottom half can be permanently closed while the top half is open.

An effective shutter scheme in a hot country – or to give you privacy round the clock – is to use a sheet of plywood with an all-over pattern cut out of it. The light can still come into the room but the view (and prying eyes) are kept out – it adds an Arabian touch to a room. Another idea is to stretch some transparent fabric over a light wooden frame and leave it permanently closed.

Blinds

Blinds provide privacy and a certain amount of warmth. They are ideal in a small room with small windows where an uncluttered look is essential.

Blinds look best when they are longer than they are wide, so if you have a large window you wish to cover, think about installing several in a row rather than one wide blind. It also means that when they are up you can keep them all at slightly different lengths, which makes for an unusual and relaxed look.

Blinds range in style from the most simple – and cheapest – roller blinds to the elaborate and sophisticated Austrian and festoon blinds. In between there are Venetian blinds, as well as blinds made out of various materials, such as wood, plastic, metal, bamboo or paper. You can make your own fabric blinds by reusing curtains that do not fit anywhere else.

ADDING A DECORATIVE DESIGN

1 Draw out your design full size on paper. Work out what you will paint freehand and what you will stencil.

2 Calculate the center line. Using dressmakers' chalk, mark out the center line onto the blind and paint it in with fabric paint.

4 Fill in the remaining areas of your design, taking care to avoid "over-painting."

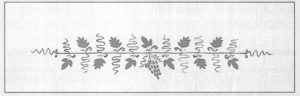

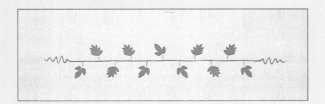

3 Cut your stencil from stiff brown paper with a craft knife. Use a stiff hog-hair brush to stencil your design onto the blind.

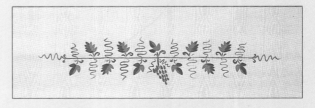

5 Following your rough design on paper, paint on your shadows with a darker shade of your two other colors.

Opposite An elegant Austrian blind with elaborate flounces provides an eye-catching window treatment in this room; its luxurious appearance contrasts with the simple style of the rest of the décor.

Furniture & soft furnishings **42–3**
Washing materials & equipment **46–7**
Hand-washing & ironing **48–9**
Stain removal **50–3**

Furniture & furnishings **92–3**
Upholstery **96–7**

CUSHIONS

Above Scatter cushions come in every shape and size and a mound of these, casually arranged along the back of a sofa, make it look much more comfortable and inviting. When choosing the fabric for your cushions, consider the covering of the chair or sofa on which they will be placed: generally, a plain background demands patterned cushions, and vice versa, but different patterns can be combined very successfully if there is some link between them, like similarities in color.

New covers for old

If your chairs and sofas are beginning to look their age, or you are getting bored with the fabrics, it is probably time for some new covers. This can be expensive, so use your imagination before you start looking for new fabrics for either loose or fitted covers.

One way of either hiding stains or distracting the eye from threadbare patches is to smother your seating with cushions – lots of them. If you have tried this and finger-smudged edges and cat-scratched arms are still staring at you, then find a beautiful piece of fabric and simply throw it over the entire seat. Any piece of fabric that suits the style and color of your room will do. A horse-blanket can be used in a bold

SCATTER CUSHIONS

Scatter cushions can be square, round, triangular, heart-shaped or any other shape that takes your fancy. The covers can be made in any fabric and can be piped, frilled or have cord stitched around the edge. They can have a large button in the middle or a tassel or you can even embroider a message on them.

setting; a kilim or other ethnic rug or blanket lends an exotic air; an old bed-spread looks warm and friendly and crisply starched white sheets draped over two or three chairs look summery and Scandinavian – great in a starkly furnished room.

Cushions can make even the most ordinary room feel luxurious. They soften stark lines, introduce new colors, turn alcoves into cosy corners and change stools, windowseats and beds into comfortable seats.

Cushions can be highly ornate: they can be overstuffed, ornamented with tassels and trimmings and covered in soft, sensuous fabrics. Or they can be angular and geometric in plain acidic colors with a simple large button in the middle for decoration. It is up to you to choose the style that will best complement your room.

Types of cushion

There are three main types of cushion: scatter, boxed and bolster. Scatter cushions are usually small and thrown onto sofas and chairs to cheer up an existing color scheme. Boxed cushions are generally found on window seats or hard chairs. They are firm and often have a decorative piped border to emphasize the cushion's square edges. Bolster cushions are tubular and can either be soft and used as decoration, like scatter cushions, or harder and used as back or arm supports on sofas or daybeds.

Cushion fillings

Cushion fillings vary in cost and firmness. Many fillings give off poisonous fumes if they catch fire. Cover them with fire-resistant material or avoid using them.

Feathers
Feathers are the most expensive but longest-lasting filling. Drawbacks are that they need to be plumped up after use, they have to be dry-cleaned and they may bring on allergies.

Kapok and Polyester
Both of these fiber fillings are cheaper than feathers and non-allergenic. Polyester fiber is washable, whereas kapok (vegetable fiber) becomes matted after a while.

Latex and foam
Latex and foam are ideal for firm cushions as they are already shaped. Foam chips are washable.

BOLSTERS

As it is usually only the ends of the bolster that you see, they should be spectacular. Even the simplest bolster should have a piping round the edge, either in the same fabric or a contrasting one to that used on the cover.

Turn bolsters into Christmas crackers. Twist the fabric round the bolster leaving enough fabric at either end so you can knot it and then cut the end of the fabric into a zig-zag pattern. Or bind the fabric with contrasting cord and scoop the ends up into a rosette or a large bow.

Right Bolsters are a very opulent form of cushion, and need trimmings to emphasize their shape. These can be simple, like the fabric-covered button on the bolster above, or sumptuous, like the beautiful tassels below.

LIGHTING & LAMPSHADES

If your room seems harsh and unwelcoming, it could simply mean that you need to rethink your lighting arrangements. Lighting a room successfully is possibly one of the most difficult things to do because every lamp, every lampshade and every lightbulb can create a different effect and a different mood – and even moving them a foot or two will change the entire effect again.

Playing tricks with light

Even if your room looks sublime in daylight, if the lighting is bad it will always look uninteresting after dark. Conversely, good lighting can make an ordinary room look marvelous. As with color, you can play tricks with light. In a tall room the light from a chandelier will make the room look lower and more intimate; wall lights will make a large room look cosier.

To make a room look larger, direct ceiling spotlights toward a wall and flood it with soft light. Highlight any good points your room may have with spotlights or uplighters and tone down any bad points. Areas of light and shade are interesting – a single light source in the middle of the room is not.

The best lighting

The best lighting is totally concealed with ample recessed spotlights tucked carefully away in the ceiling and tiny pencil spots used to highlight pictures, vases, pillars and anything else you are proud of. But this lighting is expensive to install and anyhow may be inappropriate in your home.

Instead, the easiest solution is to fit in as many table lamps as you can and try to arrange it so that they all turn on at the same time. Also attach them to a dimmer switch. The secret is to make sure you have enough lights.

Light should be soft and welcoming and never shine in anyone's eyes. Choose lower- rather than higher-wattage bulbs, unless you are using the light to read or work by. The position of a lamp is important to comfort. As a general rule, the bottom of the shade of a table lamp should be at the eye level of the seated person and the lightbulb should be invisible at all times.

Choosing lamps

As with all furniture, lamps should be the right height and size for your other furnishings. Lampshades should be neither too large nor too small for the base of the lamp they are shading. Shades that are light and flattering in color are preferable to dark ones, which can cause eye strain and may be depressing. A large pattern is suited to large shades; smaller shades should be plain or covered with a small pattern.

IDEAS FOR TABLE LAMPS

Table lamps can be made from vases, jugs, bottles – anything except priceless antiques, which will lose their value the moment you drill a hole in the bottom of them for the cord to come out of. You can leave the cord coming back out of the top but this never looks as finished.

All you need to make a table lamp is a suitable base, a bulb holder, some cord, a plug, some sand to weight the base down and a cork stopper if the base has too wide a neck to hold the bulb holder. First wire up the bulb holder, then wedge it, or the cork plus bulb holder, into the neck of the base. If you want the cord to come out of the bottom of the base, you will also need an electric drill fitted with a twist-drill bit – wear goggles when drilling and do not attempt to do this if the base is made of a particularly brittle material.

If you are simply bored with an existing china base, glue old transfers or pictures from a magazine all over it and cover the finished result with a thick layer of varnish.

REVAMPING LAMPSHADES

It is often difficult, if not impossible, to buy wire lampshade frames with which you can make your own lampshades, so start by revamping your existing ones.

You can often strip off the existing shade, but the simplest solution is to cover a lampshade with paint, fabric or paper. If part of the attraction of a particular shade is the soft, yellow light it gives out, then do not ruin this; at the most you could stencil a border around the edges of the shade. But if the shade is a dark color or made of an opaque material, there is no harm in sticking something on top – although it will, of course, look better during the day than when the lamp is lit.

Painting shades
If you use paint you can either stencil a pattern on the shade or simply draw a fine line at the top and the bottom of the shade to give it definition. You could draw a checked pattern, or some random flowers, match the pattern on your curtains or whatever else you feel like. The type of paint you use depends on the material the shade is made of.

Fabric shades
A finishing touch in a room is to cover the lampshade with the same fabric as the curtains. If the fabric is very thick it may be inappropriate, but a lighter fabric should be easy to use. Cut a length long enough to stick round the shade, leaving an even overlap both top and bottom. Then glue the fabric to the shade, folding the edges round. If you have an overlap, lay one edge over the other and with a scalpel trim the lower piece of fabric so the edges butt up against each other. If you want, you can then cover the top and bottom edge with contrasting fabric or bias binding.

Paper shades
You can use the same technique as above, sticking paper (try using a strip of leftover wallpaper) onto a cardboard or plastic frame instead of fabric.

Above Soft, diffused lighting is ideal for highlighting pictures and casting a
warm glow in a particular part of a room.

General cleaning **18–25**
Furniture & soft furnishings **42–3**
Stain removal **50–3**

Your home workshop **58–61**
Furniture & furnishings **92–3**
Veneer, gilt & leather **94–5**
Upholstery **96–7**

Furniture
MAKING CHANGES

You may well sometimes feel bored with your furniture, especially pieces you bought as a temporary measure. There are really only two options, other than keeping things as they are. The first is the simplest – throw them out. The second takes a little more time and trouble but may well be worth it – and that is to change them.

What can you change?

The easiest pieces to change are the smallest as they take the least time. Old chairs, mirrors, picture frames, bedside cabinets, occasional tables, chests of drawers, lamp stands, children's desks, can all be transformed with a little effort and imagination.

Above Painting furniture, and perhaps stenciling surfaces and picking out moldings in another color, can link disparate pieces so that they look like a set, and can give a room a very definite character.

Far right If furniture is already painted, heat-stripping the paint off is one of the easiest ways of giving a piece a new lease on life.

General principles 106–7
Fire 136–7

Making improvements 154–5
Color 168–9
Paint finishes 170–1
Stencils & borders 174–5
Painting 186–7
Improvised furniture 188–9

THE BEAUTIFUL HOME

What can you do?

Almost anything can be achieved with the use of paint and fabric. For example, a set of not very precious wooden dining-room chairs can be painted and a new cushion cover made for each of them. Alternatively, you could give them new slipcovers – one to fit over the back of the chair, another to slip over the seat and fall down to the ground. A bold gingham check looks most effective.

Why not paint an old chest of drawers with a *trompe l'oeil* of books all along the front so it looks like a book-shelf from the distance? See that the spines make interesting reading. Allow children to paint their own desks or give them a surface which looks as if it has already been "ruined" with ink spills, graffiti and scratch marks and let them stick photos of their favorite pop stars inside. Cover the surface with a thick coat of varnish to prevent scratches.

Fabric was often used in the eighteenth century to cover the intricate wooden fretwork at the top of four-poster beds. The same fabric was used for the drapery but it was simply stuck on to the wood. You could try covering your own bedstead or bedside table in the same way, using glue and tiny brass tacks – make sure the wood is smooth first or snags will rip the fabric.

The same idea could be applied to the frames of mirrors or pictures – cover a frame with the fabric used on your bedroom curtains, for example.

Before you paint . . .

Before you change the look of all your furniture you must make sure the surfaces are in the best possible condition. This can take time and is not necessarily an enjoyable task, but the finished result looks so much better that it is worth it.

New wood

New wood often has a harsh texture or a crude varnish finish. Remove any finish, fill cracks and holes with wood filler, and cover knots with shellac. Rub down with fine abrasive paper, and prime before painting.

Old wood

Remove French polish or varnish, fill cracks and treat any powder-post beetle holes. Then smooth the surfaces with a fine abrasive paper. If you want to wax the piece and parts are a different color – or wood – stain the lighter wood to match the rest by wiping on a proprietary wood stain with a soft cloth. If you are going to paint the piece, simply prime it first.

Painted wood

If the surface is in good condition and you just want to change the color, wash it and sand it down gently. If the old paint is flaking, cracked or chipped it should be stripped off. It should also be stripped first if applying extra paint is going to make a drawer or door stick.

Stained wood

If the stain is protected by varnish, you will need to remove this first, using varnish or paint stripper. Then use wood bleach to remove any stain. If you are going to paint the surface, you obviously do not need to bother about removing the stain. All you need do is sand the piece smooth, and then prime.

Metal

If the metal is in good condition all that is needed is for it to be cleaned with a sugar soap solution. If the metal is rusty or covered with flaking paint, smooth the surface with a wire brush and then treat the rust with a proprietary rust remover or with a primer containing rust inhibitor. When dry, paint in your chosen color.

STRIPPING WOODWORK

There are three main ways of removing paint, varnish or other finishes from wood. Both sanding and heat stripping can be used for removing paint. Chemicals will remove French polish and varnish as well as oil-based paints. Do not use heat to remove paint if you want a natural wood finish, as it is easy to scorch the wood.

Sanding

Flat surfaces are the easiest to sand as you can use an electric sander, but sanding can be both dusty and messy. If you are sanding moldings use a pliable abrasive block or a sheet of sandpaper.

Chemical stripping

Professional decorators rarely use chemicals to strip wood as the process can be messy, expensive and lengthy. Chemicals can also alter the color of the wood. For stripping paint and varnish, the proprietary paint or varnish stripper is painted on and then rubbed off using wire wool or scraped away with a shave hook or broad scraper. Keep your hands protected as the stripper is extremely powerful.

If you are removing French polish, use methylated spirits and fine to medium wire wool instead of paint stripper. Once the polish is removed, rub in a mixture (2 to 1) of boiled linseed oil and mineral spirits to restore the color.

Heat stripping

If you want to heat strip it is preferable to use a heat gun. Even so, work slowly and carefully as it is easy to set bits of old paint on fire. Do not use a heat gun near mirrors and use with care on window frames as the heat can crack the glass. Keep the heat source moving up and down constantly to soften the paint; at the same time scrape the paint off, using a scraper on flat areas and a shave hook on moldings and difficult corners.

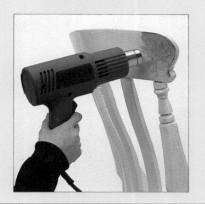

General cleaning 18–25
Furniture & soft furnishings 42–3

Furniture & furnishings 92–3

PAINTING

When you paint . . .

A professional paint finish can be achieved only through elbow grease. You will need to apply a minimum of four coats of paint, all oil-based, starting with primer, then an undercoat and followed by at least two top coats of gloss or eggshell. If you are still feeling energetic, add a coat or two of varnish on top. The important thing is to sand each coat when dry with very fine sandpaper or fine wet-and-dry abrasive paper used with soapy water to give an even, level surface for the next coat of paint. It is the careful rubbing down that makes all the difference. All the work should be carried out in a dust-free atmosphere.

A stenciled surface

If you are stenciling the surface, do this on the top coat of eggshell and then apply several coats of varnish on top – each of them rubbed down in between. You can experiment using a water-based paint instead of eggshell for a softer look, but unless you varnish the surface it will not last as long.

The surfaces of cupboards, storage chests, even chairs and tables, are fine subjects for stenciling. A unifying design worked on the various pieces of furniture in a room helps to bind them together.

GOING GRAPHIC

Try using letters and numbers to brighten up kitchen cabinets and children's chests of drawers as well as spice jars and filing cabinets. Either use giant letter stencils or copy typesetters' manuals to achieve a bold, graphic look on door and drawer fronts – the effect can look very Victorian or very Jasper Johns, depending on the type style and colors used.

Take it one step further and color coordinate shelves and drawers to match the color of lettering used.

DISTRESSING A CHAIR

Painting a chair to give a distressed look involves using two slightly different shades of the same color. Use waterproof poster paint, and try out the color first on similar wood. Polish with a wax furniture polish at the end; this has a dulling and darkening effect on the color, and also adds a sheen. A stained wax will dull colors further, so you can start bright and go progressively duller until you like the end result.

1 After sanding down the chair to provide a "key," apply a first coat of diluted poster paint.

2 When the first coat is dry, apply the second shade. Dilute it slightly more than the first to allow the first color to show through.

3 Add decorative details to the chair in a contrasting color. This paint should be slightly thicker than the second coat.

4 When dry, rub in beeswax furniture polish with a cotton cloth, until the top coat of paint is sufficiently distressed.

General principles **106–7**
Children **132–3**

Style & color **166–75**
Making changes **184–5**
Improvised furniture **188–9**

THE BEAUTIFUL HOME

DECORATING MOLDED FURNITURE

Molded legs on furniture lend themselves to being picked out in gold; use a "liquid leaf" paint, known as bronze paint, and apply it after the main paint color has dried. If you are re-covering a chair or stool at the same time, simply staple the fabric in the correct position first.

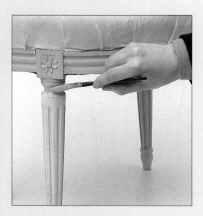

1 Sand the wood first to provide a "key" for the new paint, then apply the first coat of diluted waterproof poster paint.

2 When the first coat has dried, use a second shade of the same color. Dilute it more than the first coat, to give a glaze effect and to allow the first color to show through.

3 Apply the bronze paint carefully in the moldings and around the rosettes, as here, using a fine brush.

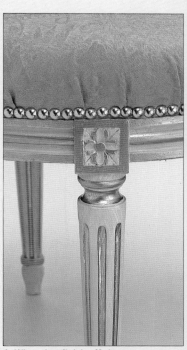

4 When dry, finish off the new seat cover by fixing upholstery nails all around the edge.

AROUND THE HOME

Many pieces of furniture and a variety of objects could benefit from a decorative paint treatment. (Before you begin, make sure that the piece you intend to paint is not a priceless antique.) Things you might consider:

In the living and dining rooms
- mirror frames
- picture frames
- coffee table
- pine chest

In the kitchen
- fitted cupboards
- kitchen table
- sideboard
- kitchen chairs/stools

In the bedroom
- bed headboard
- blanket chest
- side cupboards

In the hall
- coatrack
- side table
- side chair

Painting over tiles
If you have ceramic tiles on your walls or inset on a piece of furniture that are not particularly attractive, but too expensive to replace, you might consider painting them as a temporary solution. You will need to paint the tiles first with a metal primer, before applying your desired color. The effect may last only a matter of several years, but you will not have the expense of replacing them completely so it is worth the effort.

Adding stripes
This is not difficult, but requires careful preparation. Measure out the width of stripe you want and apply lengths of masking tape (remembering to take into consideration the width of the tape) to "frame" the areas you want to paint, i.e., the stripes. Apply two coats of your desired color and, when dry, carefully remove the tape.

IMPROVISED FURNITURE

If you like the furniture you own and it fits perfectly spatially, and proportionally, into your home then you are extremely fortunate. Equally, if you had the time, experience and money to plan everything out first you may have been lucky enough to find exactly what you wanted. Most people spend a great deal of time moving their furniture around from one room to another, trying to decide where it looks best.

Moving furniture about, at the very least, makes you reassess each piece and think about what you like and dislike about it. At best it helps train your eye so that you get used to looking at furniture in a critical way – a skill most of us have not acquired.

If it sometimes seems as if your home is never going to finish evolving, take hope. Getting the basics right and working out the overall feeling you want your home to have takes time. Meanwhile it is important to arrange the rooms so that after each change they look finished to the outside world, even though you know they are not. This is not difficult provided your furniture can be shifted around from room to room, or you improvise furniture, which will mean little extra expenditure and hopefully a lot of fun.

New ideas for occasional tables

You can never have too many small fill-in tables for coffee trays, drinks, lamps, telephones, etc. Yet, because they are mostly modern, it could take quite some time before you can find any you like enough to buy.

A large picture frame can make an excellent temporary coffee table. Two battens of 1 in by 1 in (2.5 cm by 2.5 cm) timber fixed across the back can be used to fix on the legs. These can be bought separately or removed from an existing table. Fill in the middle with a mirror or a sheet of glass covering a collage of favorite images or a piece of leftover curtain fabric for a coordinated look.

A bar stool turned upside-down with a dart board on top makes another useful small table. Drape it with fabric, making sure the fabric touches the ground all round, and you have a very cosy bedside table for the guest room.

The same idea can be used for larger tables. You can either buy a cheap plywood table and cover it with fabric or make your own board top cut to the required width with a stand for it to sit on. In either case, use lots of fabric – preferably one layer draped over another so the effect is generous. An old trunk covered with a thick layer of interlining fabric and then draped with a large tablecloth also makes an excellent addition to a room.

Seats

Use an old door to improvise a low-level sofa. Remove the hinges, lock and handle and set in four or six dowel legs. Place a thick sheet of covered foam on top, make some bolsters for the back and sides, throw plenty of scatter cushions on top and you have an extra sofa. A fitted valance around the base of the door will elegantly cover the legs.

A chest of drawers can always be cut in half horizontally and a sheet of strong plywood placed on top of the bottom half to make extra seating, especially in a child's playroom.

Pictures

If you have no pictures you may find bare walls better than a compromise. But if you feel they look too spare and intimidating you could buy some old picture frames and fit mirrors into them. Another idea is to choose some interesting wallpaper samples, ask the salesperson for decent sized samples and frame them as if they were abstract art.

For the hall, kitchen or bathroom, a painted or felt-covered board, crisscrossed with tape, can add interest if filled with your latest snapshots, children's drawings or letters which need to be answered.

STUDY FURNITURE

A decorator's trestle table makes an excellent desk, as do two filing cabinets with a sheet of formica-covered chipboard on top. Move the cabinets far enough apart so there is at least 2½ ft (76 cm) between them for your legs.

Bookshelves can be created using wooden boards supported on painted bricks, pieces of tree trunk or even books lying horizontally – make sure you will not want to read them for at least several months (or ever again).

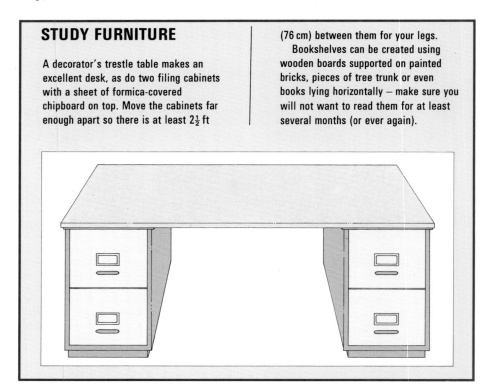

MAKING A NOTICEBOARD

You will need a sheet of corkboard 3 × 2 ft (90 × 65 cm), ½ in (1.2 cm) ribbon tape, 3½ × 2½ ft (105 × 75 cm) felt, some pins or tacks and a staple gun.

1 Cover the board with the felt, turn it over, and staple the felt on with a staple gun, or tack it on, sides before corners.

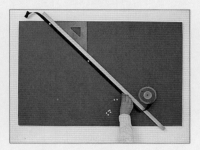

2 Mark the center of the board with a pin and set up a 45-degree line that crosses this point. On either side of the line, mark 5in (12.7 cm) gaps around the edge of the board with pins.

3 Pin the tapes tightly in position at the marked points, leaving about 4 in (10 cm) extra at each end. Repeat the process for the tapes going in the opposite direction. Thread them through the first tapes. Pin.

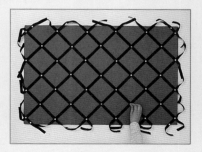

4 Press the pins into the tapes at each intersection. If you have measured the gaps correctly the tapes should cross at regular intervals.

5 Flip the board over and staple the ends of the tape to the back of the felt. The finished board can be used to hold photographs, letters, postcards, etc.

The Indoor Garden

A loose arrangement of flowering branches brings seasonal interest and a breath of fresh air to a home. An informal grouping can look stunning in any room, provided the container, and the setting, are chosen with care. The modern vase used here complements the group of ceramic bowls on the table, while the flowers reflect the floral prints on the wall.

Fresh flowers can bring any room to life by their very presence. Half a dozen roses or a large bunch of tulips or daffodils placed in a vase will probably look beautiful, no matter how they are arranged. But flower arranging is a special skill that begins with choosing the right foliage, the best flowers and an appropriate container.

Be imaginative about the container you use: glass vases come in all shapes to suit different flowers, and jugs make attractive containers for informal arrangements. A tall jug filled with spring blossom makes a lovely feature in an empty hearth.

Florist or garden?

Each flower arrangement depends on the materials available and whether you have to go to a florist to choose your stems or can simply open the door, walk into your well-stocked garden and take your pick. Taking from your garden is infinitely preferable. Not only is it cheaper, but even a few shrubs will provide you with a marvelous variety of foliage. You will probably be able to find some long spiky leaves (useful for the back and sides of displays) as well as some round furry leaves (which can be used in the middle of an arrangement).

SPECIAL-OCCASION FLOWERS

Flowers in unusual places can often be more striking than large vases of formally arranged flowers placed in expected situations.

You can do a lot with foliage; ivy comes into its own when used as decoration around the house and large branches of most trees or shrubs can be cut off and placed on a mantelpiece or table and covered with candles, baubles or other small objects.

Walls

For special occasions, take masses of ivy from your garden. Drape it generously around doorframes, hang it like a garland over mantelpieces or in a heart shape above arches, using adhesive tape or drawing pins to hold it in place. At Christmas cover the ivy with silver, gold and red baubles or pine cones; for a special birthday party interlace it with satin ribbon bows or hang crystal drops taken from broken chandeliers all over it. At Easter decorate the ivy with real eggs which you have blown and painted.

Continue the decoration up the stairs or tie a tall wooden stick to the newel-post at the bottom of your stairs and twine it with ivy and ribbons.

Mantelpieces

If you have a narrow mantelpiece that will not take a vase, buy a long, flat, plastic tray the same width as your mantelpiece and usually used for pot plants, put your Oasis (porous blocks) in and make the flowers stretch the full length of the mantelpiece.

Tables

Use a plastic tray to plant a long, low table decoration for a party. A primrose and moss planting would look enchanting in spring; hyacinths smell wonderful in winter and almost anything can be used in the summer. If bulbs are not yet open, stick small cuttings of flowering shrubs straight into the soil among the bulbs for a colorful effect and to help cover the edges of the tray.

Swags of twisted ivy

An Oasis-based decoration

It is true that you can buy almost any flower at any time of the year – even out of season – at the florist. But unless you are decorating for a formal occasion, store-bought flowers can lend an air of artificiality to a home display. Florist flowers available all year round, such as chrysanthemums, are too predictable to be worth arranging.

Never feel you need to stick to store flowers. If you want to lighten a rather heavy arrangement, for example, you could use long, feathery grasses or any other delicate garden weed. Not only will your design look original, it will also look softer.

Foliage and flowers

Always buy or pick at least twice as much foliage and flowers as you think you will need – you probably will end up using them all, but even if you have some left over they will never be wasted. They can always be used for a small table arrangement or in a pretty jug for the bedroom. There is little that looks worse than a sparse display of flowers.

You can use as much foliage as your container can hold. Any foliage will do; the more various, the better. Even dark laurel leaves will provide an excellent background for flowers to stand out against a white wall. When flowers are scarce in the garden a most effective display can be made using foliage alone or simply adding autumn berries.

When flower arranging, it is best to limit the number of colors you include. You can choose from many different varieties of flower but the result will be most effective when only two or three colors are used, for example yellow and white, or blues, pinks and whites used with predominantly silver foliage. Do not make the mistake of adding marigolds, for example, feeling you need more color – they will only kill the subtle effect you have created.

FLOWER ARRANGING EQUIPMENT

The most important equipment you will need for flower arranging is the container, be it a vase, jug, casserole or urn. Make sure you have a variety of suitable containers of all shapes and sizes. That way you can always use up flowers and foliage that are not needed in your main floral display and you will always have the right container for each place in your home.

Golden rules

It is most important when flower arranging to make sure the color scheme of your arrangement suits the room for which it is intended, so pick your flowers and foliage accordingly. No matter how warm, cheerful and autumnal an orange and yellow display looks, it will never do in a pink room. Be guided by your surroundings, rather than by the need to be seasonal.

Numbers

If you are using large flowers in your display, make sure you have an odd, rather than an even, number of them (three, five, seven, etc) and do not place them all together. Instead allow them to define the line you wish to follow up through the arrangement. Then try and repeat the color of the larger flowers in the smaller sprays around the periphery.

Height

A conventional rule is first to assess the size of your vase and then make the flowers roughly twice as high as the vase. So if the vase is 1 ft (30 cm) tall, the flowers should be 2 ft (60 cm) high above it. Then have 1 ft (30 cm) of flower spraying out to both the right and the left of the vase. This may not always be appropriate and you ultimately have to trust your own judgment, but it can be a useful rule.

Depth

Never have a flat arrangement. Poke some flowers deep among the foliage and let others come forward to give the arrangement perspective. Keep the visual weight in the base of the display and arrange shapes and color so that your eye is led up to the top of the arrangement.

Artificial flowers

Keep a few select artificial flowers – tulips, camellias, roses, etc – in reserve for the occasion when you have not got quite enough real flowers. Use them sparingly and no one should notice.

The final look

When you have finished, stand back and look critically at your display. Take a pair of scissors and ruthlessly snip out any extra foliage or flowers that have made the effect bunchy, destroying the line you were trying to create.

EQUIPMENT

You will need cutting tools such as pruning shears (1), kitchen scissors (2), and sharp knifes (3), to cut stems and twigs. Use twine (4) or florist's wire (5) to tie stems together or bend them into shape.

You also need some Oasis (6) (porous blocks) to hold the stems in place. Alternatively you could use scrunched up rabbit wire (7) or heavy metal blocks with pins, but these do not give you as much flexibility.

Before you use the Oasis you need to soak it thoroughly for an hour or so. A soggy Oasis will last for about a week – as long as your flower arrangement – without needing to be topped up. Even after use, Oasis should be kept moist, in a plastic bag. Strap the Oasis down with adhesive tape (8) before sticking the stems into it. It is often useful if the Oasis sticks out over the top of the container so that you can stick sprays into it which will trail down and hide the edge of the vase (9).

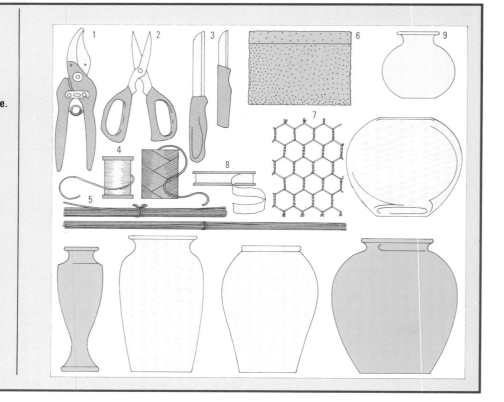

CARING FOR CUT FLOWERS

- Cut flowers in the early morning or after sundown as hot sunshine draws the moisture from the petals
- Strip all foliage from stems below the water. Water should always be kept free from decaying leaves
- Never fill vases up to the top. Only enough water just to cover the stems is necessary and top it up frequently
- Slit the stems of all flowers, except soft-stemmed (daffodils, irises, etc) and hollow-stemmed (delphiniums, etc) flowers, which need only have the ends of their stems cut off. Slitting the stems helps water soak through
- Cut soft-stemmed and hollow-stemmed flowers under water, above any film of slime that has accumulated
- Burning the end of stems of flowers such as euphorbias and poinsettias, which ooze latex (white substance), helps preserve them. Singe the stem end immediately after cutting to stop

the flow of the latex. The carbon formed is porous and will help the flowers absorb water
- Tulips and hellebores need to have their stalks pierced with a needle. Prick them right through from under the head down to the base at intervals of about 1 in (2.5 cm)
- Immediately after cutting and treating stems, place flowers in deep water overnight. Do not crowd them in or they may get damaged
- If the leaves of flowers, such as roses, are wilting, lay the flowers flat in a bath of cold water overnight
- Use a little mild disinfectant in the vase or a proprietary preservative to keep cut flowers for longer
- Glass vases are not ideal as the sunlight causes bacterial activity which quickly fouls the fresh water. Water in glass vases needs to be changed every few days to prolong life.

DRIED FLOWERS

No matter how beautiful and elegant a dried flower display is, it can never be expected to bring as much joy as a pot of living flowers. On the whole, dried flowers are best used for wreaths or garlands and for more out of the way places in your home, rather than as a traditional focal point in a living room.

They can, however, look very effective in baskets by the front door, hung upside down in bunches from the kitchen ceiling or as a dramatic display in an unused fireplace. Change them frequently as they tend to lose their colour and get dusty with age.

Below There is no reason why you should not have more than one vase of flowers on a shelf or mantelpiece, but they create a more dramatic effect if displayed in large, luxuriant masses rather than as a few stems in small vases.

HOUSEPLANTS

What can you grow indoors?

There are many plants you can grow indoors, from the easy but predictable spider plants, aspidistras, rubber plants and yuccas, etc, to more unusual species that will need some careful looking after. Or you can plant bulbs – and almost watch them growing once they emerge from the compost.

If you have a garden it is easy to bring in flowers just before they are about to flower. Almost anything can be put in a tub and brought indoors, from foxgloves, forget-me-nots, lilies and tobacco plants to larger pots of lilac and winter jasmine.

The choice

Bulbs

Bulbs are always easy and cheap to grow indoors, and a mass of flowering bulbs will make a stunning display, especially in winter when there is little else around. Plant bulbs anywhere: in soup tureens, china pots, old basins, baskets or glass vases and keep them as cool as possible. Amaryllis, narcissi and hyacinths will herald in the spring most effectively, but keep colors pure. If you are not sure of the colors of your hyacinth bulbs, plant each bulb separately – you can always group all the pots of the same color together once you can see what they are. Hyacinths also bring a wonderful scent into the room which is an added bonus.

Evergreens

Evergreen plants will, of course, look good throughout the year but they may never look stunning. The type of container you put them in will help, as will the location. It is worthwhile hunting for unusual containers, such as old birdcages, hollow china heads, decorated watering cans as well as deep china bowls and beautiful terracotta pots. It is also worth taking trouble to find an unusual spot to place the plant in and then to light it well.

Flowering plants

The most effective solution may be to use flowering plants together with evergreens. Primulas, cyclamen, violets and azaleas provide a splash of much-needed seasonal color, and when

A collection of nonflowering evergreen plants can successfully enhance a room. The variation of textures and leaf shapes – the tiny, bright green leaves of the maidenhair fern, with grass-like foliage and much larger, heart-shapes leaves – in this group of plants brings interest to the windowsill.

Going away 142–3

The indoor garden 190–1
Flower-arranging equipment 192–3
Entertaining 196–9

THE BEAUTIFUL HOME

combined with ivy, tradescantia or a vine, would make a longer-lasting arrangement. Alternatively, you can buy a stunning white-scented jasmine or bougainvillea and train it all along the wall of a bathroom.

Caring for houseplants

When buying houseplants, make sure the stems are not spindly and that the leaves are not damaged but look healthy. They should also have a "care" label which will tell you of any special requirements, and the size that you can expect them to grow.

Most houseplants are easy to look after, but they do not like drafts, changes in temperature, too much or too little water, overfeeding or too little food or too long a period in bright light or darkness. They must also be grown in special potting mixture; never place houseplants in garden soil, which can harbor pests and diseases as well as being too coarse.

Watering
Plants should almost dry out before they are watered and should be watered only when they really need it. Ideally their soil should be kept almost continually moist but not soggy. Plants naturally need more water during their period of growth, but bear in mind that over-zealous watering may damage or destroy your plants.

If you can, water plants with rain water, otherwise use tap water of room temperature and, if possible, water the soil rather than the plant with a long-spouted watering can. Fill the pot to the rim with water and then let it drain out of the bottom of the pot and collect in an outer pot or plant tray. Check the plant half an hour or so after watering and drain away any excess water that still remains in the outer tray.

Some plants, including cyclamen, African violets, miniature orange and lemon trees, can be watered from below. Stand the pot in water to just below the level of the compost and leave it to soak until the water starts moistening the soil. Let the pot drain thoroughly

before replacing it in its container. Never leave a plant that is not semi-aquatic standing in water.

Keep plants humid, especially if there are electric heaters or radiators on in the house. Spray them regularly with tepid water and leave pots of water standing around the room. A humidifier will offset the drying effect of electric heaters or radiators.

Feeding
During their growing and flowering season, plants should be fed once every two weeks with liquid fertilizer. Buy the correct feed and give too little rather than too much. Newly potted plants need not be fed for a couple of months.

Light
Most plants tend to grow toward the light, so turn them regularly for even growth unless you wish them to grow across a wall toward the window. A general rule is that plants with variegated or colored leaves need good light, plants with dark green foliage can survive in shade. Most plants like semi-shade better than direct sun, which can burn their leaves.

GOING AWAY

Before going away, move your plants away from electric heaters, radiators and windows and water them thoroughly. If you can, ask a neighbor to water them while you are away or buy a self-watering container. If neither of these is possible, place plants on trays covered with gravel and water and let them drink what moisture they need to. Alternatively, stand pots together in a waterproof container filled with moist peat.

Leaving buckets of water standing near plants will help create a humid atmosphere. After watering each plant thoroughly, wrap each one individually in a sealed plastic bag, trapping as much air inside the bag as possible and being careful not to crush the plant. Experiment before you go away and then you will know how well your plants can survive and for how long.

GROWING HERBS INDOORS

A bright, cool room or conservatory can be an excellent home for potted herbs. These are all happy to be pot grown.

Parsley   Rosemary

Thyme   Sage   Chives

Fennel   Mint

General cleaning 18–25
Dining rooms & studies 32–3
Stain removal 50–3

Carpets 88–9
Furniture & furnishings 92–3
Veneer, gilt & leather 94–5
Upholstery 96–7
Ornaments 100–1

Entertaining

Once you are satisfied with the way your home looks, you will want to invite your friends to share it with you. Entertaining should be nothing but pleasure and yet it can often feel like a terrible ordeal. The secret is to plan and prepare as much as you can in advance so that you too can relax and enjoy your party.

Dinner parties

The first decision to make is how many people to invite. Even numbers are preferable as that way there is less chance of anyone being left out of the conversation. Invite one or two talkative friends and no couple who are so in love that they will only have eyes for each other. Six to eight people ensures that there will be some general conversation – any more and guests are likely to split up into small groups. Work out your table plan and menu in advance, and always cook for a couple of extra guests as well to ensure you do not run out of food. Prepare simple meals – your guests have come to see you, not eat the latest culinary treat – and when guests arrive, serve nondrivers a few generous drinks to ease the atmosphere.

Before guests arrive
In the minutes before the guests arrive take time to check the following:
- Is the table laid?
- Have the flower arrangements started to wilt or do they still look stunning?
- Are candles and matches on the table?
- Is the main course cooked and keeping warm?
- Are the vegetables ready to be dropped into pans of boiling water?
- Are the salad and its dressing ready?
- Have the cheeses (if you are serving any) been taken out of the fridge?
- Is the dessert either in the fridge or ready to be warmed in the oven?
- Is the wine open either in the fridge or in a warm room to breathe?
- Are the predinner drinks and snacks ready in the living room for guests?
- Is there plenty of ice?
- Has the coffee been measured out ready to be made?
- Is the plastic bowl in your sink filled with hot, soapy water waiting for used plates to be soaked?
- Is the dishwasher empty and ready for its next load?

Drinks and dancing parties

If you are planning to give a large party you should start organizing it at least one month before you want to hold it. Decide how much money you have to spend, how many people you want to invite and what sort of party you want to hold.

How many people?
A rough guideline as to the amount of space you will need is as follows: an empty room will hold roughly 1 person to every 5 sq ft (0.5 sq m) of floor space. In an empty hall, allow roughly 8 sq ft (0.75 sq m) of space to a person. As a general rule, it is better to hold your party in one crowded room rather than two half-empty rooms.

What will I need?
Once you have worked out the ideal number of guests and what time of day you want the party to be held, you will have a better idea of what you need to organize. The first things to do are to rent a space (if you need one); hire caterers, barmen, etc (or enlist friends and family); book music or other entertainment; rent dishes, glasses, tables and chairs, etc; and buy the drink. Then quickly invite your friends, asking them to RSVP, and decide what you are going to wear to the party.

Shortly before the event
Keep making lists, which should get shorter and shorter, of what still needs to be done. Have you warned (or invited) your neighbors? Have you ordered soft drinks as well as hard? Have you got enough ice? Have you got enough ashtrays and garbage bags? Have you worked out the lighting and music (a trial run one night is a good idea)? Have you ordered the flowers and other decorations? Have you checked that caterers, barmen, disc jockeys, band, etc, are still coming?

On the day
Make sure the rooms are prepared. Excess furniture should be removed and remaining pieces positioned into conversation corners; flowers and other decorations should be completed; anything valuable should be removed and locked up; ashtrays, toilet paper, paper napkins, tablecloths and other details should all be attended to and lighting and music should be ready. Look around the room and give it a final critical check.

When you are convinced there is nothing left for you to do, accept it. Get yourself ready; then lie down with a drink and relax until the doorbell rings.

DRINK RULES

It is useful to have a complete set of glasses. Otherwise, collect antique ones so that everyone has a different glass. Be consistent: either give everyone the same design, or a different design so that this looks intentional.

Types of glasses
- Tumblers (for water, soft drinks and spirits)
- Red wine glasses
- White wine glasses (can be used for champagne as well)
- Sherry glasses (can be used for port and madeira too)
- Liqueur glasses (may not be necessary)
- Brandy glasses (may not be necessary)

Cocktail party
- Allow half a bottle of wine or 3 to 4 drinks per person and some extra
- Allow 16 to 20 glasses from a bottle of sherry
- Allow 18 drinks from a bottle of whisky
- Allow 20 drinks from a bottle of gin

Dinner party
- Serve white wine before red wine
- Serve a light wine before a heavy one
- Serve a young wine before an old one
- Serve dry wine before sweet wine
- Serve an expensive wine before a cheaper one

Setting the table

Any table setting can be made to look attractive with the addition of a well-folded napkin. It may take a little time – and practice – but it is well worth the effort. Both examples shown here are suitable for formal occasions. The Lazy Footman is equally good if used informally or placed across the top of each setting with a handwritten name card tucked into the fold.

THE LAZY FOOTMAN

1 First iron your napkin flat. Then fold it into a square by doubling it over twice so that it has four thicknesses.

2 Fold the left-hand edge of the napkin inwards, to about one-third of the way across the fabric.

3 Fold this edge over again; it should now reach two-thirds of the way across.

4 Now tuck the right-hand edge underneath the left-hand fold. Finally, smooth out the crease to keep it lying flat.

THE PRINCE OF WALES

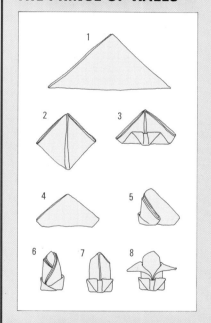

First fold the napkin to form one large triangle (1). Next join the two bottom corners to the top point, thereby creating two smaller triangles lying on their sides (2). Fold the bottom point inwards, making a crease just below the halfway mark, and then bend the tip back to the line of the fold (3). Holding this bottom edge, turn the napkin over so that it faces the table (4). Now bend the two bottom corners toward you (5) and tuck the right-hand corner into the pocket on the left-hand side (6). Now turn the napkin back over to face you (7). Finally, pull down the two outer "feathers" (8).

General cleaning **18–25**
Dining rooms & studies **32–3**
Stain removal **50–3**

FOOD PRESENTATION

No matter what type of party you are giving, the food should look even more inviting than it may taste. However delicious your meal or canapés are, if they look unappetizing, no one will feel like eating them. Adults always dress up food for children's parties so that it looks fun and colorful – there is no reason not to pay the same attention when cooking food for your peers.

Serving food

Always choose a serving dish of an appropriate shape and size, such as a long thin platter for whole fish. Serve plain food on patterned or colored plates and multi-colored and complicated food on plain plates. Similarly, use plain plates on a patterned tablecloth and patterned plates on a white

Above A beautifully laid table creates anticipation of a delicious meal to come, and heightens guests' enjoyment of the occasion. Sparkling glassware, crisp linen and a vase of fresh flowers are not beyond even the busiest host's capabilities.

damask cloth. Never present a sparsely covered plate of food to a guest, nor an overloaded one: both can be off-putting and guests can always ask for more. Pick the right size and shape plate for the food you have to offer.

Garnishes

Garnishes should heighten taste and color through either contrast or similarity. They should never just be there for decoration, unless possibly you are serving a buffet meal, but should always add an extra taste sensation. Garnishes should be fresh, edible and subdued. A salad with watercress sprinkled on it or symmetrical lines of chopped parsley or chives or placed on a red cabbage leaf for example, will not only look better but also taste better.

Soups

Before serving, pour a little cream into the center of the bowl of soup (not with consommé) and then quickly swirl the soup with a spoon. For a farmhouse effect, add *croûtons* to the soup instead.

Meat dishes

Before cooking a lamb roast, score the skin and insert sprigs of fresh rosemary in the cuts. Score the outside of a joint of ham in a criss-cross pattern, and stud each square with a clove before cooking. Before serving a meat loaf, sprinkle alternate lines of sieved hard-boiled egg yolk and chopped parsley on top of it. Pipe mashed potato in a swirl on top of a thick stew and brown it quickly in the oven or under the grill.

Desserts

A lemon or orange mousse decorated with whipped cream could have lemon rind finely grated over it or finely sliced and draped over it – remember to boil the rind for a few minutes first to remove the bitter taste. Scatter the crystallized petals of edible flowers like violets, freesias or roses over creamy desserts. You can buy these or make your own by painting petals with beaten egg white, sprinkling with castor sugar and leaving to dry. Even simpler is to decorate desserts with fresh flowers. Slices of star fruit or kiwi fruit make another simple but effective decoration.

CHILDREN'S PARTIES

Children's parties are inevitably messy affairs. It helps if you buy disposable tablecloths, plates, cups and cutlery (or use plastic) and equip yourself with large garbage bags.

Until children start school and have to invite their entire class, there is no need to invite a lot of children, so keep the party small and short – a few hours at the most – and get as much help as you can for the hectic occasion.

- Keep rooms safe: remove all breakable objects, trailing lamp cords and furniture that is precious or easy to trip over. Decorate the room with lots of balloons, streamers, etc
- Buy ready-made cake and instant desserts and save your creativity for decorating them. A theme is fun, providing you get the right one for your child's age group. You could ask the guests to come in fancy dress, but make it clear that this should be simple. Other parents won't thank you if they have to spend hours making elaborate costumes
- Have every minute pre-planned. Make sure you have a game or activity for when guests arrive, to help break the ice. Work out a program of games (active games before the meal and quieter ones afterwards), and, if you are hiring professional entertainers, arrange to have them perform directly after the meal so that there is no time for children to get overexcited
- Keep a first-aid box and stain-removal kit handy and a spare bed prepared in case one of the guests gets overcome with excitement
- Make sure you have enough sweets, balloons, crayons, etc so that each guest can win a prize and take a little gift home
- Have refreshments available for any adult helpers

Left Children's party food should always look colorful and festive. Apart from one large birthday cake, keep items of food small – dainty cakes and sandwiches are more appealing to little guests.

199

CONVERSION TABLES

OVEN TEMPERATURES

Electric °C	70	80	100	110	120	140	150	160	180	190	200	220	230	240
°F	150	175	200	225	250	275	300	325	350	375	400	425	450	475

Gas			Low	$\frac{1}{4}$	$\frac{1}{2}$	1	2	3	4	5	6	7	8	9

LENGTHS

inches	millimeters	millimeters	inches
$\frac{1}{8}$	3·2	5	0·20
$\frac{1}{4}$	6·4	10	0·39
$\frac{3}{8}$	9·5	15	0·59
$\frac{1}{2}$	12·7	20	0·79
$\frac{5}{8}$	15·9	25	0·98
$\frac{3}{4}$	19·0	30	1·18
$\frac{7}{8}$	22·2	40	1·58
1	25·4	50	1·97
$1\frac{1}{4}$	31·7	60	2·36
$1\frac{1}{2}$	38·1	70	2·76
$1\frac{3}{4}$	44·4	80	3·15
2	50·8	90	3·55
3	76·2	100	3·94
4	101·6	500	19·70
5	127·0	1,000	39·40
10	254·0		

feet	meters	meters	feet/inches
1	0·30	1	3 3
2	0·60	2	6 7
3	0·91	3	9 10
4	1·21	4	13 1
5	1·52	5	16 5
10	3·05	10	32 10

miles	kilometers	kilometers	miles
1	1·6	1	0·6
2	3·2	2	1·25
3	4·8	3	1·75
4	6·4	4	2·5
5	8·0	5	3·1
10	16·1	10	6·2
50	80·5	50	31·1
100	160·9	100	62·1
200	320	200	125

WEIGHTS

ounces	grams	grams	pounds/ounces	
$\frac{1}{4}$	7·08	25	–	$\frac{7}{8}$
$\frac{1}{2}$	14·17	50	–	$1\frac{3}{4}$
$\frac{3}{4}$	21·26	75	–	$2\frac{1}{2}$
1	28·35	100	–	$3\frac{1}{2}$
2	56·69	125	–	$4\frac{1}{2}$
3	85·04	150	–	$5\frac{1}{4}$
4	113·39	175	–	6
5	141·74	200	–	7
6	170·09	300	–	$10\frac{1}{2}$
7	198·44	400	–	14
8	226·79	500	1	$1\frac{1}{2}$
12	340·19			

pounds	kilograms	kilograms	pounds/ounces	
1	0·45	1	2	$3\frac{1}{4}$
2	0·90	2	4	$6\frac{1}{2}$
3	1·36	3	6	$9\frac{3}{4}$
4	1·81	4	8	13
5	2·26	5	11	$\frac{1}{4}$
6	2·72	6	13	3
7	3·17	7	15	7
8	3·62	8	17	10
9	4·08	9	19	13
10	4·53	10	22	$\frac{3}{4}$
14	6·35	25	55	2
56	25·22	50	110	3

LIQUIDS

Metric	Imperial	USA
5 ml	$\frac{1}{8}$ fl oz	1 tsp
15	$\frac{1}{2}$	1 tbsp
25	1	$\frac{1}{8}$ cup
50	2	$\frac{1}{4}$ cup
65	$2\frac{1}{2}$	$\frac{1}{3}$ cup
100	4	$\frac{1}{2}$ cup
150	5	$\frac{2}{3}$ cup
175	6	$\frac{3}{4}$ cup
225	8	1 cup ($\frac{1}{2}$ pt)
300	10	$1\frac{1}{4}$ cups
350	12	$1\frac{1}{2}$ cups
400	14	$1\frac{3}{4}$ cups
475	16	2 cups (1 pt)
600	20	$2\frac{1}{2}$ cups
750	24	3 cups
900	32	4 cups (2 pts)
1 liter	35	$4\frac{1}{4}$ cups
1·14 liters	40	5 cups

To convert liters to pints, divide by 0·473
To convert pints to liters, multiply by 0·473

METRIC SYMBOLS

length	liquids
mm millimeter	**ml** milliliter
cm centimeter	**l** liter
m meter	
km kilometer	

weight	area and volume
g gram	**m²** square meters
kg kilogram	**m³** cubic meters

IMPORTANT INFORMATION

NAME	**CARPENTER** . . . .
ADDRESS	. . . .
. . . .	**LOCAL GARAGE** . . . .
. . . .	. . . .
TELEPHONE NO.	**VET** . . . .
	. . . .
LOCAL POLICE	**GARDENER** . . . .
. . . .	. . . .
AMBULANCE SERVICE	**LOCATION OF:**
. . . .	Supply valve . . . .
FIRE DEPARTMENT	Gas meter . . . .
. . . .	Gas mains switch . . . .
DOCTOR	Electricity meter . . . .
. . . .	Electricity mains switch . . . .
	Boiler . . . .
PLUMBER	Water tanks . . . .
. . . .	Furnace . . . .
EMERGENCY PLUMBER	**OTHER NUMBERS**
. . . .	. . . .
ELECTRICIAN	. . . .
. . . .	. . . .
EMERGENCY ELECTRICIAN	. . . .
. . . .	. . . .

Index

Photo Credits

The publisher would like to thank the following photographers and organizations for their kind permission to reproduce the photographs in this book:

1 Yves Duronsoy; 2 R. Beaufre/Stylograph; 6 Camera Press; 8 Paul Ryan /J. B. Visual Press; 11 above Camera Press; 11 below Derry Moore; 12 above Derry Moore; 12 below Camera Press; 13 above Gilles de Chabaneix; 13 below Guy Bouchet; 14 Roland Beaufre/Agence Top; 15 Jean-Paul Bonhommet; 20 Camera Press; 23 Camera Press; 26 left IPC Magazines/World Press Network; 26 right Annet Held; 28 Richard Bryant/Arcaid; 29 Rodney Hyett/Elizabeth Whiting and Associates; 30 Dennis Krukowski/Conran Octopus (Mr. & Mrs. John H. Winkler); 31 Annet Held; 32 Camera Press; 33 Camera Press; 34 Paul Barker; 35 Michael Crockett/Elizabeth Whiting and Associates; 37 Fritz von der Schulenburg (Mimi O'Connell/Peter Farlow); 38 Rene Stoeltie; 39 left Mike Nicholson/Elizabeth Whiting and Associates; 39 right Richard Bryant/Arcaid; 40 La Maison de Marie Claire/Hussenot/Belmont; 42 Paul Ryan/J. B. Visual Press; 47 Andreas von Einsiedel/Elizabeth Whiting and Associates; 48 Picture Colour Library; 56 Jean-Paul Bonhommet; 58 Camera Press; 65 Camera Press; 66 Houses & Interiors; 68 Ron Sutherland/Elizabeth Whiting and Associates; 71 Spike Powell/Elizabeth Whiting and Associates; 72 Aqua Maison Ltd. (Aqua Ware Range); 74 Andreas von Einsiedel/Elizabeth Whiting and Associates; 76 Guy Bouchet; 80 left J. P. Godeaut/Stylograph; 80 right Derry Moore; 84 above IPC Magazines/World Press Network; 84 below Andreas von Einsiedel/Elizabeth Whiting and Associates; 85–6 Camera Press; 88 Houses & Interiors; 90 left Fritz von der Schulenburg (Andrew Wadsworth); 90 right Richard Bryant/Arcaid; 93 Jean-Paul Bonhommet; 94 Fritz von der Schulenburg (Suky Schellenberg); 95 S. Cossu/Stylograph; 96 Paul Ryan/J. B. Visual Press; 98 Vogue Living (Geoff Lung); 100 Fritz von der Schulenburg (Andrea de Montal); 101 Guy Bouchet; 102 Camera Press; 103 left Paul Ryan/J. B. Visual Press; 103 right Tom Leighton/Elizabeth Whiting and Associates; 104 Richard Bryant/Arcaid; 107 Smallbone of Devizes; 110 Camera Press; 111 Michael Dunne/Elizabeth Whiting; 113 above Shona Wood/Conran Octopus (Polly Powell); 113 below Smallbone of Devizes; 115 The Anthony Blake Photo Library; 116 Rene Stoeltie; 118 Camera Press; 119 Michael Crockett/Elizabeth Whiting and Associates; 120 Richard Bryant/Arcaid; 122 Gilles de Chabaneix; 123 IPC Magazines/World Press Network; 124 Jon Bouchier/Elizabeth Whiting and Associates; 127 Brigitte Thomas; 130 IPC Magazines/World Press Network; 132 above Tim Woodcock; 132 below Sally and Richard Greenhill; 133–4 Bubbles/Loisjoy Thurstun; 140 Paul Ryan/J. B. Visual Press; 141 Rodney Hyett/Elizabeth Whiting and Associates; 143 IPC Magazines/World Press Network; 144 Fritz von der Schulenburg (Richard Mudditt); 152 Paul Ryan/J. B. Visual Press; 155 Camera Press; 156 Peter Woloszynski/Elizabeth Whiting and Associates; 159 Houses & Interiors; 160 Dennis Krukowski/Conran Octopus (Mr. & Mrs. John H. Winkler); 161 Camera Press; 162 Di Lewis/Elizabeth Whiting and Associates; 163 Spike Powell/Elizabeth Whiting and Associates; 165 Jessica Strang (Rye Tiles); 166 Michael Dunne/Elizabeth Whiting and Associates; 167 Ed Ironside/Elizabeth Whiting and Associates; 169 IPC Magazines/World Press Network; 170 Ed Ironside/Elizabeth Whiting and Associates; 171 Gilles de Chabaneix; 172 Ed Ironside/Elizabeth Whiting and Associates; 173 Davies, Keeling and Trowbridge; 174 Jacqui Hurst/Conran Octopus; 175 Tim Street-Porter/Elizabeth Whiting and Associates; 176 Spike Powell/Elizabeth Whiting and Associates; 178 Dennis Krukowski; 180 IPC Magazines/World Press Network; 183 Jean-Paul Bonhommet; 184 Houses & Interiors; 190 John Hollingshead; 193 Guy Bouchet; 194 Camera Press; 198 Tim Street-Porter/Elizabeth Whiting and Associates; 199 Julie Fisher/Conran Octopus.

Special Photography for Conran Octopus by Geoff Dann: 177, 179, 181, 185, 186, 187, 189, 197.